ARCHAEOLOGICAL MAP OF NYMPHAION (CRIMEA)

ACADEMIA SCIENTIARUM POLONA

BIBLIOTHECA ANTIQUA

ALEKSANDRA WĄSOWICZ

EDITOR

JANUSZ STĘPNIEWSKI

EDITORIS ADIUTOR

vol. XXIII

INSTITUTE OF ARCHÆOLOGY AND ETHNOLOGY
POLISH ACADEMY OF SCIENCES

T. Scholl and V. Zin'ko

Archæological Map
of Nymphaion (Crimea)

WITH CONTRIBUTIONS BY
I. AČKINAZI, M. BEDNARZ, N. FEDOSEEV,
R. KARASIEWICZ-SZCZYPIORSKI,
M. MAZZUCHELLI, K. MEYZA, E. ZIN'KO
EDITED BY
ALEKSANDRA WĄSOWICZ

WARSAW 1999

Translated by Sylwia Twardo

Editorial Office
00-140 Warszawa, Al. Solidarności 105

The book is published by the financial support
of the State Committee for Scientific Research

ISBN 83-85463-82-8
ISSN 0208-5631

The cover design is based on a Russian map from 1852

Cover design
Jerzy Grzegorkiewicz

Typesetting and printing
Letter Quality
01-216 Warszawa, ul. Brylowska 35/38, tel. 631 41 37, 631 45 18
PUIP Jachranka 94

CONTENTS

СОДЕРЖАНИЕ

PREFACE

The *Archaeological Map of Nymphaion* is just one of the results of a five–year–long period of (1993–1997) Polish–Russian–Ukrainian cooperation carried out within the terms of reference of the project: "Nymphaion: the History and Structure of a Greek polis."

International studies of this Greek colony, probably established by Miletus in the 6th century B.C.,[1] were begun in 1993 at the suggestion of the then director of the Kerč Museum, professor Eleonora Jakovenko.

Within the boundaries of international agreements subsequently reached, the participants in the project were: the Archaeological Museum in Kerč and the Hermitage Museum in Saint Petersburg (from 1993), the State Committee for the Protection of Historical Monuments of Crimea in Simferopol' (from 1994), the Centre National de la Recherche Scientifique in Nantes (from 1994), and, from the very beginning, as one of the parties initiating the cooperation, the Institute of Archaeology and Ethnology at the Polish Academy of Sciences, Warsaw. Without a special agreement the work was shared out between other institutions, especially the Institute of Archaeology at Warsaw University (from 1993) and, as the necessity arose, by employees of the Institute of History at the University of Wrocław, the Insitute of Geological Sciences at Polish Academy of Sciences, and the Arbeitsgruppe Archäometrie der Freien Universität, Berlin.

The aim of the Project was to study the history and structure of a Greek colony, Nymphaion[2] in its totality. This embraced the investigation of both the town and its rural hinterland (chora), as well as various aspects of the life of its inhabitants in Antiquity, i.a., economy, culture, and social and ethnic relations. For this end various categories of source material were used: archaeological, iconographic, literary, epigraphic, and palaeozoological ones, as well as various methods: field survey, excavation, geophysical and underwater survey, cartography, and analysis of satellite pictures. It was intended to carry out parallelly various forms of research work, i.a., field work, studies of source materials, studies of selected historical problems, preparation of publications, and working conferences (of the round table type).

It seems appropriate to explain why Nymphaion, a relatively small, but important colony located to the south of Kerč (ancient Pantikapaion), on the western shore of the Kerč Strait (Bosphorus Cimmericus), was selected as a subject of the investigation. Nymphaion became the focus of our interest because it provided optimum conditions for the accomplishment of the aims of the Project. Firstly, it was a relatively small colony (in comparison to, e.g., Pantikapaion or Olbia), and thus it was easier to study the problems involved in their totality. Secondly, the neighbourhood of the Ancient town is not covered with buildings and this made it possible to study the chora. Finally, and perhaps most importantly for our part, the excavations conducted in the area of the town since 1939 by the Hermitage Museum have yielded impressive results, which offered further interesting research prospects. So far a large section of fortifications, numerous sanctuaries, residential buildings, and other structures have been uncovered.

During the 5 year long research, the ambitious (as we had realised from the very beginning) plans were carried out to a different extent: some topics have been thoroughly examined, other ones shall soon be presented in publications, some have been abandoned. The current state of these various avenues of research is presented in recent publications and literature.[3]

---

[1] For information on the history of Nymphaion and archaeological excavations at the area of that colony see: CHUDJAK 1962; GRAČ 1989; N. KUNINA, T. SCHOLL, O. SOKOLOVA, A. WĄSOWICZ, *The Bibliography of Nymphaion*, Archeologia (Warszawa) 45, 1994 (1995), pp. 79–89.

[2] See A. WĄSOWICZ, *Nymphaion Project*, Archeologia 45, 1994 (1995), pp. 69–72.

[3] Nymphaion Project I, Archeologia 45, 1994 (1995), pp. 69–89; Nymphaion Project II, ibidem, 46, 1995 (1996), pp. 71–91; Nymphaion Project III, ibidem, 47, 1996 (1997), pp. 85–112; Nymphaion Project IV, ibidem, 48, 1997 (1998), pp. 55–72; Nymphaion Project V, ibidem, 49, 1998 (1999), pp. 85–98; KARASIEWICZ-SZCZYPIORSKI 1995; KARASIEWICZ-SZCZYPIORSKI 1996; STĘPNIEWSKI 1994; SCHOLL, ZIN'KO 1996; ZIN'KO 1997d.

From the very beginning, one of the main objectives of the Project was to carry out the exploration of the chora. However, it was necessary to select a research method which would allow us to obtain concrete results and reach a certain stage of completion within the limited period of five years. It was decided to prepare an archaeological map of the area of Nymphaion on the basis of a field survey. Unfortunately, although the territories of many Greek colonies either on the Black Sea littoral or in the Mediterranean have been subject to advanced investigation, no method suitable for application to our conditions was found in the existing literature. Moreover, no such method could be found in publications presenting archaeological maps of the Greek mainland.[4] For that reason it was decided to adapt for our research in Crimea the model elaborated for the field survey carried out in Poland for the purposes of preparing the so-called Polish Archaeological Record [*Archeologiczne Zdjęcie Polski (AZP)*, cf Introduction, pp. 10]. Clearly, this idea may be criticised. However, it seems, in the light of the studies carried out for several years at Nymphaion, that the method we adopted has worked. The next step should be the further investigation of the rural hinterland of Nymphaion carried out by archaeologists, historians, and geographers in conjunction. The results presented in this book are, it should be strongly emphasised, the first steps along that path.

The archaeological map of Nymphaion is a product of team work. Viktor Zin'ko, the Curator of Archaeological Monuments from Kerč, knows the area and the monuments existing in it perfectly, and has studied the rural settlement in the European part of the Bosporan Kingdom[5] for several years. He holds the excavation and survey permit issued by the local authorities, which has made our joint investigations possible. Tomasz Scholl from the Institute of Archaeology at Warsaw University, having considerable experience of excavations and field surveys from various sites in Poland, Syria, Egypt, and Jordan, undertook a thorough study of the methods used in preparing the Polish Archaeological Record. He adapted the principles applied in Poland for the purposes of our work at Nymphaion. The painstaking, metre by metre, penetration of the area was carried out under the guidance of the two above-mentioned archaeologists in mixed Polish-Ukrainian teams, and, in the first two years of research, also with Russian colleagues (under the guidance of S. Solov'ev from the Hermitage Museum).

The results of the survey of the Nymphaion area will be assessed by our readers, especially the specialists dealing with the history of Greek colonisation and settlement in Antiquity. However, I would like to make some general statements, which I am entitled to do as the Director of the Project on the Polish part, having initiated the work on the Archaeological Map of Nymphaion.

Our research has proved that there probably existed an organised and well-run rural hinterland of Nymphaion (i.e., the chora) integrally connected with the city. The hinterland had an area of ca 70 square kilometres having mainly natural limits (Lake Čurubaš to the north, the Kerč Strait to the east, and Lake Tobečik to the south). It is assumed to have existed from the 6th century B.C., i.e., in parallel with the origins and development of the colony. It is possible to draw conclusions about the way the area was run and stages in its development, which would be a subject of a separate study.

Moreover, this book may prove relevant for the further discussion on methods of studying Greek colonies, or even more broadly, poleis. It proposes a method of studying the chora – acknowledged by the majority of historians as an integral part of the Greek state – which consisted of the urban centre and the connected with it rural hinterland. Inasmuch as the majority of the specialists agree upon the existence and importance of these two components, systematic and methodical research on the chora is in its initial stages. This concerns both the colonies, which have little worthwhile written source material (as is also the case with Nymphaion) and the Aegean Greece, where the literary and epigraphic sources have shed some light on the problems of rural areas.

Let me conclude this presentation of our common work by expressing my gratitude to those who contributed to the preparation of this book. I would like to thank all the participants in the Nymphaion Project who fostered our cooperation over the consecu-

---

[4] The Black Sea littoral was first presented in a work by I.V. FABRICIUS, *Archeologičeskaja karta Pričernomor'ja Ukrainskoj SSR*, Kiev 1951. Both this and the later publications aiming, in the intention of their authors, at preparing archaeological maps of, e.g., Olbia, Tyras, Chersonesus, European Bosporus, were not preceeded by a systematic and exhaustive field prospection and did not present locations of the discovered sites on detailed maps. The work by Ja. M. Paromov, about the Taman Peninsula, is a notable exception, yet it has not been published so far and is stored in the Archives of the Institute of History of Material Culture at the Russian Academy of Sciences in Saint Petersburg (Archiv Leningradskogo Otdelenija Instituta Archeologii Akademii Nauk SSSR, fond 35, opis' 2–D, delo nr 518). – The survey conducted in southern Italy by J.C. Carter, e.g., in Metapontion and Crotone, has not been published, either. The results of prospections conducted in Greece and on the Aegean Islands have been recently issued by M. BRUNET, *Les territoires ruraux en Grèce: archéologie, géographie et histoire*, in: Les Nouvelles de l'Archéologie, 69, automne 97, pp. 19–23 (with literature).

[5] See, e.g., ZIN'KO 1986; V.N. ZIN'KO, *Sel'ske poselenija i mogil'niki Bospora i Chersonesa IV–III vv. do n.è. (opyt sravnitel'nogo analiza)*, Leningrad 1991, Ph.D.thesis.

tive years: the successive Directors of the Archaeological Museum in Kerč, first Eleonora Jakovenko, Ph.D., then Piotr Ivanenko, M.A., the Director of the Hermitage Museum in Saint Petersburg, Professor Michail Piotrovskij, the supervisor of the excavations of the town of Nymphaion, Olga Sokolova, M.A., and the other specialists from that Museum, who have worked upon Nymphaion, the Director of the State Committee for the Protection of Historical Monuments in Crimea from Simferopol', Jurij Mogaričev, Ph.D., and Viktor Zin'ko, Ph.D., from that Committee, as well as Loïc Ménanteau, Ph.D., from the CNRS in Nantes.

I should not fail to mention the competent and well-knit team of Polish participants in the Nymphaion Project who, frankly speaking, were the core of that international undertaking, and among them my friends and colleagues: Tomasz Scholl, Ph.D. and Radosław Karasiewicz-Szczypiorski, M.A., from the Institute of Archaeology at Warsaw University, Krzysztof Domżalski, M.A., Tomasz Herbich, M.A., and Krzysztof Misiewicz, Ph.D., from the Institute of Archaeology and Ethnology, Polish Academy of Sciences, Małgorzata Mycke-Dominko, Ph.D. and Ewa Pilich, M.A., from the Institute of Geography at Warsaw University, Krzysztof Nawotka, Ph.D., from the Institute of History at the University of Wrocław (the author of the works on graffiti), Tomasz Nowicki, M.A., from the Institute of Geological Sciences in Warsaw at the Polish Academy of Sciences, Professor Małgorzata Biernacka-Lubańska (consultant on the subject of the pipeline), and the group of students from Warsaw University: Mr Robert Horosz (the photographer), Miss Magdalena Nowakowska (the draftsman), and others.

Separate thanks should be extended to the Polish archaeologists who provided us with valuable information, advice, and encouragement on the subject of field survey and work on the Polish Archaeological Record: Danuta Jaskanis, M.A., Marek Konopka, M.A., Professor Elżbieta Kowalczyk, and Eudoksia Papuci-Władyka, Ph.D., who we consulted on the subject of pottery.

We are also grateful to the yearly, *Archeologia*, for publishing, with considerable effort, large portions of material from the Nymphaion Project and the Institute of Archaeology and Ethnology, PAS, for bringing this book to print.

Our participation in the multinational Nymphaion Project was possible due to the financial aid of the State Committee for Scientific Research in Warsaw (grants for the years 1996 and 1997), and of the Batory Foundation (financing the conference "Nymphaion II"), and, especially, due to the financial help and friendly interest of our private sponsor, Mr Jerzy Buława.

Aleksandra Wąsowicz

INTRODUCTION

One of the main ways of preserving information about the past is to record the visible on the ground traces of the past activities of man, before industry, building, agriculture, and tourism, which all destroy the occupation layers, develop. Therefore, the tasks accomplished within the guidelines of the international research project: "Nymphaion – the History and Structure of a Greek polis" included making an Archaeological Map of Nymphaion,[1] the aim of which was to put together the data useful for studying the chora of the Ancient town (see Map 2).

In order to achieve this goal, experience drawn from the long-lasting application of the method of field survey used to prepare the so-called Archeologiczne Zdjęcie Polski (AZP) [Polish Archaeological Record (PAR)][2] was utilised. The method consists in a systematic field survey carried out by groups of up to 7 people walking in an extended line at a distance of between 5 and 15 m (depending on the local conditions), as a result of which every accessible square metre of the area is investigated. The other features of the method are:

– use of a topographical map (scale 1 : 25 000) divided into quadrangles, which facilitates recording of the sites found in their boundaries;

– use of unified Record Charts of sites;

– collecting all the artefacts found on the surface and recording them on the maps (scale 1 : 10 000);

– recording all the data in a computer and making them accessible.

Furthermore, in the compilation of an Archaeological Map, the study of the archival material plays a vital role.

Of course, the project would have been impossible to implement without the help of the experience and scientific achievements of Russian and Ukrainian archaeologists in field work, especially that carried out in the area of the Crimean Peninsula.[3] On the basis of that experience, necessary corrections to the Polish system were made to work out a common method to study a definite goal – Nymphaion's hinterland.

Changes in the form of Site Record Charts as well as a system of recording them in the computer were elaborated. Uniform principles of making charts for special finds, in line with those applied in the National Museum in Warsaw, were adopted. It was decided that non-diagnostic pottery fragments would not be described but only their find-spots would be recorded on the maps.

It was assumed that the Archaeological Map was to be prepared by representatives of many disciplines: besides archaeologists, geographers (including a specialist in analysing satellite pictures and topographical maps), geologists, specialists in underwater research, paleobotanists, geophysicists, anthropologists, and osteologists, were to participate. For a variety of reasons not all aspects of the project have been accomplished.

The field work was to be carried out in mixed Polish (Tomasz Scholl, Ph.D., Institute of Archaeology at Warsaw University, Warsaw) – Russian (Sergej Solov'ev, Ph.D., the Hermitage Museum, St Petersburg) – Ukrainian (Viktor Zin'ko, Ph.D., State Committee for the Protection of Crimean Monuments of History and Culture, Simferopol' – Kerč) teams, exploring the whole area under investigation on foot. Ultimately, the task was carried out

[1] SCHOLL, ZIN'KO 1997 (including literature on our common work). On the principles of the Nymphaion Project see: A. WĄSOWICZ, *Nymphaion Project*, Archeologia 45, 1994 (1995), pp. 69–72. For a short resume of the results of respective seasons see: Polish reports Nymphaion, Arch. 1993 (1994); Nymphaion, Arch. 1994 (1995); Nymphaion, Arch. 1996 (1997); Nymphaion, Arch. 1997 (1998); Ukrainian reports ZIN'KO, Arch. 1994; ZIN'KO, Arch. 1995.

[2] *Archeologiczne Zdjęcie Polski – metoda i doświadczenia. Próba oceny* [Polish Archaeological Record – Method and Experiences. An Attempted Assessment], Warszawa 1996; M. KONOPKA, *Instrukcja ewidencji stanowisk archeologicznych metodą badań powierzchniowych (Archeologiczne Zdjęcie Polski)* [Directions for Recording Archaeological Sites by Means of Field Survey (Polish Archaeological Record)], Warszawa 1984; R. MAZUROWSKI, *Metodyka archeologicznych badań powierzchniowych* [Methodology of Archaeological Field Survey], Warszawa 1980.

[3] See, e.g., V.D. BLAVATSKIJ, *Antičnaja polevaja archeologija*, Moskva 1967; A. N. ŠČEGLOV, *Razvedki i raskopki antičnych sel'skich poselenij i agrarnych sistem. Instrukcija*, in: *Metodika polevych archeologičeskich issledovanij*, Moskva 1983, pp. 12–30.

by the Polish-Ukrainian team, and the Russian group worked only during the first two seasons.

Also present in the Polish group doing the field work were Tomasz Herbich, M.A. (in 1993, 1994)[4] and Krzysztof Misiewicz, Ph.D. (in 1997),[5] both geophysicists, responsible for the geophysical surveys and their descriptions in this publication (both from the Institute of Archaeology and Ethnology, Polish Academy of Sciences, Warsaw), Tomasz Nowicki, M.A. (1997, Institute of Geological Sciences, Polish Academy of Sciences, Warsaw),[6] a geologist and topographer, the author of the geological and geographical passages in this volume as well as of maps of the majority of barrow groups and two plots, Krzysztof Domżalski, M.A., an archaeologist (1996, Institute of Archaeology and Ethnology, PAS), Radosław Karasiewicz-Szczypiorski, an archaeologist (from 1994), and Robert Horosz, a photographer (1996, 1997) (both from the Institute of Archaeology, Warsaw University), as well as a large group of students from the Institute of Archaeology, Warsaw University.[7] In the 1994 season, geographers from Warsaw University: Małgorzata Mycke-Dominko,[8] Ph.D., and Ewa Pilich, M.A., took part. During that season, an underwater survey was carried out by a group of Polish divers.[9]

The Ukrainian team participating in the field work included: Igor' Ačkinazi, Ph.D. (1995),[10] author of some of the topographical drawings (archaeologist, Krymskoe otdelenie Instituta Vostokovedenija Nacional'noj Akademii Nauk Ukrainy, Simferopol'), Aleksandr Avetikov, M.A. (archaeologist, Bosporskij Archeologičeskij Centr Goskomiteta po ochrane i ispol'zovaniju pamjatnikov istorii i kul'tury – BAC, Kerč, 1995), Leonid Ponomarev (archaeologist, BAC, 1996, 1997), and a draftsman, Lidija Berezovskaja (BAC, 1995). The permission to conduct the

field work was held by Viktor Zin'ko, Ph.D., who also identified and dated the finds. The Ukrainian team carried out trial excavations and archival research.

We were also aided by Loïc Ménanteau, Ph.D., from the Centre National de la Recherche Scientifique, Nantes, France, who analysed the pictures obtained from the SPOT satellite.[11]

The Project was carried out under the scientific guidance of professor Aleksandra Wąsowicz (Institute of Archaeology and Ethnology, PAS).

The preliminary work was began in 1993. It focused on two goals: 1) testing the possibilities of conducting the field survey; 2) elaborating the system of documentation and field work. In 1993 and 1994, several reconnaissance expeditions were made in order to learn about the field and weather conditions (this concerned especially the Polish group) as well as to meet the population of the area to be investigated.

It was established that the studies were to embrace an area of ca 70 square kilometres, delimited on the north, south, and east by natural water boundaries, on the basis of an a priori assumption that this area ought to correspond to that of the Nymphaion chora. The area of the town itself was not included in the investigations. The duration of one season (1 month) was determined by the financial possibilities of the parties and the time the participants had at their disposal. It was decided that early autumn (especially the month of September) would be the most suitable to carry out the field work, as at that time agricultural activities (harvesting and ploughing) are mostly finished and the sun has killed grass and weeds. Moreover, at that time employees and students of Warsaw University had a break between terms. Unfortunately, over consecutive years the weather conditions were very unfavourable: frequent rains caused unexpected growth of vegetation and loess soils became very muddy.

One of the greatest problems was to obtain a detailed topographical map of the appropriate scale, i.e., 1 : 25 000. It was made available to us in 1994, thanks to S. Solov'ev. The map bears the date of November 13, 1972. It was made on the basis of materials from 1966–1967 and issued by Glavnoe upravlenie geodezii i kartografii pri Sovete Ministrov SSSR. It had many inaccuracies both due to the changes which have taken place in the area after its preparation and to intentional distortions probably made for military reasons. Eventually we used maps,

[4] T. Herbich carried out research at the following sites: II.1.1.; II.1.12.; II.1.19.; II.1.22.; II.2.1.

[5] K. Misiewicz investigated the following sites: II.1.17.; II.1.20.; II.1.42.; II.4.1.; II.4.10.

[6] T. Nowicki worked at the following sites: II.1.17.; II.1.20.; II.1.42.; II.2.10.; II.2.11; II.2.14; II.2.15.; II.2.16.; II.3.1.; II.3.3.; II.4.1.; II.4.2,3.

[7] In 1995 the following students of the Institute of Archaeology at Warsaw University: Małgorzata Majcher, Maciej Ner, Teresa Witkowska, and Maciej Wołosiak took part in the field survey and in 1997, Magdalena Nowakowska.

[8] M. Mycke-Dominko redrew the map obtained from S. Solov'ev for our purposes.

[9] In 1994, under the guidance of a specialist from Kerč, A. Šamraj, underwater survey was conducted by divers from Warsaw: from the Pathfinders' Diving Club „Wanda" and from the Students' Club for Underwater Research at the Institute of Archaeology, Warsaw University.

[10] I. Ačkinazi worked at the necropolises located along the Kerč Strait, at sites along the banks of Lake Tobečik and in the north-western part of the investigated area.

[11] Due to his work we are able to compare the topographical-archaeological maps with satellite pictures, especially at sites II.3.5. and II.4.1. As a result it was possible to tentatively delineate the course of ancient pathways (sites II.4.2.1–6.). Also the ancient natural environment can be partially reproduced by analysing satellite pictures and topographic maps from various periods.

scale 1:10 000, which were enlarged fragments of the above-mentioned map, scale 1:25 000. The study area was divided into squares each with sides 1 km long and the sites were numbered independently within each square. Due to the configuration of the area (the Kerč Strait to the east and open space to the west) the squares were numbered from the north to the south and from the east to the west so as to be able to continue their numeration towards the west.

During the field work all the sites were carefully recorded on maps, record charts of sites were filled in, and full descriptions and topographical drawings were made. Also those places which should, for a variety of reasons, be investigated once again were recorded. Thanks to this it was possible, i.a., to locate the earlier excavations. Moreover, during our survey all the changes observed in the area were recorded on the map. The old natural environment can be partly reproduced on the basis of satellite pictures and old topographical maps.

Our base was located in the village of Èl'tigen, situated more than 8 km away beyond the farthest limits of the investigated area. Because of this it was necessary to use a car to get to the places from which the field work was carried out on foot. The artefacts collected every day, consisting mainly of diagnostic amphorae fragments, were washed, drawn (altogether more than 500 drawings were made) and photographed (altogether more than 1 200 photographs of artefacts and field structures were made). More than 50 charts of special finds were drawn.

From the first season onwards the geophysicists: T. Herbich and K. Misiewicz, conducted their investigations. They used a resistivity meter specially constructed for archaeological purposes. Geophysical surveys were carried out with the use of the electro-resistivity method. The twin-probe array with different distances between the electrodes (AM = 1 m, BN = 5 m and AM = 0.5 m, BN = 0.25 m) was applied to the measurements in the field. In selected points of the settlement Čurubaš Južnoe also geoelectrical soundings were performed. The measurements were taken at a one metre (regular) and alternating (every 2 m in profile) grid. During the first season the aim of the geophysical survey was to learn whether it was possible to locate archaeological remains by means of observing changes in ground resistivity. It also enabled us to collect data about the resistivity characteristics of the litology of the milieu, and ways in which structures can be distinguished in the existing conditions.

K. Misiewicz also used geoelectrical measurements as the main method. The choice of the method depended on the task. Specialist computer programmes allowed to prepare an introductory report on the results of the resistivity surveys made during the field work and to establish where trial pits should be made to obtain key data to interpret the resistivity maps. Altogether 90 geoelectrical soundings were made and ca 8 000 readings of profiles, on an area of ca 1 ha in four places.

In the last season, i.e., 1997, a complete field documentation of part of the barrow necropolises and plots (some of them were recorded in 1995 by I. Ačkinazi) was elaborated. The limestone outcrops in this area often resemble barrows. At the same time, many of the actual barrows have been levelled by intensive ploughing (to a depth of 0.7 m), natural erosion, or by plundering (some of the barrows were dug out as early as the 19th century, and other ones, later). Therefore, in order to make precise records of the barrows a special group was formed, composed of a Ukrainian archaeologist with experience in studying barrow necropolises, L. Ponomarev, and a geologist from Poland, T. Nowicki, a specialist in the Quaternary period, particularly interested in the phenomena of Karst. Due to their help it was possible to establish which of the elevations are, or may be, barrows, and which are natural. This will probably allow us to make a more precise record of the barrows.

The complete documentation of the field work is stored in Warsaw in the Institute of Archaeology and Ethnology, PAS, and in the BAC in Kerč.

T. Nowicki's studies enable us to state that the investigated area is mainly located in a region composed of Tertiary marine sedimentary rocks, mainly Oligocene and Miocene ones. The rock layer is overlaid by dark Oligocene clays, the so-called Majkopian deposits, covered with Miocene and Pliocene deposits. These are mainly strongly diagenetic shelly conglomerates, becoming a loose mollusc sediment towards the top. Quaternary layers of Pleistocene loess beds rest on Neogene sediments. Outcrops of Sarmatian limestones: fossil reefs and bryozoan bioherms form a characteristic relief pattern of sharp, rocky bluffs. These are the remains of Middle and Upper Miocene lagoons (Upper Sarmatian) and are particularly pronounced in the north-western part of the investigated area as well as along the shore of the Strait. The Lower Sarmatian is represented by soft silt which, being most susceptible to erosion, forms hollows surrounded by carbonate hills. Reef structures formed a barrier protecting the internal parts of the lagoon from the open sea. In the Pliocene, in the internal zone of the lagoon, in a shallow pool, first carbonate and then carbonate-iron sedimentation occurred. It produced oolite and siderite iron ores. Erosion brought ferruginous salts to the pool from the organic soils rich in iron and phosphorus during a period of hot and humid climate. The last stage in the shallowing of the pool was the sedimentation of carbonates in the centre of the pool and of marls and silts in the littoral and outside the reef barriers of the lagoon. In the glacial Pleistocene this was covered with loess deposits. The Kerč Peninsula owes its morphology to large-radius synclines. The axes of these synclines are parallel and contain i.a., lake Tobečik, lake Čurubaš and the town of Kerč. Both lakes were probably sea bays which became shallower as a result of the large-scale uplifting of the Kerč Peninsula in the Quaternary. As a result, bryozoan and coral fossil reefs can be seen ca 100 m above sea level. The sand bars created by sea currents cut the bays off from the open sea. Such a sand bar is easily visible to the north of Nymphaion: beach sediments – carbonate (shelly) sands close the outlet of the former bay, which probably used to be the outlet of an overground stream. As a result of evaporation deposits of salt have formed in the lakes. As the sub-loess layers of the investigated area were very diversified, the thickness of the loess cover is also variegated. It is completely missing on the summits of fossil reefs and has the depth of up to ca 15 m in a cliff found near the village of Čeljadinovo. The loess contains shells, roots, and bones of vertebrates which inhabited the steppe and tundra zones once found in the central part of the area. Loess underlies fertile *černozem* soils and its yellow hue is caused by the oxidized iron content. Stretches of overground water in this area occur in depressions falling below the water table. Also in flat zones or on gentle slopes one may observe shallow pools without outlets. There are a few areas with small springs whose flow presumably fluctuates, depending on the rainfall. The loess is mainly drained on the surface, especially intensively during storms. As a result small, dry valleys with gentle slopes and clearly eroded profiles are formed. Their slopes undergo the same processes of drainage. During less heavy rainfall, seepage of water through the loess layers to the water table plays a more important role. Ground water levels are seasonal in this area, i.e., the depth of the water table changes depending on the rainfall. As a result of that water appears in wells periodically. The natural level limiting the water bearing zone is the depth at which the Oligocene silts of the so-called Majkopian series occur. The drainage layers are constituted by shelly conglomerates or loess. In the latter case the appearance of ground water above the loess is dependent upon the amount of infiltrating water. Reef structures, due to their considerable porosity, may be excellent reservoirs of water, which, however, is difficult to draw. Wells were dug mainly in loess soils. Also natural outflows of water were utilised, in places where the water table was cut by erosion or by man in a pit dug in a dry valley. The drainage pattern

flows towards Lake Tobečik (southwards), Lake Čurubaš (northwards), and the Kerč Strait (northwards).

In the studied area the major part of the land belongs to three state farms and the rest is occupied by a few private plots located in the south-eastern corner. The population lives in three villages belonging to the state farms: Èl'tigen (Geroevka), Tobečik (Čeljadinovo), and Ortel' (Ogon'ki). The village names are of Tartar and Russian origin, respectively. The change of the names took place in 1944, together with a complete exchange of population (thus the present inhabitants of the area know very little about its history). Today some names are used interchangeably. From the north-west the area embraced by the survey is adjoined by the structures of the modern village of Priozernoe (Tartar Čurubaš). Furthermore, along the shore of the Strait there is a narrow band of holiday centres. The remaining area is free of permanent structures which hinder our field work so much.

After a preliminary but detailed survey the whole area utilized in establishment and exploitation of an opencast iron ore mine (dumps, access roads) was intentionally excluded from further archaeological research. A survey of the pit-tips also yielded negative results. No traces of human activity could be detected over the whole of existing ground surface.

The mine and its infrastructure has caused disturbances in the natural environment: in particular, considerable changes in the drainage pattern relative to the landscape.

Studies of the rural settlement of the Kerč area, including the neighbourhood of Nymphaion, have a long tradition.[12] The first to take an interest in the area located to the south of the town of Kerč was P. Dubrux, in the early 19th century. It was only in the 1920s, however, that a Russian archaeologist, Ju. Marti, carried out a first reconnaisance and small-scale excavations in the rural area. Since 1953 systematic field works, both excavations and surveys, have been conducted. At that time a team operating under the auspices of the East-Crimean Department of the Black Sea Expedition of the Institute of Archaeology at the Academy of Sciences of the Soviet Union began its work there. This resulted in the best and largest monograph of the rural territory of European Bosphorus written by I. Kruglikova.[13] In 1991, complex investigations of the area were began by the Bosporan Rescue and Archaeological Expedition from Kerč, under the guidance of V. Zin'ko.

Work on the Archaeological Map of Nymphaion has resulted in the recording on a topographical map of all finds connected with human activity in this area

---

[12] For the history of research see: SOLOV'EV, ZIN'KO 1995.
[13] KRUGLIKOVA 1975.

14

from the earliest to modern times, i.e., from the 2nd millenium B.C. to the first half of the 20th century. Focusing on the main aim of the Project, particular attention has been paid to the Ancient period. Traces of previous archaeological excavations were also recorded.

The book has the following structure: Part I contains a catalogue of all archaeological sites recorded in the investigated area and numbered within their respective squares (see Map 1). During the preparatory work for this volume some of the numbers were eliminated (some sites were amalgamated with others or rejected as sites after additional survey),[14] hence the discontinuities in the numbering. Short descriptions present the following information: site, dating, numbers of the field register with the season indicated (finds only from the joint field survey from 1995–1997). Lack of field register number means no drawn finds. If the site is described in greater detail in further parts of the book the appropriate part is indicated. The names of settlements and necropolises are used according to the existing terminology, validated by V. Zin'ko.

Part II of the book contains descriptions of the main sites in respective categories: settlements, necropolises, plots, wall, pathways, pipeline, quarries, underwater structures. After each name the square and number of site from the catalogue of sites is given. Each description is accompanied by a fragment of a map (scale 1 : 10 000, for technical reasons the scale is changed but each side of the square is 1 km) presenting the square with the location of the described site; moreover, plans of the site and special finds are illustrated (if they exist).

It should be added that the term "settlement" is a convention used to denote a site discovered by means of a field survey, without any trial excavations. The term is used to mean a site with an area of more than one are (a hundred square metres) where, besides the obviously dominating presence of pottery (mainly fragments of amphorae and roof tiles) other artefacts, e.g., small stones not connected with the local geology, were found; also important is the location of the site. Moreover, the same site could have various functions in different periods.

Part III discusses certain groups of special finds, which can be published at the present stage of research. The most precious (for a variety of reasons) artefacts found during the field survey are presented. This includes introductory studies of stone artefacts from the 2nd millenium B.C., stamps on ancient amphorae, rock fragments untypical for the Nymphaion area, ancient sculpture, and Mediaeval pipes.

The Tables present mainly the diagnostic artefacts, used for dating.

The sites (parts I and II) are presented in alphabetical order, except for the town and necropolis of Nymphaion, which have been intentionally discussed at the beginning. No survey work has been carried out at the area of the town, which has been described on the basis of the existing literature. The town merits a separate monograph and thus a separate season of field survey. Similarly, the necropolis of Nymphaion requires much more time and attention.

Results of excavations conducted in the discussed area so far have also been used in our publication. The results so-far unpublished, or published only in the form of short communiqués, are presented in greater detail. For that reason, in Part II, after the description of each newly discovered site, its full literature and archival information are presented, whereas after better known sites, only selected literature is mentioned.[15] All geographical names and personal names are presented according to the international principles of transliteration.

The footnote system is identical to that used in the other publications of the Nymphaion Project, issued mainly in the yearly *Archeologia*, volume 45, 1994 (1995) onwards. Three general maps and smaller maps included in the descriptions of respective sites were produced on the computer by Alina Nowak. The artefacts were drawn by Magdalena Nowakowska (all from the 1997 season) and Olga Berezovskaja; some of them were re-drawn by Hanna Zaborowska. The drawings from the 1996 season were mainly made by Radosław Karasiewicz-Szczypiorski. Plans of some of the sites were produced on the computer by Tomasz Nowicki. Nearly all the photographs were taken by Robert Horosz.

The Authors would like to extend the gratitude to the Director and the staff of the Institute of Archaeology and Ethnology, Polish Academy of Sciences for the help in preparing this book for publication and for providing financial support.

---

[14] The numbers of sites remained unchanged intentionally so as not to change the field records and, especially the field numbers of artefacts.

[15] For full literature about the investigated area see: N. KUNINA, T. SCHOLL, O. SOKOLOVA, A. WĄSOWICZ, *The Bibliography of Nymphaion*, Archeologia 45, 1994 (1995), pp. 79–89, with later supplement in Archeologia 46, 1995 (1996), pp. 89–91.

I. CATALOGUE OF THE SITES

SQUARE   02–07

1. Pottery fragment; handle of a Mediaeval amphora (10th–12th century?). Field Register N/95/283p.

2. Remains of a wall made from vertical, unworked limestone slabs. Traced for more than 50 m.

SQUARE   02–08

1. Pottery fragments from an area of more than 10 ha; mainly Mediaeval (9th–16th century); fragments of flint from the 2nd millenium B.C (see III.1.1) and of a Bosporan roof tile; remains of a building and ash-pits. N/95/267 – 8p, 270 – 3p, 295 – 8p. See II.1.3.: the settlement of Čurubaš – 2.

SQUARE   02–09

1. Pottery fragments from an area of nearly 1 ha, including amphorae dated to the 4th–3rd century B.C (a few Heraclean and Chersonesian), and to the 8th–9th century. Visible traces of stone structures. N/95//226 – 7p. See II.1.2.: the settlement of Čurubaš – 1.

2. Pottery fragments; handle of an amphora, Late Antiquity; handle of a jug from the 12th–14th century. N/95/280 – 1p.

3. Pottery fragments from an area of nearly 2 ha; amphorae from the 4th–3rd century B.C (a few from Heraclean, Chian, and Thasian ones), Bosporan roof tile. N/96–19 – 23p. See II.1.4.: the settlement of Čurubaš – 3.

4. Pottery fragments; amphorae from the 4th–3rd century B.C, Sinopian roof tile. N/96/10p.

5. Remains of a structure made of large unworked limestone blocks. Middle Ages?

6. Limestone water through (reused?), height 0.23 m, width 0.42 m, length 0.42 m, depth 0.07 m. Antiquity?

8. Two barrows. See II.2.4.: the kurgan necropolis at the settlement of Čurubaš – 3.

9. Pit necropolis. Middle Ages? See II.2.3.: the pit necropolis of Čurubaš.

SQUARE   03–06

1. Pottery fragments from an area of nearly 0.5 ha; amphorae from the 4th–3rd century B.C. (i.a., Chersonesian). N/95/327p, 329p.

2. Pottery fragments; Late Hellenistic amphorae: Thasian and south-Pontic.

3. Two barrows.

SQUARE   03–07

1. Pottery fragment; handle of a Heraclean amphora, 4th–3rd century B.C. N/95/275p.

2. Pottery fragments from an area of nearly 15 ha; amphorae and other vessels from the 4th century B.C to the 1st–2nd century A.D., a few pottery fragments from the 8th–9th century. N/95/258–66p, 290–2p. See II.1.10.: the settlement of Čurubaš – 9.

3. Pottery fragments from an area of nearly 0.5 ha; amphorae from the 4th–3rd century B.C. Remains of walls made of worked limestone blocks. See II.1.9.: the settlement of Čurubaš – 8.

4. Remains of plot enclosures. See II.3.1.: plots near the settlement of Čurubaš – 9.

5. Worked depressions in rock. Press-beds? See II.3.1.: plots near the settlement of Čurubaš – 9.

SQUARE   03–08

1. Pottery fragments from an area of nearly 0.2 ha; a few fragments of vessels from the 12th–16th century, some with green glaze. See II.1.8.: the settlement of Čurubaš – 7.

2. Remains of plot enclosures. See II.3.1.: plots near the settlement of Čurubaš – 9.

3. Pottery fragments from an area of nearly 0.1 ha; amphorae from the 1st–3rd century A.D. See II.1.7.: the settlement of Čurubaš – 6.

4. Traces of stone quarrying. Antiquity? See II.4.8.: quarry no. 1.

SQUARE   03–09

1. Pottery fragments from an area of nearly 0.5 ha; mainly from the 2nd millenium B.C., as well as from the 4th–3rd century B.C., the 8th–9th century, and other finds, including i.a., stone fragments – see III.1.2–5. N/95/246–56p. See II.1.6.: the settlement of Čurubaš – 5.

2. Pottery fragments from an area of nearly 1 ha; pottery and flint fragments from the 2nd millenium B.C. (see III.1.5.), fragments of Thasian amphorae

from the 4th century B.C., Hellenistic (including amphorae from the Thasian circle), 1st–2nd century A.D., and the 8th–9th century. N/95/209 – 14p, 223 – 5p. See II.1.5.: the settlement of Čurubaš – 4.

SQUARE   03–10

1. Pottery fragments; handle of a Thasian amphora from the 4th–3rd century B.C., amphorae from the 8th–9th century.

2. Pottery fragments; amphorae from the 4th century B.C.: Heraclean, Solokha type. Remains of the funeral rite connected with barrow 03–10, site 3. N/96/3–5p.

3. Barrow partly destroyed by a structure used for storing chemical substances, now abandoned. A limestone slab from a cist grave can be observed on the existing surface of the mound.

SQUARE   03–11

1. Pottery fragments; i.a., Sinopian and Heraclean amphorae from the 4th–3rd century B.C. N/96/6–7p.

2. Pottery fragments; amphorae from the 4th–3rd century B.C. and 1st–2nd century A.D. N/95/24p.

SQUARE   03–12

1. Fragments of walls of a modern structure covering an area of 0.1ha; i.a. fragments of so-called Marseilles tiles, limestone rubble.

2. Barrow. Height 0.4 m, diameter, 10 m.

3. Pottery fragments; foot of a Sinopian amphora, 4th–3rd century B.C.

SQUARE   04–02

1. Fragments of pottery dated to the 4th–3rd century B.C. Material collected by V. Zin'ko in 1973.

SQUARE   04–03

1. Fragments of marble with traces of working. See III.3.1.

2. Plundered burial. Antiquity. See. II.2.1.: the pit and kurgan necropolis of Nymphaion. Two fragments of porphyry nearby (see III.3.2.).

3. Two plundered pit burials; nearby, i.a., a fragment of a Thasian amphora, 4th–3rd century B.C. See II.2.1.: the pit and kurgan necropolis of Nymphaion.

SQUARE   04–04

1. Pottery fragments from an area of nearly 0.8 ha; amphorae: Chian, Thasian, Sinopian, and Heraclean from the 4th–3rd century B.C.; amphorae from the 1st–2nd century A.D., fragment of a terra sigillata jug from the 2nd–1st century B.C., fragments of a Sinopian mortarium from the 4th century B.C., fragments of Bosporan and Sinopian roof tiles, fragment of a terracotta figurine. N/95/313p, N/97/28 – 39p,

51–6p. See II.1.17.: the settlement of Čurubaš Nižnoe – 2 (Nižne Čurubašskoe – 2).

2. Pottery fragments from an area of nearly 2 ha; amphorae from the 4th–3rd century B.C., the 1st–2nd century A.D., the 8th–9th century. See II.1.16.: the settlement of Čurubaš Nižnoe – 1 (Nižne Čurubašskoe – 1).

3. Five barrows, one with a triangulation marker 47.9. See II.2.16.: kurgan necropolis.

4. Two plundered cist graves. The northwestern-most graves can be linked with the Nymphaion necropolis. See II.2.1.: the pit and kurgan necropolis of Nymphaion.

5. Pipeline. N/97/65p. Antiquity (?). See II.4.10.

6. Fragment of a retouched flint blade, 2nd millenium B.C. N/97/63p. See III 1.6.

SQUARE 04–05

1. Pottery fragments from an area of nearly 0.5 ha; amphorae, i.a., Hellenistic Chian ones.

2. Modern well made of limestone slabs. Internal diameter of 1.70 m. Modern depth of the water table – 5 m.

SQUARE 04–06

1. Pottery fragments; Chian, Thasian amphorae from the 4th–3rd century B.C., jug made of red clay from the 1st–2nd century A.D. N/95/287 – 8p.

2. Pottery fragments from an area of nearly 5 ha; amphorae dated to the 4th century B.C.: Heraclean, Chersonesian, Mendean, and other ones (the material dated to the 6th century B.C comes from excavation). See II.1.12.: the settlement of Čurubaš Južnoe (Južne Čurubašskoe).

3. Pottery fragment; Hellenistic Chian amphora.

4. Remains of plot enclosures. See II.3.5.: plots near the settlement of Čurubaš Južnoe (Južne Čurubašskoe).

5. Barrows. See II.2.5.: the kurgan necropolis of Čurubaš Južnoe (Južne Čurubašskij). See also II.3.5. (plan of plots) for the distribution of the barrows (western group).

6. Plundered pit burials, stone cist graves. The finds include, i.a., two stamps on handles of Heraclean amphorae, see III.2.1,4. N/97/2 – 3p, 5p, 72p, 98 – 9p, 103p. See II.2.6.: the pit necropolis of Čurubaš Južnoe (Južne Čurubašskij).

SQUARE 04–07

1. Pottery fragments: amphorae, Late Antiquity. N/95/183 – 4p.

2. Pottery fragments from an area of nearly 0.5 ha; amphorae from the 1st–2nd century A.D.: pseudo-Coan, south-Pontic, Rhodian, from red clay. N/95/284 – 6p.

3. Pottery fragments from an area of more than 4 ha; mainly amphorae from the 1st–3rd century A.D., terra sigillata. A few Hellenistic fragments. Visible remains of walls, ash-pit. N/95/293 – 4p, N/97/82p. See II.1.11.: the settlement of Čurubaš Citadel'.

4. Pottery fragment; rim of a Hellenistic Thasian amphora. N/95/289p.

5. Scythian stone statue. See III.4.1.

6. Barrows. See II.2.11.: the kurgan necropolis of Skal'nyj.

7. Pottery fragments from an area of nearly 0.5 ha; fragments of hand thrown pottery, amphorae and jugs from the 4th–6th century. N/97/7–8p.

8. Plots near the settlement of Čurubaš Citadel'. See II.3.2.

SQUARE 04–08
1. Pottery fragment; belly of an amphora, 8th–9th century.

2. Pottery fragment; foot of a Hellenistic Chian amphora.

SQUARE 04–09
1. Pottery fragments; amphorae (i.a., Colchian), Late Antiquity. N/95/217p.

3. Pottery fragments from an area of more than 1 ha; amphorae: Chian, Thasian, from the 4th century B.C.; 1st–2nd century A.D., 8th–9th century. Fragments of hand-thrown pottery. N/95–216p, 218p, 220p.

4. Pottery fragment; handle of an amphora from the 14th–16th century.

SQUARE 04–10
1. Pottery fragment; belly of a Heraclean amphora, 4th–3rd century B.C.

SQUARE 04–11
1. Pottery fragment; belly of a Hellenistic Chersonesian amphora.

2. Pottery fragments; two handles of Hellenistic Thasian amphorae.

4. Pottery fragments from an area of ca 1 ha; numerous Bosporan roof tiles, amphorae from the 4th century B.C. and the Hellenistic period. Visible concentrations of stones. N/96/11 – 5p. See II.1.13.: the settlement of Čurubaš Majak – 1.

SQUARE 04–12
1. Pottery fragments from an area of ca 3 ha; amphorae: from the 4th–3rd century B.C and Hellenistic periods (Heraclean, Thasian, Chian, Mendean; Sinopian: with stamps, see III.2.8–9, 11, 13–16), fragments from the 1st–3rd century A.D. (amphorae, jugs, cups, roof tiles), the 8th–9th cen-

tury; concentrations of stones. N/96/26 – 37p, N/97/1p, 40–50p, 57–62p. See II.1.14.: the settlement of Čurubaš Majak – 2.

2. Pottery fragments from an area of nearly 0.5 ha; 1st–3rd century A.D.: amphorae, roof tiles, tableware (including handles of a terra sigillata jug, Bosporan, 1st century A.D.). N/97/4p. See II.1.15.: the settlement of Čurubaš Majak – 3.

3. Fragment of a whetstone (?), sandstone. N/97/6p.

4. Pottery fragment; handle of a Chian amphora, 4th–3rd century B.C.

5. Pottery fragment; handle of a Chian amphora, 4th–3rd century B.C.

6. Concentration of stones in an area of 3 m × 2 m, visible north-east corner of a wall.

7. Concentration of stones in an area of 3 m × 2 m, some of the stones bear traces of working.

8. Pathway. See II.4.5: pathway no. 4.

SQUARE 05–02
1. Modern well. Diameter, 1.4 m. Made of limestone slabs.

2. The ancient town of Nymphaion. See II.1.1.

SQUARE 05–03
1. Pottery fragments from an area of more than 5 ha; Bosporan and Sinopian roof tiles; amphorae: 3rd–1st century B.C. (including pseudo-Coan), 8th–9th century. N/95/319 – 24p.

2. Pottery fragments from an area of nearly 0.5 ha; amphorae, jugs, pithoi: 4th–3rd century B.C. (including Rhodian, Thasian, pseudo-Coan), mainly the 1st century B.C. – 1st century A.D. N/95/338 – 43p, 346p.

3. Plundered stone tombs. See II.2.1.: the pit and kurgan necropolis of Nymphaion.

4. Fragments of two round limestone querns with a diameter of 0.55 m (thickness, 0.075 m, round opening in the centre, diameter: 0.02 m) and 1.10 m (thickness, 0.16 m). Antiquity (?).

5. Fragments of Hellenistic pottery from an area of nearly 0.5 ha; amphorae: Thasian and Chersonesian; fragment of limestone quern, ca 0.5 m in diameter.

6. Pottery fragments from an area of over 1 ha; fragment of a black-gloss cup, late 5th century B.C., amphorae from the 4th century B.C. to 1st–2nd century A.D.: Heraclean, Sinopian, Chersonesian, Bosporan, Thasian, fragments of a Hellenistic mortarium. N/95/349p.

7. Pottery fragments from an area of 0.4 ha; amphorae from the 4th–3rd century B.C (Chian, Heraclean, Sinopian), Hellenistic (Chersonesian), fragments of high-quality tableware (including Attic black-gloss vessels from the second half of the 5th century B.C.), Saltovo-Majak fragments from

the 8th–9th century. N/95/348p, N/97/85 – 91p, 100 – 1p. See II.1.20.: the settlement of Èl'tigen Zapadnoe.

8. Anthropomorphic stele, 1st–2nd century A.D. See III.4.5.

9. Ancient pathways. See II.4.2,3: pathways no. 1 and 2.

10. Plundered cist tomb, next to it a bronze coin from the 4th century B.C. N/95/347p. See II.2.1.: the pit and kurgan necropolis of Nymphaion.

11. Pit and kurgan necropolis of Nymphaion. See II.2.1.

12. Early Mediaeval settlement, 7th–10th century. See II.1.18.: the settlement of Èl'tigen Jugo-Zapadnoe.

13. Traces of a quarry. See II.4.9.: quarry no. 2.

SQUARE 05–04

1. Pottery fragment; handle of south-Pontic amphora, 1st–2nd century A.D. N/95/325p.

2. Pottery fragment; foot of Chian amphora, the first half of the 4th century B.C. N/95/328p.

3. Pottery fragment; handle of a Hellenistic Chersonesian amphora.

4. Pottery fragment; handle of a Rhodian amphora, late 3rd–2nd century B.C. N/95/326p.

5. Barrows. See II.2.16.: the kurgan necropolis with the triangulation marker 47.9.

6. Pathway. See II.4.7.: pathway no. 6.

SQUARE 05–06

1. Pottery fragments from an area of 0.01 ha; amphorae: Thasian, Rhodian, and Chersonesian, from the 4th–3rd century B.C. (a barrow?). Nearby two similar, ploughed up elevations.

2. Barrows. See II.2.5.: the kurgan necropolis of Čurubaš Južnoe (Južne Čurubasskij). See also II.3.5. (plan of plots) for the distribution of the barrows (western group).

SQUARE 05–07

1. Pottery fragments; early Mediaeval amphorae. N/95/180 – 2p.

2. Pottery fragments; amphorae: Chian and Heraclean, from the 4th–3rd century B.C., from the 1st–2nd century A.D. N/95/229 – 30p.

3. Pottery fragments from an area of over 1 ha; Hellenistic amphorae; and fragments from the 8th–9th century; fragment of a flint blade (see III.1.7.). N/95/222p, 257p. See II.1.33.: the settlement of Ogon'ki – 7.

4. Pottery fragments; amphorae: Thasian and Chersonesian from the Hellenistic period. N/95/215p.

5. Wall fragments.

6. Four barrows. See II.2.15.: the kurgan necropolis with the triangulation marker 97.9.

SQUARE 05–08

1. Pottery fragments; i.a., amphorae: Thasian from the Hellenistic period, and from the 8th–9th century. N/95/193 – 5p.

2. Fragment of a pipe. N/95/197p. See III.5.1.

SQUARE 05–09

1. Pottery fragment; foot of a Sinopian amphora from the 4th–3rd century B.C.

SQUARE 05–10

1. Pottery fragments; Hellenistic Heraclean and Chian (?) amphorae.

2. Barrow.

SQUARE 05–11

1. Ruins of a modern building; i.a., fragment of a so-called Marseilles roof tile.

2. Pottery fragment; foot of a Mendean amphora, 4th century B.C. N/96/1p.

3. Pottery fragments from an area of nearly 0.5 ha; amphorae: Heraclean, Sinopian, Bosporan, Chersonesian, and Cnidian from the 3rd–1st century B.C. N/96/2p.

4. Fragments of flint blades; 2nd millenium B.C. N/96/25p. See III.1.8.

5. Pottery fragments; Thasian amphorae from the 4th–3rd century B.C.

6. Remains of plot enclosures. See II.3.4.: plots near the settlement of Čurubaš Majak – 1.

7. Pottery fragment; handle of a Hellenistic Chian amphora.

SQUARE 05–12

1. Pottery fragments; amphorae: Hellenistic Chian and Sinopian, and ones from the 8th–9th century. N/96/9p.

2. Scythian stone statue. See III.4.2. See also II.2.14.: kurgan necropolis, near the triangulation marker 93.6.

3. Pottery fragments from an area of nearly 0.5 ha; amphorae, i.a., Hellenistic Sinopian and ones from the 1st–2nd century A.D., fragment of a so-called Marseilles roof tile. N/96/18p.

4. Barrows. See II.2.14.: kurgan necropolis near the triangulation marker 93.6.

5. Pottery fragment; handle of Hellenistic Chian amphora.

6. Pottery fragment; amphora handle, 8th–9th century.

7. Pottery fragments; two belly fragments of Hellenistic Chian amphora.

8. Pottery fragments from an area ca 500 × 150 m; late Mediaeval; stone remains, so-called Marseilles roof tiles.

9. Pottery fragment; foot of Hellenistic Chian amphora.

10. Pathway. See II.4.6.: pathway no. 5.

SQUARE 05–13

1. Pottery fragments; amphorae: Chian, 4th–3rd century B.C., pseudo-Coan, 1st–2nd century A.D. See II.4.5, 6.: pathway no. 4 and 5.

2. Pottery fragment; foot of Hellenistic Thasian amphora. N/96/8p.

3. Barrows.

SQUARE 06–02

1. Two amphorae from the 9th century. See II.5.2. settlement no. 1.

2. Pottery fragments from an area of nearly 0.4 ha; amphorae: 4th–3rd century B.C., 1st–2nd century A.D.; a concentration of limestones; stone altar. See II.5.2.: settlement no. 1.

3. Anchorage; 15 anchor stones; fragments of amphorae, 4th–3rd century B.C., 8th–9th century. See II.5.5.: anchorage.

SQUARE 06–03

1. Fragment of a limestone funerary stele, semi-figure, 1st–2nd century A.D. N/95/345p. See III.4.4.

2. Pottery fragments from an area of nearly 0.5 ha; amphorae, 3rd–2nd century B.C. (including Rhodian ones), 1st–2nd century A.D. (including, i.a., a Sinopian one). N/95/314 – 8p. See II.1.19.: the settlement of Èl'tigen Muzej.

3. Fragments of Late Mediaeval pottery; vessels, roof tiles.

4. Pottery fragments from an area of nearly 0.5 ha; 8th–9th century; remains of walls.

5. Barrows. See II.2.1.: the pit and kurgan necropolis of Nymphaion.

6. Pottery fragments from an area of nearly 0.5 ha; amphorae: 4th–3rd century B.C.; remains of walls. See II.5.3.: settlement no. 2.

SQUARE 06–04

1. Faience bead, the first centuries A.D. (?) N/95/127p.

SQUARE 06–07

1. Pottery fragments; amphorae: Chian and Thasian, 4th–3rd century B.C. N/95/228p.

2. Pottery fragments; amphorae: Heraclean, 4th–3rd century B.C. N/95/207 – 8p.

3. Basalt grinder. Modern times? N/95/312p.

4. Remains of plot enclosures. See II.3.5.: plots near the settlement of Ogon'ki – 6.

SQUARE 06–08

1. Pottery fragments from an area of nearly 1.5 ha; amphorae: Heraclean from the 4th–3rd century B.C., and from the 8th–9th century. See II.1.32.: the settlement of Ogon'ki – 6.

2. Pottery fragments; Hellenistic and Late Antique amphorae. N/95/191 – 2p.

3. Pottery fragments; amphorae: Thasian and Sinopian from the 4th–3rd century B.C. N/95/219p.

4. Pottery fragments; amphorae: Late Hellenistic Rhodian (?) amphorae, others from the 8th–9th century.

5. Two barrows. See II.2.9.: kurgan necropolis near the settlement of Ogon'ki – 6.

SQUARE 06–09

1. Pottery fragments from an area of more than 3 ha; mainly from the 4th–3rd century B.C., a few from the 8th–9th century. N/95/177p. See II.1.31.: the settlement of Ogon'ki – 5.

2. Pottery fragments; amphora: Heraclean from the 4th–3rd century B.C., handle of jug, 1st–3rd century A.D.

SQUARE 06–13

1. Pottery fragments; 1st–2nd century A.D. (including mouth of south–Pontic amphora). N/96/16 – 7p.

SQUARE 07–03

1. Pottery fragments from an area of 0.4 ha; amphorae: 4th–3rd century B.C.; concentration of stones. See II.5.4.: settlement no. 3.

SQUARE 07–04

1. Pottery fragments from an area of ca 0.3 ha; amphorae: from the 4th–3rd century B.C. (including Thasian examples), and from the 8th–9th century. N/95/108 – 14p.

2. Pottery fragments from an area of more than 3 ha; 4th–3rd century B.C. (including i.a., a stamp on a handle of a Sinopian amphora – see III.2.10), 1st–3rd century A.D., mainly 8th–9th century. N/95/330 – 7p. See II.1.26.: the settlement of Geroevka – 6.

3. Pottery fragments; 7th–8th century; remains of stone foundations.

4. Russian cemetery; tombstones from the first half of the 20th century.

5. Barrow.

SQUARE 07–05

1. Pottery fragments from an area of ca 0.5 ha; amphorae, i.a., Chian and Heraclean, 4th–3rd century B.C., Bosporan, 1st–2nd century A.D. N/95/125 – 6p.

SQUARE 07–08

1. Pottery fragments from an area of ca 1 ha; mainly from the 4th–3rd century B.C., a few from the 1st–2nd century A.D., remains of walls, ash–pit. N/95/150 – 72p. See II.1.30.: the settlement of Ogon'ki – 4.

SQUARE 07–09

1. Fragment of a pipe. N/95/179p. See III.5.2.

2. Pottery fragments from an area of more than 1 ha; amphorae: Hellenistic Thasian, Sinopian, and Chersonesian; ones from the 8th–9th century. N/95/173 – 6p.

3. Pottery fragments; Hellenistic Chian amphorae. N/95/196p.

4. Earthen wall. See II.4.1.: wall.

SQUARE 07–10

1. Fragment of hand-thrown pottery, flint blade, the 2nd millenium B.C.; N/96/39p. See III.1.9.

2. Pottery fragments; Hellenistic Bosporan amphorae, the 8th–9th century.

SQUARE 08–04

1. Pottery fragments from an area of ca 3 ha; 4th–3rd century B.C., 8th–9th century; concentrations of stones. N/95/41 – 2p. See II.1.23.: the settlement of Geroevka – 3.

2. Pottery fragments from an area of nearly 0.5 ha; 1st–3rd century A.D. (including Colchian and Bosporan examples), mainly 8th–9th century. N/95/68 – 70p, 85p.

3. Pottery fragments from an area of nearly 0.5 ha; amphorae and jugs from the 8th–9th century. N/95/81p.

4. Pottery fragment; Sinopian amphora, 4th–3rd century B.C. N/95/80p.

5. Pottery fragments from an area of ca 3 ha; 4th–3rd century B.C. (including a stamp on a handle of a Heraclean amphora, see III.2.2.), 8th–9th century A.D. N/95/67p. See II.1.24.: the settlement of Geroevka – 4.

6. Barrows near the settlement of Geroevka – 3. See II.2.8.

7. Barrows near the settlement of Geroevka – 2. See II.2.7.

SQUARE 08–05

1. Pottery fragments from an area of ca 0.5 ha; amphorae: from the 4th–3rd century B.C. (including Thasian ones), 1st–2nd century A.D., and the 8th–9th century. N/95/278 – 9p. See II.1.40.: the settlement of Tobečik – 7.

SQUARE 08–08

1. Pottery fragments from an area of ca 1 ha; amphorae, i.a., Thasian and Rhodian, roof tile: 4th– 2nd century B.C.; mainly Late Mediaeval vessels, fragments of the so-called Marseilles roof tiles. N/95/142p.

SQUARE 08–09

1. Pottery fragments; Hellenistic amphorae from the Thasian circle.

2. Barrows. See II.2.10.: the kurgan necropolis of Ogon'ki.

SQUARE 08–10

1. Pottery fragments from an area of ca 2 ha; hand thrown from the 2nd millenium B.C., Hellenistic amphorae (including Thasian ones), a few from the 8th–9th century. See II.1.29.: the settlement of Ogon'ki – 3.

2. Pottery fragments from an area of nearly 1 ha (to the south of triangulation point 60.5); fragment of flint blade (see III.1.10); fragment of stone grinder; amphorae: one Lesbian fragment from the 5th century B.C., but mainly Hellenistic Heraclean, Chian, Thasian, and a few from the 1st–2nd century A.D., some pieces from the 8th–9th century. N/96/38p, 40–7p.

3. Barrow. Height 2 m. Diameter ca 50 m.

SQUARE 09–03

2. Pottery fragments; amphorae: from the 4th–3rd century B.C. (inculding Heraclean and Bosporan), but mainly from the 8th–9th century. N/95/28 – 9p, 32 – 7p.

3. Pottery fragments from an area of nearly 4 ha; Late Antique and Early Mediaeval amphorae and jugs (from excavations: pottery from the 6th–3rd century B.C. as well as from the 4th–6th and 8th–9th centuries), other artefacts; concentrations of stones N/95/21 – 7p, 145 – 9p. See II.1.22.: the settlement of Geroevka – 2.

5. Barrows. See II.2.2.: kurgan necropolis Čeljadinovo Vostočnoe.

6. Site of a shipwreck; 17th–18th century (?). See II.5.1.

SQUARE 09–04

1. Pottery fragments; amphorae and jugs from the 8th–9th century. N/95/118 – 21p.

2. Pottery fragments from an area of 200 m^2; amphorae from the 4th–3rd century B.C. (including Heraclean ones), 1st–2nd century A.D. (including south-Pontic ones), 8th–9th century; Bosporan roof tile with a fragment of a stamp. N/95/198 – 202p.

3. Pottery fragments from an area of nearly 0.5 ha; amphorae and jugs, 8th–9th century.

4. Pottery fragment; foot of Hellenistic amphora.

5. Fragment of hand thrown pottery and of a flint blade, the 2nd millenium B.C. N/97/64p. See III.1.11.

SQUARE 09–05

1. Remains of a stone weir.

2. Pottery fragments from an area of nearly 1 ha; amphorae: Chian, Chersonesian, and Thasian from the 4th–3rd century B.C., Hellenistic examples from the Thasian circle. N/95/115–7p. See II.1.39.: the settlement of Tobečik – 6.

3. Pottery fragment; belly of Hellenistic amphora, Thasian circle.

4. Pottery fragment; belly of a black-gloss bowl, the late 5th century B.C. N/95/282p.

SQUARE 09–06

1. Pottery fragments from an area of nearly 1 ha; 1st–3rd century A.D., 8th–9th century, Late Middle Ages. N/95/186–90p.

2. Pottery fragments from an area of nearly 0.5 ha; Mediaeval and Late Mediaeval.

3. Remains of foundations from limestone slabs, 6.08 m × 8.03 m.

5. Pottery fragments from an area of nearly 1 ha; 1st–3rd century A.D., 8th–9th century. See II.1.37.: the settlement of Tobečik – 4.

6. Pottery fragments from an area of ca 0.5 ha; amphorae: Thasian, Chersonesian, Cnidian, 4th–3rd century B.C. N/95/231 – 4p. See II.1.38.: the settlement of Tobečik – 5.

7. Russian cemetery from the 19th century.

SQUARE 09–07

1. Pottery fragments; amphorae from the 8th–9th century.

SQUARE 09–08

1. Three disturbed barrows. See II.2.13.: the Trechbratnye barrows.

SQUARE 09–09

1. Pottery fragments; Sinopian amphorae, 4th–3rd century B.C., Late Antiquity. N/95/140 – 1p.

SQUARE 09–10

1. Pottery fragments from an area of ca 0.5 ha; a few fragments of hand thrown pottery from the 2nd millenium B.C., Hellenistic Bosporan roof tiles, fragments of amphorae from the 1st–3rd century A.D.; stone sling missiles, concentrations of stones. N/95/134 – 5p. See II.1.28.: the settlement of Ogon'ki – 2.

2. Pottery fragments from an area of nearly 0.4 ha; amphorae from the 4th–3rd century B.C. and the 8th–9th century. See II.1.27.: the settlement of Ogon'ki – 1.

3. Pottery fragments; south-Pontic amphorae made of light-coloured clay, 1st–3rd century A.D.

SQUARE 09–11

1. Pottery fragment; belly of an amphora made of light-coloured south-Pontic clay, 1st–3rd century A.D.

SQUARE 10–03

1. Pottery fragments; two handles of Heraclean amphorae, 4th–3rd century B.C. N/95/8 – 9p.

2. Pottery fragments from an area of ca 0.3 ha; amphorae from the first half of the 4th century B.C. to the 1st–2nd century A.D. N/95/1 – 6p, 15–20p. See II.1.25.: the settlement of Geroevka – 5.

3. Pottery fragment; belly of Bosporan amphora; 1st–2nd century A.D. N/95/30p.

4. Pottery fragments from an area of more than 6 ha; from the 6th century B.C. to the 8th–9th century. See II.1.21.: the settlement of Geroevka –1.

SQUARE 10–04

1. Pottery fragments; Hellenistic Bosporan roof tile, amphorae from light-coloured clay, south-Pontic, 1st–2nd century A.D. N/95/12p.

2. Pottery fragments: Hellenistic Chian and Heraclean amphorae; ones from the 8th–9th century.

3. Pottery fragment; handle of Hellenistic Chersonesian amphora. N/95/221p.

4. Pottery fragment; belly of an amphora, 8th–9th century.

5. Pathway. See II.4.4.: pathway no. 3.

SQUARE 10–05

1. Pottery fragments from an area of 0.12 ha; bellies of amphorae, 4th–3rd century B.C. (including Thasian and Heraclean), 1st–2nd century (including Colchian), concentrations of stones. N/95/7p. See II.1.34.: the settlement of Tobečik – 1.

2. Pottery fragment; handle of a Chersonesian amphora, 4th–3rd century B.C. N/95/38p.

3. Pottery fragments from an area of more than 1 ha; bellies of amphorae from the 4th–3rd century B.C. (including Heraclean, Sinopian, and Chersonesian ones). N/95/44, 82 – 4p, 86p. See II.1.35.: the settlement of Tobečik – 2.

4. Pottery fragment; belly of a Hellenistic Chian amphora.

SQUARE 10–06

1. Pottery fragments from an area of more than 5 ha; amphorae from the second half of the 5th century to the 3rd century B.C. (including Cnidian ones), Bosporan roof tiles, pottery from the 13th–14th century, a pipe (see III.5.3.). N/95/203 – 6p. See II.1.36.: the settlement of Tobečik – 3.

2. Pottery fragments from an area of nearly 15 ha; amphorae and other vessels (including black-gloss ware) from the early 5th century B.C. to the

3rd century A.D., and from the 8th to the 9th century. Concentrations of stones. N/95/6p, 45–52p, 54–64p, 71–9p, 94–8p, 102–3p, 106p, 144p, 185p, 235–45p. See II.1.41.: the settlement of Tobečik – 8.

3. Fragment of a marble relief. N/95/311p. See III.4.3.

SQUARE 10–07

1. Pottery fragments from an area of ca 5 ha; amphorae (some with stamps: see III.2.3, 5, 6, 16) and other vessels from the 5th to the 2nd century B.C. (including Aeolian, Chian, Heraclean, Mendean, Thasian, Chersonesian, Sinopian, and Rhodian) and a few from the 1st to the 3rd century A.D., fragments of tableware (including black gloss vessels), stone balls, a spinning whorl, concentrations of stones. N/95/7 – 8p, 10 – 11p, 87 – 93p, 100 – 1p, 104p, 107p, N/97/9 – 27p, 66 – 71p, 73 – 81p, 83 – 4p, 92 – 7p, 102p. See II.1.42.: the settlement of Tobečik – 9.

3. Pottery fragments from an area of 0.3 ha; amphorae: Hellenistic (including, i.a., Thasian and Chersonesian), Late Antiquity, from the 8th–9th century. N/95/178p.

4. Pit and kurgan necropolis. See II.2.12.: the pit and kurgan necropolis of Tobečik.

SQUARE 10–10

1. Pottery fragments from an area of more than 6 ha; amphorae: from the 4th–2nd century B.C., Bosporan roof tiles, amphorae: from the 1st–4th century A.D., the 8th–9th century, and Late Mediaeval. N/95/128–30p, 136p. See II.1.27.: the settlement of Ogon'ki – 1.

2. Tartar cemetery. See II.2.10.: the kurgan necropolis of Ogon'ki.

3. Four barrows. See II.2.10.: the kurgan necropolis of Ogon'ki.

SQUARE 11–03

1. Pottery fragments from an area of 0.2 ha; Late Mediaeval; modern roof tiles. N/95/10–1p.

SQUARE 11–07

1. Pottery fragment; belly of Chersonesian amphora from the 1st–2nd century A.D. N/95/53p.

2. Pottery fragment; Chersonesian amphora from the late 4th century B.C. N/95/99p.

3. Remains of a stone structure, 8.2 m × 3.5 m; modern.

SQUARE 11–09

1. Pottery fragment; Chian amphora from the first half of the 4th century B.C. N/95/143p.

II. SITE DESCRIPTIONS

II.1. SETTLEMENTS (NOS. 1–42)

II.1.1. THE TOWN OF NYMPHAION
(SQUARE 05–02, SITE 2) [Photo A, B, 1]

The town is located on the rocky promontory of Kara-Burun (Kamyš-Burun) and today occupies an area of 9.5 ha. It was first described by P. Dubrux in the early 19th century. In the second half of the 19th century it was excavated by A. Ljucenko, N. Kondakov, and S. Verebrjusov. Systematical archaeological works were started in 1933 by the Expedition of the Hermitage Museum conducted by V. Skudnova and M. Chudjak, who is the author of the only monograph on the Ancient town (Chudjak 1962). From 1966 the excavations were directed by N. Grač, and since 1991, by O. Sokolova.

The area of the later city of Nymphaion probably was first settled by the Ionians. In the south-eastern part of the town V. Skudnova uncovered remains of dug-outs and storage pits with pottery dating to the 6th century B.C. During further excavations foundations of several houses from the first phase of settlement were discovered. On the northern slope of the promontory, in a fissure in the rock, a temple of Demeter was located. This structure was rebuilt several times. Originally, it had walls of mud brick, erected on stone foundations, and its roof was covered with tiles. In the mid-6th century B.C. it occupied an area of 10 m². In the late 6th century B.C. the temple was destroyed by fire. In the 5th century B.C. a new temple of Demeter was built, with a temenos of an area of ca 50 m² surrounded by a wall. In the mid-5th century B.C. a third temple of Demeter was constructed.

In recent years archaeological work has been concentrated on the southern slope of the hill: the so-called "temple part" of the town, where, on three terraces, a number of structures interpreted as temples have been discovered. The first altars and temple structures were erected in this part of Nymphaion at the turn of the 6th and 5th century B.C. In the Hellenistic period the temples were rebuilt and enlarged and in the south-eastern part of the excavated sector a monumental stone staircase with a step altar on the top was constructed. To the west of the altar a wall made from rusticated ashlars, preserved to a height of 2 m, and

dating to the late 4th century, was uncovered. The wall was probably part of the ancient city fortifications. To the west of the wall remains of steps joining the terraces together, have been preserved as well as buildings bearing traces of numerous reconstructions. On each of the terraces remains of altars, architectural details, and numerous fragments of statues were found. In one of the rooms a large number of plaster fragments with graffiti and drawings was uncovered. The largest drawing (1.20 m long) represents a ship with the name of "Isis" written on it. Altogether, ca 15 m² of decorated wall surface have been recovered.

In the 3rd century B.C. there was a strong earthquake which did significant damage to Nymphaion and its "temple part." In the second half of the 3rd century B.C., wine presses were constructed in the same place. In the Roman period several large storage pits were located there. The above-mentioned presses, however, were not the first ones in the town; the earliest wine press in Nymphaion was probably made in the early 4th century B.C.

In the late 3rd and early 2nd century B.C. a new defense wall was erected on the southern slope of the hill, in the above-described part of the town. The 2.5–3 m wide wall had two facings made of large, lightly worked limestone blocks. In some places these blocks were moved to a distance of 1 m away from the wall, probably by the earthquake of 63 B.C.

A large complex of structures uncovered by N. Grač, remains of streets, and alleys together with some preserved fragments of sewage system, dates to the 2nd–3rd century A.D.

The last phase of the town is dated to the first centuries of our era. To that period, i.a., foundations and floors paved with stones as well as a number of storage pits are dated.

The artefacts excavated during archaeological works conducted in the area of Nymphaion are stored in the Hermitage Museum in St Petersburg and in the Museum in Kerč.

CHUDJAK 1962; SKUDNOVA 1964; GRAČ 1989. For a complete bibliography see N. KUNINA, T. SCHOLL, O. SOKOLOVA, A. WĄSOWICZ, *The Bibliography of Nymphaion*, Archeologia 45, 1994 (1995), pp. 79–89.

II.1.2 THE SETTLEMENT OF ČURUBAŠ – 1
(02–09, SITE 1) [Fig. 1–3]

The settlement is located on a hill at the southern edge of the village of Priozernoe, near a deserted farm. In a 1 m deep pit located there the remains of stone walls can be seen. The walls of an ancient structure, made of medium-sized limestone rocks are situated immediately under the turf. The occupation layer is scarcely perceptible and has the form of a thin (up to 0.15 m deep) vein of ashy-grey soil containing few artefacts. In this layer amphora fragments dating to the 4th–3rd century B.C., a fragment of a fish-plate (N/95/226p), a fragment of black-gloss kantharos from the first half of the 3rd century B.C., and a fragment of a Bosporan roof tile were found. Pottery dating to the 8th–9th century also comes from the area of the settlement.

The site has not been excavated.

ZIN'KO, Arch. 1995, 1. 33; KARASIEWICZ-SZCZYPIORSKI 1996, p. 465.

II.1.3. THE SETTLEMENT OF ČURUBAŠ – 2
(02–08, SITE 1) [Fig. 4–6]

The settlement is located on a turf-covered elevation resembling a promontory, also near the southern edge of the village of Priozernoe. Remains of Mediaeval pottery are scattered over an area of more than 10 ha. A large number of fragments of Mediaeval vessels, some with green glaze (i.a., amphorae with round bottoms) were found. Moreover, frag-

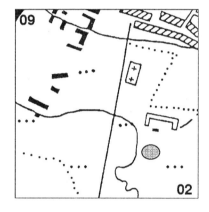

Fig. 1. Map of square 02-09 with the location of the site

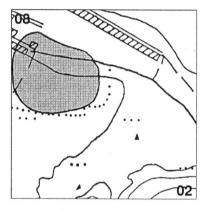

Fig. 4. Map of square 02–08 with the location of the site

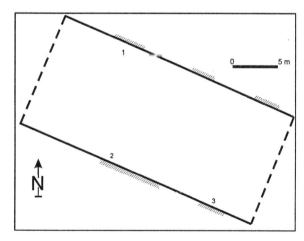

Fig. 2. Plan of site.
Place of discovery: 1 – fish-plate; 2 – rim of black-gloss kantharos; 3 – amphora fragments (by I. Ačkinazi)

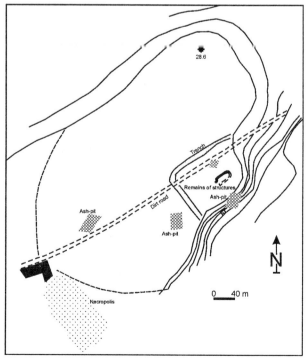

Fig. 3. Fish-plate – N/95/226p (by L. Berezovskaja)

Fig. 5. Plan of site (by I. Ačkinazi)

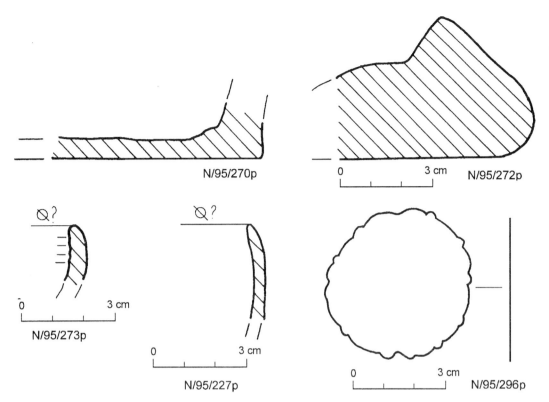

Fig. 6. Selected artefacts: N/95/270p – fragment of bowl, the 14th–16th century; N/95/272p – fragment of Bosporan tile, Hellenistic period; N/95/273p – fragment of glazed bowl, the 14th century; N/95/227p – rim fragment of kantharos, Attica, the 1st half of the 3rd century B.C.; N/95/296p – bronze appliqué plaque

ments of ancient Bosporan roof tiles (N/95/272p) and few fragments of hand thrown pottery from the 2nd millenium B.C., as well as a flint chip were also collected (see: III.1.1.). The south-eastern part of the "promontory" is separated from its remaining parts by a ca 2 m deep trench. In the thus delineated area of ca 1 ha 0.6 m thick stone foundations of a structure measuring 23 m × 11 m are visible. Also in the south-eastern part of the "promontory," on its steep slope, among ash pits the remains of a structure with foundations made from vertical limestone slabs can be seen. In that place, among pottery fragments, a bronze ornament (N/95/296p) was found. In the area of the settlement several ash-pits are visible.

This is a large, Mediaeval settlement, tentatively dated to the 9th–16th century, with traces of earlier material.

To the west the settlement is adjoined by a pit necropolis. See II.2.3.: the pit necropolis of Čurubaš.

The site has not been excavated.

The finds are stored in the Museum in Kerč.

ZIN'KO, Arch. 1995, 1.34.

II.1.4. THE SETTLEMENT OF ČURUBAŠ – 3
(02–09, SITE 3) [Fig. 7]

The site is located on a wide, flat "promontory" like the settlement of Čurubaš – 2. Part of the settle-

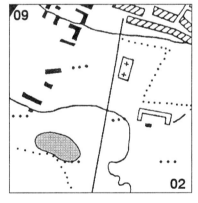

Fig. 7. Map of square 02–09 with the location of the site

ment is covered with turf and part is ploughed. Pottery fragments can be found at an area of ca 2 ha; in some places there are visible concentrations of it. Fragments of amphorae (Heraclean, Sinopian, Chian, and Thasian) and vessels of red clay dating to the 4th–3rd century B.C., as well as Bosporan and Sinopian roof tiles were collected. A few fragments of Mediaeval pottery were also found.

At the south-western limit of the settlement two barrows were discovered.

The site has not been excavated.

ZIN'KO, Arch. 1995, 1. 34.

II.1.5. THE SETTLEMENT OF ČURUBAŠ – 4
(03–09, SITE 2) [Fig. 8]

The site is located on a low bank of a pond, resembling a promontory, and occupies an area of more than 1 ha. Part of the site is ploughed. Among

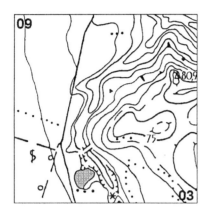

Fig. 8. Map of square 03–09 with the location of the site

small stones fragments of Chian and Thasian amphorae dating to the 4th–3rd century B.C., fragments of amphorae from the first centuries A.D., numerous fragments of early Mediaeval pottery were found, as well as a flint blade, a fragment of a polished battle-axe made of crystalline rock and few fragments of hand thrown pottery from the 2nd millenium B.C..

The site has not been excavated.

ZIN'KO, Arch. 1995, 1. 34.

II.1.6. THE SETTLEMENT OF ČURUBAŠ – 5
(03–09, SITE 1) [Fig. 9–10]

The site is located on a low bank of a small lake, gradually rising to the north. In a ploughed field, at an area of ca 0.5 ha, a large number of small fragments of hand thrown pottery was found (N/95/250p). Flint blades, a fragment of a basalt

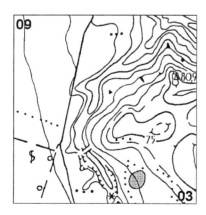

Fig. 9. Map of square 03–09 with the location of the site

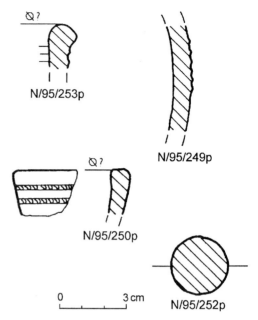

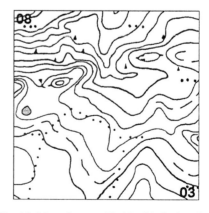

Fig. 10. Selected pottery fragments: N/95/253p – rim fragment of a vessel, the 11th century; N/95/249p – belly fragment of a vessel with grooved decoration; N/95/250p – rim fragment of vessel, Bronze Age; N/95/252p – fragment of handle, the 4th century B.C.

hammer, and a fragment of a flint fabricator (see III.1.2–5.) were collected. These finds can be dated to the 2nd millenium B.C.

The northern part of the site is covered with turf in which a few amphora fragments, dating to the 4th–3rd century B.C. (N/95/252p) and 8th–9th century (N/95/249p), were found.

The site has not been excavated.

ZIN'KO, Arch. 1995, 1. 34.

II.1.7. THE SETTLEMENT OF ČURUBAŠ – 6
(03–08, SITE 3) [Fig. 11]

The site is located at the highest point of the Čurubaš Skal'ki range, 0.25 km to the south-east of triangulation marker 80.9. From a flat, 30 m × 20 m, area,

Fig. 11. Map of square 03–08 with the location of the site

among rocky projections, few fragments of amphorae dating to the first centuries A.D. were collected. The whole area of the settlement is covered with turf.

The site has not been excavated.

ZIN'KO, Arch. 1995, 1. 35.

II.1.8. THE SETTLEMENT OF ČURUBAŠ – 7
(03–08, SITE 1) [Fig. 12]

The site is located at the western edge of a valley surrounded by rocky outcrops, overlooking a small ravine. The area of the settlement is covered with steppe grasses. At an area of 80 m × 20 m frag-

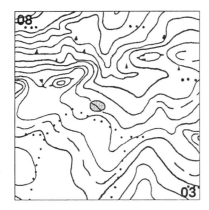

Fig. 12. Map of square 03–08 with the location
of the site

ments of Mediaeval pottery were found, i.a., ones with green and light brown glaze, dating to the 12th–16th century.

The site has not been excavated.

ZIN'KO, Arch. 1995, 1. 35.

II.1.9. THE SETTLEMENT OF CURUBAŠ – 8
(03–07, SITE 3) [Photo 2, Fig. 13]

The site is located at a northern slope of the rocky range of Čurubaš Skal'ki, on a southern bank of a brook. A ravine between natural outcrops of lime-

stone is partitioned by the remains of a wall visible along ca 60 m. A large part of the wall is covered with turf, but in some places large, lightly worked stones are visible. At the bottom of the ravine, in the central part of the wall, the remains of a rectangular tower (ca 6 m × 4 m), built of vertical limestone blocks, can be seen. The tower, with the walls ca 1 m thick, has a north-south orientation. The western part of the structure is well preserved.

Amphora fragments dating to the 4th–3rd century B.C. have been collected.

The site has not been excavated.

ZIN'KO, Arch. 1995, 1. 35; Zin'ko 1996, p. 32.

II.1.10. THE SETTLEMENT OF ČURUBAŠ – 9
(03–07, SITE 2) [Fig. 14–15]

The site is located in the Čurubaš Skal'ki range. It was discovered by V. Gajdukevič in 1938. In 1963, I. Kruglikowa opened 5 trenches, each covering 25 m². At the area of the settlement several elevations with limestone outcrops, overgrown with steppe grasses, are visible. On a flat top of one of them, with an area of nearly 800 m², I. Kruglikowa studied the structures and distinguished three construction phases. The earliest one, dating to the 3rd–2nd century B.C., was preserved only in depressions, where the rock is under the soil. In these places fragments of Bosporan tiles (both pan and ridge), amphorae, wheel thrown vessels, both ordinary and black-gloss ones, as well as hand thrown pottery were found. At the southern edge of the elevation, remains of stone walls dating to the 1st century B.C. – 2nd century A.D. were discovered. The walls were made of small limestone rocks bound with clay; larger stones were found only in the foundation layer. A fragment of a paved yard made of limestone slabs was preserved; also fragments of terra sigillata bowls from the 1st–2nd century A.D., and of Bosporan roof tiles were found.

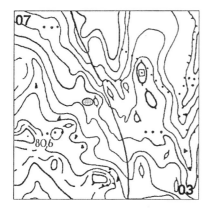

Fig. 13. Map of square 03–07 with the location
of the site

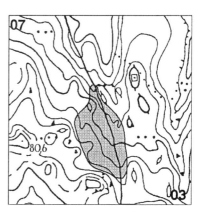

Fig. 14. Map of square 03–07 with the location
of the site

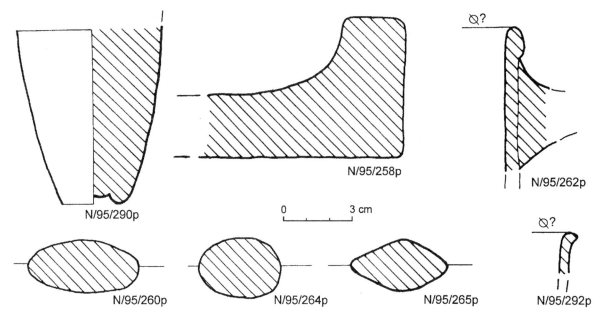

Fig. 15. Selected artefacts: N/95/290p – foot of Chian amphora, the 1st half of the 4th century B.C.; N/95/265p – amphora handle, south Pont, the first centuries A.D.; N/95/292p – rim of black-gloss bowl, the 4th/3rd century B.C.; N/95/262p – rim fragment of Chian amphora, the 4th century B.C.; N/95/258p – fragment of Bosporan roof tile, Hellenistic period; N/95/260p – handle of Colchian amphora, Hellenistic period; N/95/264p – fragment of amphora handle, Hellenistic period

In the area of the settlement, I. Kruglikowa recorded the remains of several free-standing structures, which had separate plots of land. Drawings of two such plots were made (see II.3.1.: the plots near the settlement of Čurubaš – 9).

The earliest material obtained during the field survey from 1995 is represented by fragments of Chian amphorae from the first half of the 4th century B.C. The ceramic material is scattered over an area of more than 10 ha, and especially along a dirt road, and dates to the period from the 4th century B.C. to the first centuries A.D. Moreover, a few fragments of amphorae dating to the 8th–9th century were found.

GAJDUKEVIČ 1940, p. 317; KRUGLIKOVA 1975, pp. 130–131, 269, no. 174; ZIN'KO, Arch. 1995, 1. 35–36.

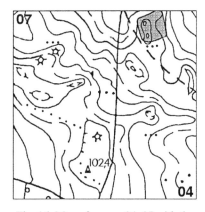

Fig. 16. Map of square 04–07 with the location of the site

II.1.11. THE SETTLEMENT OF ČURUBAŠ CITADEL' (04–07, SITE 3) [Photo 3, Fig. 16–19]

The site is located on tall, rocky elevations in the Čurubaš Skal'ki range. The settlement had a square plan with 200 m long sides. In its north-western cor-

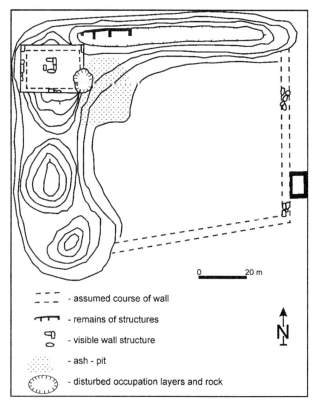

- - - - assumed course of wall

⊤⊤⊤ - remains of structures

- visible wall structure

.... - ash - pit

- disturbed occupation layers and rock

Fig. 17. Plan of site (by V. Zin'ko)

ner, at the top of the elevation, the remains of a rectangular structure (35 m × 25 m) and of a square tower adjoining it to the west can be seen. The foundations were built from large limestone blocks. To the southeast of the fortifications there is a large ash-pit. In the northern part, on an elongated limestone outcrop, the remains of several smaller structures have been recorded. The rock makes up their northern wall. To the east and south, in the lower part of the settlement, there are walls. Near the eastern wall there is a rectangular structure. In the lower part of the settlement few pottery fragments were found. In the upper part, especially from the ash-pit area, a large number of amphorae fragments, vessels of red clay, and terra sigillata, dating to the 1st–2rd century A.D., were collected.

I. Kruglikova has included this site within the settlement of Čurubaš. 100 m to the south of the site, a plot enclosure is visible (see II.3.2.: plots near the settlement of Čurubaš Citadel').

KRUGLIKOVA 1975, p. 268, no. 174; ZIN'KO, Arch. 1995, 1. 36; Zin'ko 1996, p. 13.

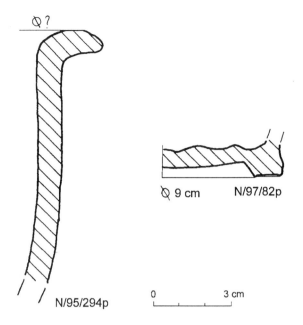

Fig. 18. Selected pottery fragments: N/95/294p – rim fragment of mortarium, the 1st–2nd century A.D.; N/97/82p – bottom fragment of a jug (by L. Berezovskaja)

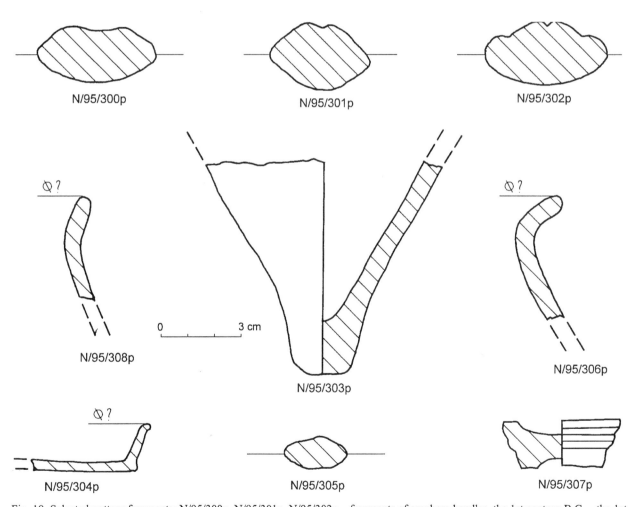

Fig. 19. Selected pottery fragments: N/95/300p, N/95/301p, N/95/302p – fragments of amphora handles, the 1st century B.C. – the 1st century A.D; N/95/303p – foot fragment of amphora, the 1st century B.C. – the 1st century A.D.; N/95/308p, N/95/306p – rim fragments of hand thrown vessels, fragments of terra sigillata vessels, the 1st century A.D.; N/95/305p – handle of a cup, N/95/304p – rim of bowl; N/95/307p – foot of black-gloss kantharos, the 4th century B.C., secondarily used as a saucer or miniature vessel (by L. Berezovskaja)

II.1.12. THE SETTLEMENT OF ČURUBAŠ JUŽNOE
(JUŽNO ČURUBAŠSKOE) (04–06, SITE 2) [Fig. 20–23]

The site is located on a small elevation resembling a promontory, with a north-south orientation, located on the south-eastern slope of the Glubokaja ravine. The occupation layer is visible at an area of 5 ha. The eastern part of the settlement is ploughed up and the rest is covered with steppe vegetation. The settlement was discovered in 1938 by V. Gajdukevič and re-recorded in 1960 by I. Kruglikova, who excavated it in 1963–1964.

In the central trench (III) which has an area of 428 m², remains of standing structures dating from the late 6th to the 3rd century B.C. were uncovered. The unearthed artefacts included painted black-gloss vessels and fragments of Lesbian and Rhodian amphorae. Three structures dating to the 5th–4th century

B.C. were preserved. House No. 2, dating to the late 5th century, consisted of two rooms with an area of 29 m² and 36 m² respectively. The entrance, in the form of a 1.6 m long corridor formed by two small walls projecting in antis was located in the western part of the structure. The whole width (1.3 m) of the corridor floor was covered by a stone threshold. The door to the other, larger room was also located in the western side, opposite the main entrance.

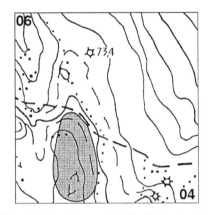

Fig. 20. Map of square 04–06 with the location
of the site

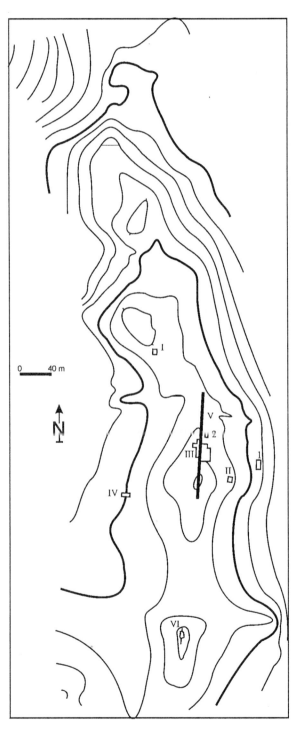

Fig. 22. Topographic plan of the site with trenches: I–VI – excavated by I. Kruglikova, 1963–1964, 1–2 – trial pits from 1994
(plan after Kruglikova 1975, fig. 3)

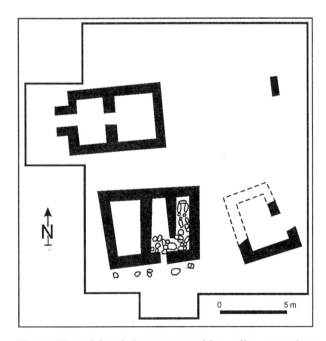

Fig. 21. Plan of foundations uncovered by earlier excavations
(after Kruglikova 1975, fig. 14)

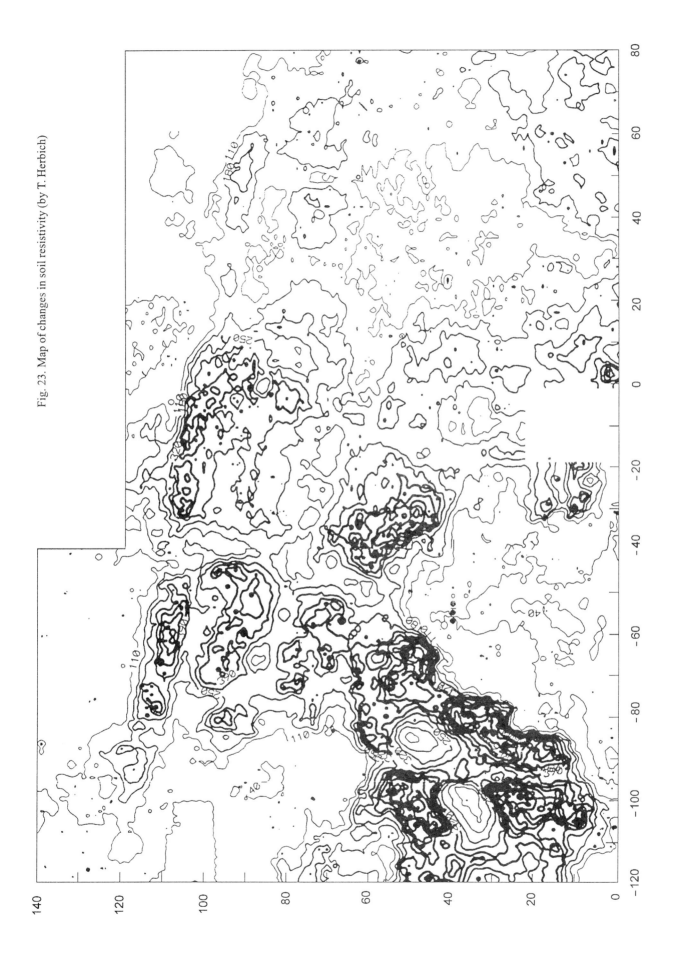

Fig. 23. Map of changes in soil resistivity (by T. Herbich)

32

The building was probably thatched. In the 4th century B.C., 2.80 m to the south of House No. 2, House No. 1 was erected. It also had two rooms with an area of 16 m² and 13 m². The floors were partly covered with paving and the roof was made of tiles. To the south of House No. 2 there was a paved yard. Between the southern wall of the building and the yard flat stones were uncovered, which probably served as foundations for posts. To the east of House No. 1, parts of the foundations of a wall of a farm building, made of stone chips bound with clay, were found.

This complex of buildings was adjoined by an enclosed plot of an area of more than 1 ha (see II.3.3.: plots near the settlement of Čurubaš Južnoe). In the discussed area several such "country house" complexes have been discovered.

Among the pottery remains found at this site there were fragments of amphorae (Chian, Thasian, Heraclean, Sinopian, Bosporan, Coan with peculiar ringed foot, etc.), black and red figure vessels, black-gloss wares, vessels made of red and of grey clay, and few fragments of fish-plates. Moreover, parts of terracotta statuettes representing a sitting goddess have been collected.

In 1994, in the western part of the settlement, geophysical prospecting was carried out over an area of 2.5 ha. A pattern of resistivity with a high amplitude (from 20 to 1 000 ohm) was obtained. The map (Fig. 23) presents several areas with increased resistivity exceeding 200 ohm, with irregular shapes and dimensions no smaller than 20 m x 20 m. In the central part these areas are separated by zones of lower resistivity, in the northern part, they form complexes. In the southern part the subsoil has lower values of resistivity. In the eastern part the high resistivity area ends sharply along a line slightly oblique to the eastern limit of the survey. The interpretation of the geophysical survey suggested that the central part of the investigated area was the most interesting. Two trial trenches were made (excavations were supervised by S. Solov'ev and V. Zin'ko). The trenches covered areas of both higher and lower resistivity. It turned out that the highest anomalies are connected with limestone outcrops, which can often be found at a depth of 0.5–0.8 m.

Lower resistivities reflected the lowered bed-rock floor, and thus a greater thickness of material with lower resistivity – the soil. The rock floor could have been lowered either by a change in the natural conditions or by human activity.

Trial trench 1 (5 m × 10 m) was located to the east of I. Kruglikova's Trench III and had a north-south orientation. It revealed the following stratigraphy: at the top there was a 0.3 m thick layer of topsoil containing ash and a few pottery fragments

dating to the first half of the 4th century B.C. Below it there was a 0.4 m thick layer of grey clay with considerable inclusions of ash, dried clay, small stones, pottery fragments, and animal bones. This layer rested on bedrock. In the south-western part a 0.45 m wide cutting in the rock for the foundations of an overground structure was uncovered. The structure had a south-east – north-west orientation. To the south of the structure there were remains of a mud brick wall. In the north-eastern corner of trial trench 1, a 0.88 m deep, 2.0 m long, and 1.0 m wide pit cut in the rock, which is considered to be a dug-out, was unearthed. The pit was filled with soil mixed with ash, fragments of mud bricks, and few pottery fragments dating mainly to the second half of the 5th century B.C. The potsherds included fragments of swollen neck Chian, Lesbian, and proto-Thasian amphorae, as well as black-gloss and hand thrown vessels.

Trial trench 2 (4 m × 4 m) was located to the north of Trench III and had a southward orientation. The 0.6 m thick occupation layer rested on bedrock. On the surface of the rock a cutting with the remains of a dilapidated wall preserved to a height of 1 row of stones could be seen. The wall was probably a field enclosure. The pottery material from this trench is dated to the period between the late 5th and the 1st half of the 4th century B.C. It consisted mainly of fragments of Chian, Heraclean, and other amphorae, and vessels of red clay.

GAJDUKEVIČ 1940, p. 317; KRUGLIKOVA 1975, pp. 28, 46–49, 92–93, 269, no. 173; Nymphaion, Arch. 1994, pp. 3–4, 6, 17, fig. 2; ZIN'KO, Arch. 1994, pp. 19–24; KARASIEWICZ-SZCZYPIORSKI 1995, pp. 546, 548; ZIN'KO 1996, pp. 18–19; ZIN'KO 1997d.

II.1.13. THE SETTLEMENT OF ČURUBAŠ MAJAK – 1 (04–11, SITE 4) [Fig. 24]

The site is located on the eastern slope of a flat, broad depression, interpreted as one of the pathways

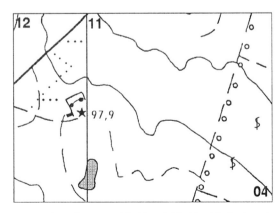

Fig. 24. Map of squares 04–11 and 04–12 with the location of the site

(see II.4.5.: pathway no. 4), to the south-east of the lighthouse of Curubaš. Today the whole area is ploughed intensively. The occupation layer is hardly visible, and pottery fragments are scattered over an area of ca 1 ha. In the southern part traces of stone constructions making up the border of a settlement composed of at least five elevations can be seen. In the pottery material fragments of Bosporan tiles (both pan and ridge) predominate. Moreover, few belly fragments of Heraclean, Bosporan, Rhodian, and Sinopian amphorae dating to the 4th century B.C. and the Hellenistic period, as well as a few bones, were found.

The site has not been excavated.

II.1.14. THE SETTLEMENT OF ČURUBAŠ MAJAK – 2
(04–12, SITE 1) [Fig. 25–26]

The site is located at the edge of a ploughed field to the south west and west of the Čurubaš lighthouse. The western part is covered with turf and

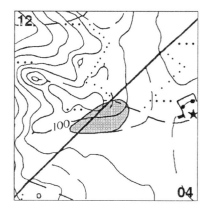

Fig. 25. Map of square 04–12 with the location of the site

adjoins a large hill (triangulation marker: 101.6) with visible rock outcrops. At an area of ca 3 ha, the remains of six structures, in the form of low elevations with the diameter of ca 50 m, with a large number of stones and pottery fragments, have been

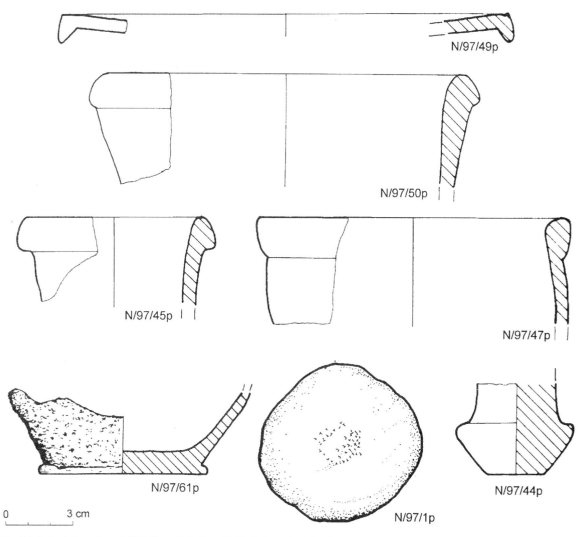

Fig. 26. Selected artefacts: N/97/49p – fish plate, Hellenistic period; rim fragments of amphorae: N/97/50p – unidentified centre, the first centuries A.D.; N/97/45p – Thasian, the 4th–3rd century B.C.; N/97/47p – Chian, the 4th–3rd century B.C.; N/97/61p – fragment of hand thrown vessel; N/97/1p – sling missile; N/97/44p – foot of Thasian amphora, the 4th–3rd century B.C.

recorded. The pottery is represented mainly by fragments of amhporae (Heraclean, Sinopian, Mendean, Chian, and other ones), black-gloss wares, vessels made of red clay, and fragments of Bosporan and Sinopian tiles. Moreover, seven Sinopian stamps have been found (see III.2.8–9, 11, 13–16). The pottery is dated mainly to the 4th–3rd century B.C., but Hellenistic sherds and ones from the 1st–3rd century A.D. were unearthed as well. The finds also include a stone ball. The ancient pottery collected from the northernmost structure consisted of fragments of Saltovo-Majak type amphorae and vessels, dating to the 8th–9th century. The scatter of the Mediaeval pottery extends up to 100 m to the north and ends sharply to the west of the lighthouse, at the edge of a marshy hollow with a north-south orientation. This pottery was also spotted to the south of the large hill with rock outcrops.

In a washed out pathway heading southwards, pottery is visible for a length of 100 m. In an area of wasteland between the pathway and the main dirt road going north-south, forms resembling corners of stone foundations were recorded, as well as loose stones of various sizes.

The site has not been excavated.

II.1.15. THE SETTLEMENT OF ČURUBAŠ MAJAK – 3 (04–12, SITE 2) [Photo C, Fig. 27]

The site is located on the top of a hill with a triangulation marker 112.3 as well as on its north-west slope ending in a high plateau. To the west and south traces of cuttings in the rock, which may be the remains of fortifications, can be seen. To the north the hill is delimited by a deep valley; to the west it slopes down sharply towards a flat plain. Pottery is visible only in animal burrows and pits. It includes few and very small fragments dating to the 1st–3rd century A.D.

The site has not been excavated.

II.1.16. THE SETTLEMENT OF ČURUBAŠ NIŽNOE – 1 (NIŽNE ČURUBAŠSKOE –1) (04–04, SITE 2) [Fig. 28]

The site is located on the low southern slope of Lake Čurubaš. In 1989, in a ploughed field, V. Zin'ko and N. Fedoseev recorded a small, square elevation (25 m × 25 m) with a few potsherds

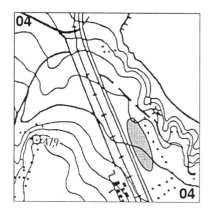

Fig. 28. Map of square 04–04 with the location of the site

dating to the first centuries A.D. and fragments of Bosporan tiles. In 1995, over an area of nearly 2 ha a large number amphora fragments were found, dating to the 4th–3rd century B.C., 1st–2nd century A.D., and numerous fragments of pottery dating to the 8th–9th century.

The site has not been excavated.

II.1.17. THE SETTLEMENT OF ČURUBAŠ NIŽNOE – 2 (NIŽNE CURUBAŠSKOE – 2) (04–04, SITE 1) [Photo 5, Fig. 29–31]

The site is located close to a small ravine near the Kerč – Èl'tigen asphalt road and is probably connected with the pipeline (see II.4.10.). During the field survey of 1995, only a few fragments of Chian amphorae dating to the 4th century B.C. were found at this site.

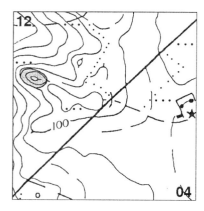

Fig. 27. Map of square 04–12 with the location of the site

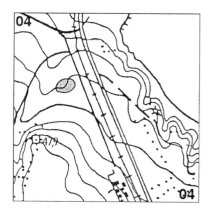

Fig. 29. Map of square 04–04 with the location of the site

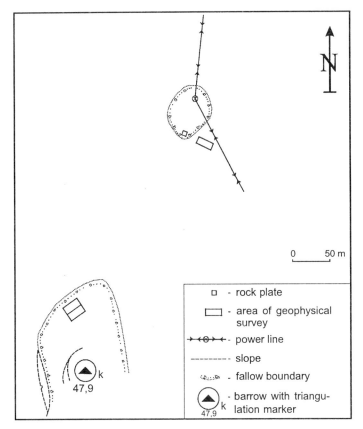

Fig. 30. Plan of site with marked area of geophysical survey
(by T. Nowicki)

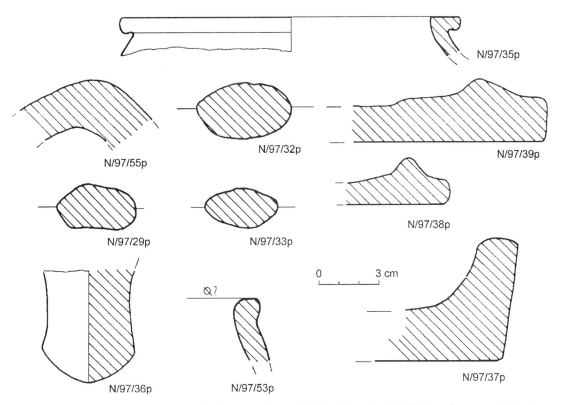

Fig. 31. Selected pottery fragments: N/97/35p – rim fragment of vessel, Hellenistic period; N/97/55p – fragment of Sinopian roof tile; N/97/32p – handle fragment of Heraclean amphora, the 4th–3rd century B.C.; N/97/39p – fragment of Bosporan roof tile; N/97/29p – handle fragment of Sinopian amphora, the 4th–3rd century B.C; N/97/33p – handle fragment of Sinopian amphora, the 1st–2nd century A.D.; N/97/37p – fragment of Bosporan roof tile, Hellenistic period; N/97/53p – rim fragment of Heraclean amphora, the 4th century B.C.; N/97/36p – foot of Sinopian amphora, 4th–3rd century B.C.; N/97/38p – fragment of Bosporan roof tile

During the survey of 1997 it was found that the area had been ploughed up. Over an area of 80 m × 100 m numerous potsherds were collected. They mainly included amphora fragments dating to the 4th–3rd century B.C. (Chian, Thasian, Sinopian, and Heraclean), numerous fragments of Bosporan and Sinopian roof tiles, a fragment of a terra sigillata jug from the late 2nd – early 1st century B.C., and a fragment of a terracotta figurine. Few fragments from the first centuries A.D. have also been recorded. In the field limestone rubble can also be seen, particularly in the northeastern part. In the centre of the settlement stands a steel electricity pylon on a concrete base. In its vicinity, in an unploughed part of the field, several large, worked limestone slabs have been recorded.

The concentration of power lines made geophysical survey impossible in this area.

II.1.18. THE SETTLEMENT OF ÈL'TIGEN JUGO-ZAPADNOE (05–03, SITE 12) [Fig. 32–34]

The site is located at the area of the necropolis of Nymphaion, on a gentle slope of an elevated plateau, to the west and south-west of the modern settlement of Èl'tigen.

Concentrations of Mediaeval pottery were noticed in this area in 1956 by I. Kruglikova. In 1963, A. Gadlo carried out excavations at this site, which he called "Geroevskoe selišče". He also noticed that the remains of an early Mediaeval settlement could be seen over an area of ca 160 ha. Traces of the settlement extended along more than 3.5 km running from north to south along the shore of the Strait. The northern part, ca 1500 m × 800 m in area, was located on a slope of the plateau. The southern part extended along the shore, forming a rather narrow (ca 200 m wide) zone. According to A. Gadlo, the settlement can be dated to the period between the late 7th to the turn of the 9th and 10th centuries, although its density of population decreased a century earlier.

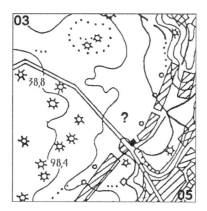

Fig. 32. Map of square 05–03 with the location of the site

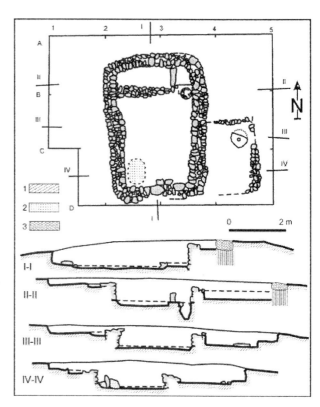

Fig. 33. Plan of trench III and sections of the uncovered structure: 1 – topsoil, 2 – bedrock, 3 – burnt clay (after Gadlo 1968, fig. 20)

In 1963, A. Gadlo sank three trenches on the plateau. In trench I (at the south-west edge of the northern part) stone remains of a rectangular standing structure, divided into two rooms when in use, were uncovered. The internal dimensions of the structure are 7 m × 4.5 m.

In trench III located in the central part of the settlement, a rectangular (3.93 m × 2.52 m) semi-dug-out with rounded corners was uncovered. The bottom of the semi-dug-out was 1.1–0.63 m below the modern ground level. Two periods of use have been distinguished: in the first one the walls of the dug-out were made of earth, then the room was extended and the walls lined with one row of small stones to the height of the then occupation level. Above it walls consisting of two rows of stones with a filling between them were erected.

In trench II–IV, A. Gadlo distinguished 3 construction periods. The first one was represented by a rectangular (4.8 m × 3.1 m) dug-out with rounded corners, dug into the bedrock to the depth of 0.7–0.8 m. The walls and the floor were covered with a layer of clay, darkened with soot in places. The entrance was in the southern wall and consisted of 1 m wide earthen steps. In the north-western corner there was a stone hearth (1.4 m × 0.9 m), raised 0.5 m above the floor level. In the central part of the hearth a post was located, supporting a thick, flat

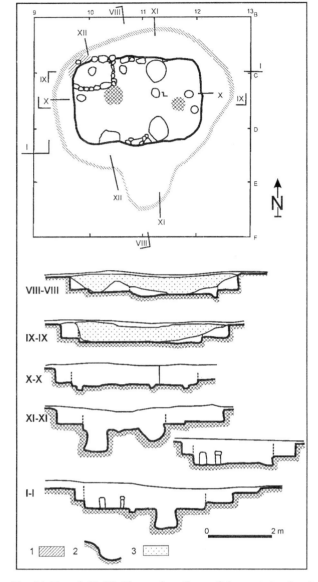

Fig. 34. Trench II–IV. Plan and sections of dug-out: 1 – level of preserved Ancient layer, 2 – burnt clay, 3 – ash pit (after Gadlo 1968, fig. 21)

0.5 m. Its northern and southern walls were lined with stones. In the centre of the floor there was a stone which served as the base for the main post supporting the roof. In the north-western corner there was a hearth.

It should be added that remains of early Mediaeval dwelling-houses were found during excavations carried out at the pit necropolis of Nymphaion by N. Grač, A. Avetikov, and S. Solov'ev.

During the field survey of 1995–1997, over the whole area more than 120 concentrations of pottery were recorded, dating to the 8th–9th century, mixed up with limestone rubble. This has allowed us to draw a hypothetical map of the extent of Mediaeval settlement along the Kerč Strait (see map III).

KRUGLIKOVA, Arch. 1956b, p. 7; GADLO 1968; GRAČ 1989, p. 65; Nymphaion, Arch. 1995, p. 4.

II.1.19. THE SETTLEMENT OF ÈL'TIGEN MUZEJ (06–03, SITE 2) [Fig. 35–36]

The site is located on a low (up to 1.5 m) bluff along the sea shore. Part of the settlement has been destroyed by the sea. The preserved part is covered with sand and overgrown with bushes and grass. In the northern part there is a small elevation. An occupation level is visible for more than 100 m, abruptly ending in the sea. At the depth of 0.9–1.1 m it consists of a 0.3 m thick, grey, clayey occupation level containing fragments of amphorae dating to the 3rd–2nd century B.C. including one with a Rhodian stamp from the early 2nd century B.C. In many places remains of walls constructed from medium-sized limestone rocks can be seen. Above it there is a 0.35 m thick layer of sand and sandy silt, devoid of artefacts. Above that, stretching up to the level of the turf, a 0.2 m thick ashy-clayey layer is visible. It contains fragments of amphorae and other vessels dating to the 1st–2nd century A.D.

fire-clay brick slab, which had a round opening – a smoke hole – in its eastern part. The dug-out had a gable roof. On the floor, i.a., decorated vessels of the Saltovo-Majak type were found. Near the northern wall of the dug-out there was a 0.7 m deep storage pit for grain. In the second and third period of utilization the dug-out served as a rubbish dump.

The second period of the trench currently under discussion is represented by two surface structures, which once co-existed with the dug-out, and survived after the dug-out was abandoned. Their remains were dismantled during the construction of the structures belonging to the third period of occupation.

The third period is represented by three structures. Two of them were overground one-room dwelling-houses, and the third one was a 5.1 m × 3.2 m semi-dug-out, dug into the ground to a depth of

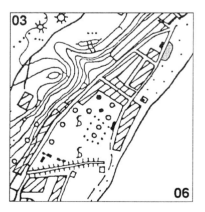

Fig. 35. Map of square 06–03 with the location of the site

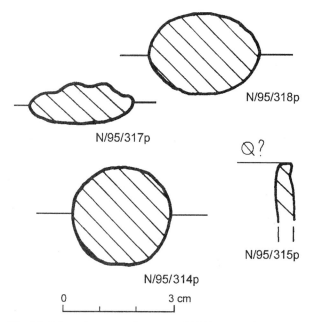

Fig. 36. Selected pottery fragments: N/95/318p – fragment of amphora handle, unidentified centre from the turn of the eras; N/95/317p – fragment of jug handle, 1st century B.C.; N/95/314p – handle fragment of pseudo-Coan amphora, Roman period; N/95/315p – rim fragment of cup, Roman period

(see II.4.2.). On its other side there is a small gully with a north-south orientation. These natural conditions limited the dimensions of the settlement (50 m × 80 m). At the northern edge of the elevation there is an ash-pit. In 1992, V. Zin'ko collected the following pottery material in a field survey: feet of Heraclean and Chian amphorae, small fragments of black-gloss vessels, fragments of Bosporan roof tiles. The material is dated to the 4th–3rd century B.C. Over the whole area of the elevation numerous concentrations of stones of various sizes, sometimes bearing traces of working, can be seen. Today the site as well as the whole surrounding area is divided into allotments.

During the survey of 1995, besides pottery from the 4th–3rd century B.C., fragments of amphorae dating to the 1st–2nd century A.D. were found.

In 1997 a 30 m × 70 m large part of the area (Fig. 38) was subjected to geophysical survey by means of resistivity profiling with a twin-probe array; the distance between probes being: AM = 1 m and BN = 5 m. This allowed us to follow the resistivity changes in layers up to ca 1 m deep. The

In 1993 an attempt was made to conduct a resistivity survey in this area. Due to the type of soil – strongly salinated sand – the results can not be considered reliable.

The site has not been excavated.

II.1.20. THE SETTLEMENT OF ÈL'TIGEN ZAPADNOE (05–03, SITE 7) [Photo F, 6, Fig. 37–44]

The site is located within the territory of the pit and kurgan necropolis of Nymphaion, on a small elevation. The elevation is delimited on one side by an elongated ravine with an east-west orientation, along which an ancient pathway used to run

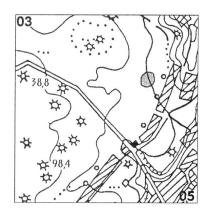

Fig. 37. Map of square 05–03 with the location of the site

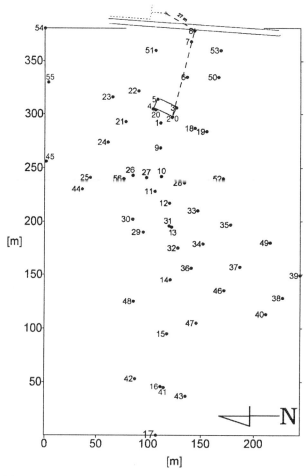

Fig. 38. Location of measurement points on pathways 1 and 2, and the settlement Èl'tigen Zapadnoe with marked place of geophysical survey (by T. Nowicki)

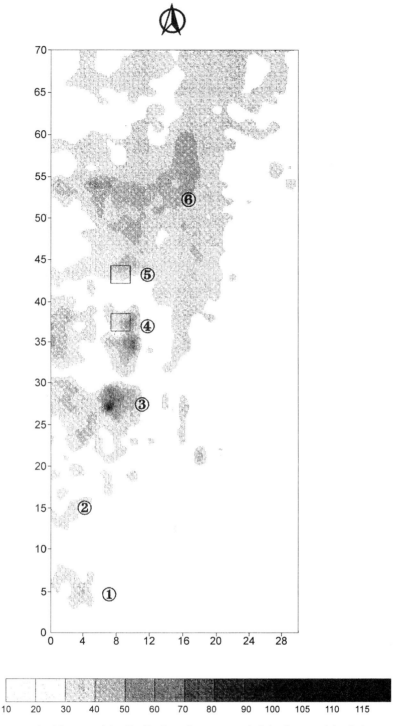

Fig. 39. Map of the distribution of apparent resistivity (by K. Misiewicz)

survey was based on a 1 m × 1 m grid. The results of the survey were presented on coloured printouts of isolines representing points of equal resistivity (Photo F) and a three dimensional model of resistivity changes (Fig. 40). The resulting picture does not differ much from that obtained for the site Tobečik – 9. The resistivity in both places ranged between 10 and 100 ohm. It was possible to distinguish zones of disturbance of the natural arrangement of strata most probably caused by man-made structures. In Photo F, the edges of these zones are marked in yellow. They are located mainly in the western part of the investigated area. Within these zones, places where archaeological remains in the form of walls or their foundations have been preserved are indicated. They cause narrow, linear anomalies in resistivity distribution, forming closed structures, as can be seen in Figure 39, Photo F.

Six main groups of anomalies caused by the structures have been distinguished. Anomaly 1 and 2

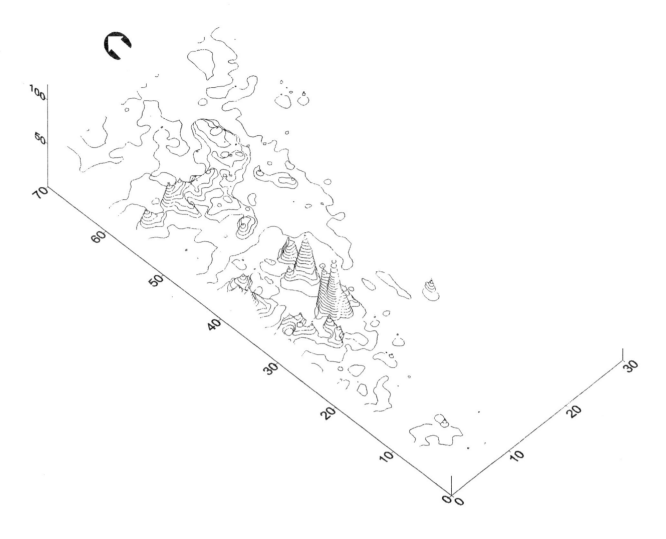

Fig. 40. 3–D model of the changes of resistivity (by K. Misiewicz)

are small increases in resistivity, creating regular, narrow, linear anomalies. They may be caused by single wall foundations probably located at a depth of more than 1 m. The registered picture of resistivity distribution results from disturbances in water transpiration in places where archaeological remains are located. One needs to interpret the results gathered in large zones in areas 3, 4, and 5, slightly differently. These zones embrace an area of 10 m × 15 m and it seems that here we may be dealing with remains of structures located in a layer of rubble. This is proved by linear anomalies which enclose this zone from the south, east, and west. It is not clear whether this zone continues to the north, joining anomaly complexes 5 and 6 or if the disturbances are caused by one or two structures. It can not be clearly stated either, whether an oblong anomaly, which forms the boundary of an area of increased resistivity to the east is caused by the foundations of one or two different walls. It may be, however, supposed that the extension of the anomaly on its southern edge is characteristic for an image obtained from the remains of corners of buildings[1].

A more complex image of resistivity distribution was obtained in zone 6 of increased resistivity. The disturbances appear here over an area of 25 m × 25 m and, as it can be seen in the model of resistivity changes distribution, they form two separate, parallel, linear anomalies at metres E8 and E16. Between them there is a vertical anomaly, running slightly obliquely between metres N50–N60. Such an arrangement of narrow zones of increased resistivity may indicate that we may also be dealing with the remains of a complex of structures in this area.

At the site Èltigen Zapadnoe it was impossible to apply resistivity probing to establish the probable depth of the discovered remains. The site is located

---

[1] T. HERBICH, K. MISIEWICZ, O. TESCHAUER, *Multilevel resistivity prospecting of architectural remains: the Schwarzach Case Study*, in: Archaeological Prospection, 1997, 4, pp. 105–112.

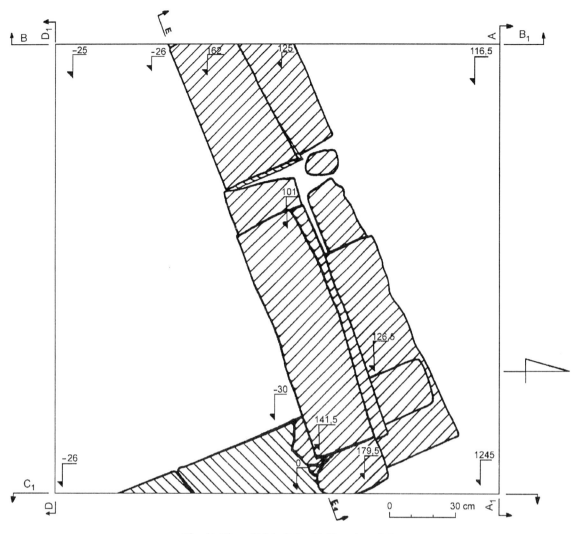

Fig. 41. Plan of trial pit (by M. Nowakowska)

at the top and along the slope of a hill and the gradients running in all directions influence the readings of the values of resistivity. They require complex calculations to obtain the actual depth of the current penetration. Therefore it was decided to obtain data about the actual depth of the archaeological structures by digging a trial trench in the place where the clearest anomalies in resistivity distribution were located. The 2 m × 2 m trench was located at the borderline of zones 3 and 4 – metres E8 – 10, N32–34. As a result a fragment of a corner of a monumental structure was uncovered. The uncovered wall was made from limestone ashlars. One upper block has been preserved suggesting the existence of a vault. Among the recovered archaeological material a stamp on the neck of a Chian amphora of the 5th century is particularly worthy of mention (see III.2.7.).

Nymphaion, Arch. 1994, pp. 7, 19, fig. 6; ZIN'KO, Arch. 1994, 1. 19; KARASIEWICZ-SZCZYPIORSKI 1995, p. 546; Nymphaion, Arch. 1997, pp. 4, 17.

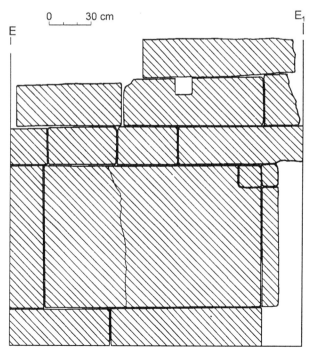

Fig. 42. Southern face of wall (by M. Nowakowska)

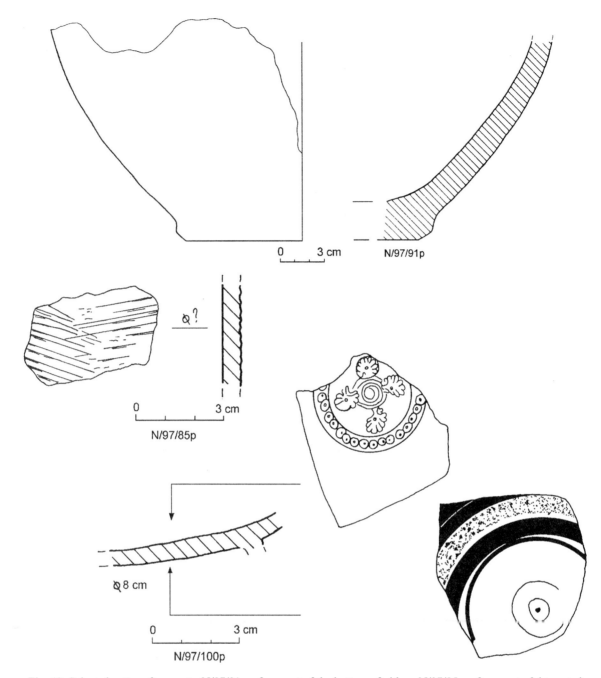

Fig. 43. Selected pottery fragments: N/97/91p – fragment of the bottom of pithos; N/97/85p – fragment of decorated belly of a Saltovo-Majak vessel, the 8th–9th century A.D.; N/97/100p – bottom fragment of kantharos, Attica?, the 6th/5th century B.C.

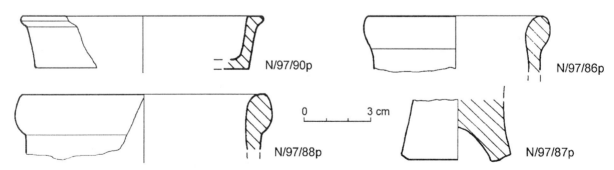

Fig. 44. Selected pottery fragments: N/97/90p – rim fragment of kantharos, Attica ?; N/97/86p – N/97/88p – rim fragments of amphora, unidentified centre; N/97/87p – foot fragment of Heraclean amphora

II.1.21. THE SETTLEMENT OF GEROEVKA – 1
(10–03, SITE 4) [Photo 7, Fig. 45–46]

The site is located on a high, abraded shore of the Strait. It extends from the north to the south for a length of ca 1 km; the occupation level constitutes a ca 60 m wide zone. Excavations have revealed that the eastern part of the settlement has been destroyed by the sea, although it can not be stated to what extent. The occupation level forms separate concentrations of various sizes. The settlement was discovered in 1956 by I. Kruglikova. In 1956–1957 and in 1963 excavations were conducted by I. Kruglikova, and in 1986–1994, by V. Gorončarovskij. Altogether, 1750 m² have been uncovered. 350 m² of an area excavated by I. Kruglikova, have been destroyed by the sea.

The earliest occupation level which comes from the period when the settlement was founded, dates to the late 6th – early 5th century B.C. Dug-outs and storage pits also come from that period. V. Gorončarovskij uncovered a 4 m × 3 m oval-shaped dug-out dating to the last quarter of the 6th century B.C. In the early 5th century B.C. there appeared structures with hearths and 0.4 m thick walls made of stone and mud brick. In storage pits objects of Scythian origin: bronze and bone *psalia*, an *akinakes*, and a plaque representing a lion's head have been found. The excavations revealed that in its first phase the settlement was small, not fortified, and consisted of a few detached dwelling structures with storage pits. Unlike I. Kruglikova, V. Gorončarovskij did not discover any traces of fire in layers from the 5th century B.C.

In the layer dating to the 5th century B.C. a dug-out belonging to the second quarter of that century was discovered. On the shoreline I. Kruglikowa cleared a rectangular water tank measuring 1.6 m × × 1.8 m and preserved to a depth of 8 m, constructed of large blocks of stone. The tank was in use from the late 6th/early 5th to the 3rd century B.C. In the late 5th century a 14 m² stone structure and storage pits were built.

In the first half of the 4th century B.C. the next period of the settlement began. In the first quarter of that century a fortified structure of the «country house» type, with 1.4 m thick external walls and ca 30 m in length was erected. In its north-west corner there was a 3 m × 2.8 m tower with 1.7 m thick walls. The central point of the «country house» was a yard adjoined by several rooms, three of which, located in the southern part, each had an area of 12 m².

In the late 4th – early 3rd century B.C. a new «country house» was erected. Its rooms adjoined the remains of the western wall of the earlier structure. The new rooms had areas between 5 m² and 8 m².

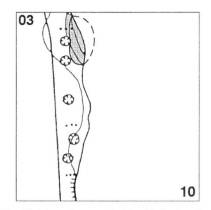

Fig. 45. Map of square 10–03 with the location of the site

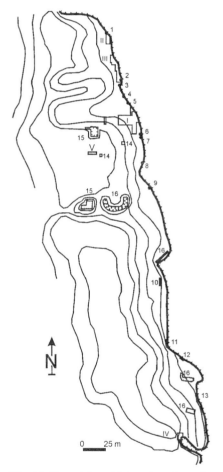

Fig. 46. Plan of site with location of trenches:
1–4, 6–9 – pits, 5 – stone and pit, 10 – wall fragment, 11–12 – dug-outs, 13 – pottery dump, 14 – trial pits, 15–16 – shelter and trenches from the 2nd World War, I–V – trenches (after Kruglikova 1975, fig. 10)

The pavement of the new «country house», uncovered over an area of 24 m², can be dated to the late 3rd – early 2nd century B.C. Stamps and coins were found. Moreover, during I. Kruglikova's excavations, building complexes dating to the 1st century B.C. were unearthed.

44

The settlement was also inhabited in the first centuries A.D. V. Gorončarovskij excavated a structure dating to the late 4th – early 5th century. Moreover, loose finds and constructions from the 8th–9th century were discovered.

The finds from the excavations are stored in the Institute of Archaeology, Russian Academy of Sciences (Moscow), IIMK Russian Academy of Sciences (St. Petersburg) and in the Kerč Museum.

KRUGLIKOVA 1960, pp. 69–72; KRUGLIKOVA 1975, pp. 40–44, 269, no. 169; GORONČAROVSKIJ 1991, pp. 23–24; GORON-ČAROVSKIJ 1993, pp. 22–23; KARASIEWICZ-SZCZYPIORSKI 1995, p. 547.

II.1.22. THE SETTLEMENT OF GEROEVKA – 2 (09–03, SITE 3) [Photo E, 8, 9, Fig. 47–53]

The site is located on a high, bluff shore of the Strait. Concentrations of a disturbed occupation level (pottery, scattered stones) appear over an area of up to 4 ha. To the north the settlement is delimited by a deep ravine, and to the south, by a vaguely outlined gully. Nearly the whole area of the site, with the exception of a narrow, 20 m wide zone adjoining the sea is subject to intensive cultivation. The settlement was discovered in 1956 by I. Kruglikova. Excavations were conducted by V. Zin'ko in 1992–1996.

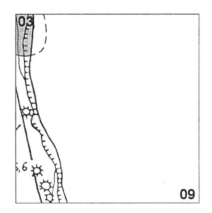

Fig. 47. Map of square 09–03 with the location of the site

Altogether, an area of more than 1200 m² along the shore was uncovered. The settlement consisted of two layers, the occupation level extending to a depth of 0.9–1.7 m. Dwelling-houses, farm buildings, and burials from two periods: Antiquity and the early Middle Ages, were found.

The first period is represented by a complex dated to the early 5th century B.C. It was located in the southern part of the settlement in a small pit with ash fill which contained scorched fragments of a black figure kyathos, Rhodian-Ionian painted amphorae, and amphorae made of grey clay. The settlement was most intensively occupied between the late 5th and 3rd century B.C. In the central part of the trench two dug-outs and eight storage pits were revealed. The bottom of dug-out 1 was 2.3 m deep in the bedrock, and its eastern part was destroyed by the sea. The preserved remains of the dug-out had dimensions of 6.5 m × 5.5 m. In the western and southern part the walls, made of clay, rested on a stone foundation. The walls and floor were covered with clayey daub. The dug-out had two hearths. The entrance, consisting of 1 m wide steps, was located in the northern part and the uppermost step was at the same

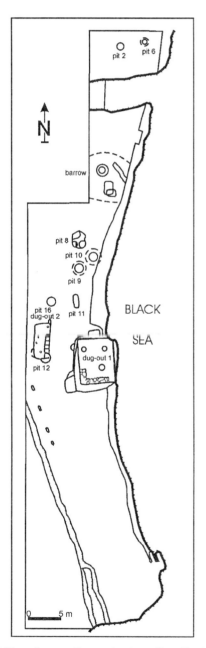

Fig. 48. Plan of excavations – structures from the Ancient period (by L. Berezovskaja)

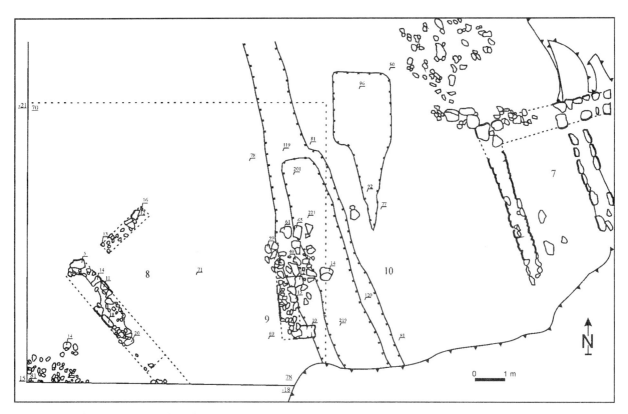

Fig. 49. Area investigated in 1995 – view of structures from Ancient and Mediaeval times (by V. Zin'ko)

level as the edge of the trench. The fill was composed of alternate layers of clay and rubbish. Of the pottery fragments collected, amphorae made up 90.4%, wheel thrown vessels (black gloss and red clay), 7.1%, and hand thrown pottery, 2.5%. Moreover, a large number of fragments of Bosporan roof tiles were discovered. The fill was dated to the 2nd–3rd quarter of the 4th century B.C.

Nearby, dug-out 2 (5.5 m × 2.5 m) was uncovered. Its entrance consisted of a staircase of 5 steps cut in the bedrock (sandy clay), located along the eastern side of the building. In the fill there were found fragments of 12 amphorae (i.a., Chian, Heraclean, Thasian, Sinopian), fragments of Bosporan and Sinopian roof tiles, table ware (i.a., black gloss) and kitchen ware, a terracotta figurine of Attis, a lead weight, and a bronze ring. The dating of these items is analogous to those found in dug-out 1.

In the central and southern part of the excavated area a more than 30 m long trench was found, probably used for draining dung. The southern end of the trench reached a rectangular pit – a tank. The major part of the ancient settlement has been destroyed by the sea. During the underwater excavations of 1994, ancient querns and fragments of amphorae dating to the 4th–3rd century B.C. were collected. In the southern part of the investigated area, at a depth of up to 0.5 m, a concentration of and limestone slabs and blocks, probably the remains of some monumental structure, were discovered.

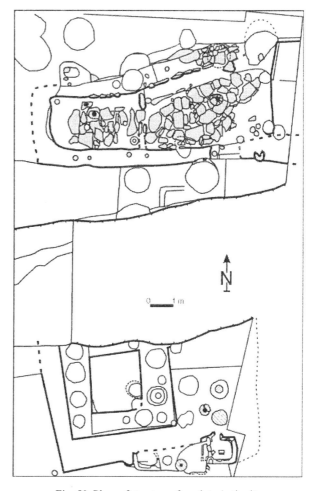

Fig. 50. Plans of structures from late Antiquity
(by S. Solov'ev)

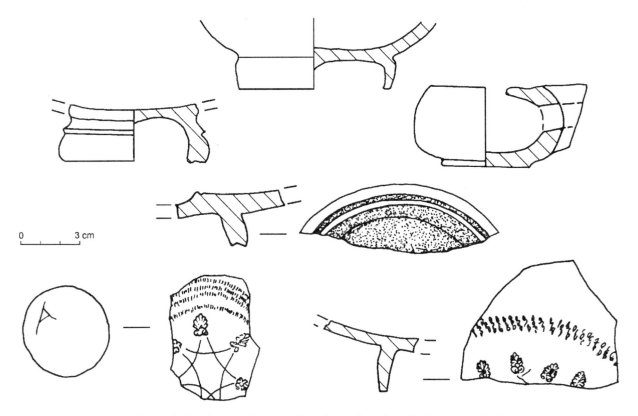

Fig. 51. Selected pottery fragments from the Ancient phase (by L. Berezovskaja)

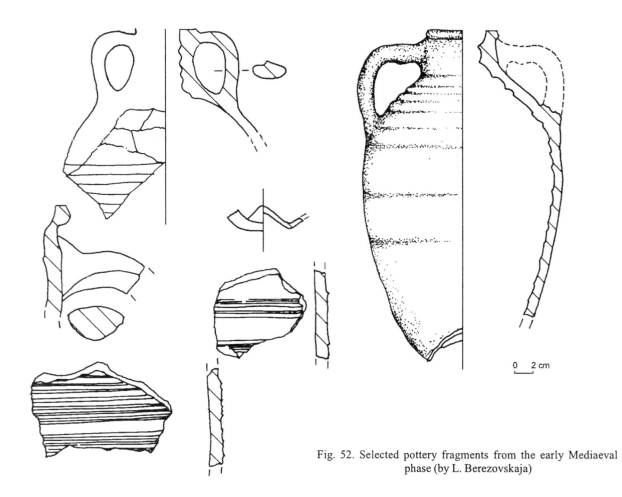

Fig. 52. Selected pottery fragments from the early Mediaeval phase (by L. Berezovskaja)

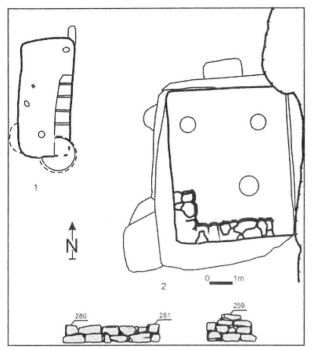

1 - wall face - southern view
2 - wall face - eastern view

Fig. 53. Ancient dug-outs (1, 2) – plan, sections, and stone structures of dug-outs (by S. Solov'ev)

The early Mediaeval layer contained structures from two periods: the first, dates to the 4th–6th century, while the second one, dates to the 8th–9th century. In the northern part of the excavated area a «country house» from the 4th–6th century, erected on a slope of a ravine, was discovered. A dwelling-house measuring 11 m × 4.1 m to 2.3 m adjoined the northern slope. The house had three rooms, of which only the central one (5.7 m × 3.3 m) was open to the courtyard. In the eastern room there was an oven with a stone chimney built into the wall. To the south of the house there was a small yard (10 m × 3 m). A farm house (9.3 m × 5.9 m) was cut into the southern slope of the ravine and was used mainly for the initial treatment of and for storing grain. This building also had two stone ovens. The artefacts included numerous fragments of amphorae and hand-thrown pottery, as well as a few fragments of terra sigillata vessels, numerous stone and metal artefacts. Moreover, a Byzantine coin from the 6th–8th century, dated by A. Gilevič, was discovered. The «country house» had been destroyed by fire.

The structures dating to the 8th–9th century consist of a house with two rooms, remains of farm houses, and several storage pits (for storing grain), uncovered in the southern part of the excavated area. Moreover, stone socles of four large, oval cattle pens were found. The house has been destroyed by abrasion except for its north-western corner. The

artefacts are represented by fragments of amphorae with small horizontal ribbing and incisions of the Saltovo-Majak type.

In 1996, near the north-eastern edge of the settlement, at the side of a barrow (see II.2.7.: barrows near the settlement of Geroevka – 2), V. Zin'ko cleared the remains of a tower (2.1 m × 1.95 m on the inside) partly disturbed by a bulldozer. The entrance to the tower was on its north-eastern side. The fill contained a few fragments of amphorae and hand thrown pottery dating to the 8th–9th century.

In 1994 a geophysical survey was conducted with the aim of testing the usefulness of this method in studying the remains of stone constructions located at the depth lesser than 0.5 m. The results of this test carried out over an area of 400 m² were negative.

The artefacts from the excavations are stored in the Kerč Museum.

KRUGLIKOVA 1975, p. 269, no. 170; Nymphaion, Arch. 1994, pp. 4–5, 20; ZIN'KO 1994a, pp. 124–129; ZIN'KO 1994b, pp. 18–20; ZIN'KO, SOLOV'EV 1994, pp. 159–163; KARASIEWICZ-SZCZYPIORSKI 1995, pp. 546, 548; ZIN'KO 1996, pp. 12–20; ZIN'KO 1997a, pp. 85–94; ZIN'KO 1997b, pp. 40–41; ZIN'KO 1997d; FEDOSEEV, ZIN'KO 1998.

II.1.23. THE SETTLEMENT OF GEROVEKA – 3
(08–04, SITE 1) [Fig. 54–55]

The site, 3 ha in area, is located on the high, steep shore of the Kerč Strait. It was discovered by I. Kruglikova in 1956 and dated by her to the Hellenistic period. Today, separate concentrations of limestone rocks and amphora fragments dating to the 4th–3rd century B.C. can be seen running alongside the shore for a length of 250 m (between a deep ravine to the south and a gully to the north) and in a 15–20 m wide zone. To the west, in a ploughed field, pottery dating mainly to the 8th–9th century with few Ancient fragments, can be found.

In 1996 V. Zin'ko opened a 60 m² trench on the northern slope of the ravine, 150 m to the west of the

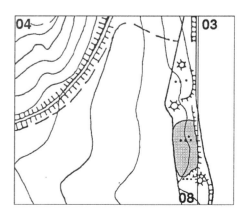

Fig. 54. Map of square 08–04 with the location of the site

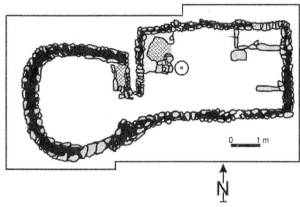

Fig. 55. Plan of structure dated to the 8th–9th century
(by V. Zin'ko)

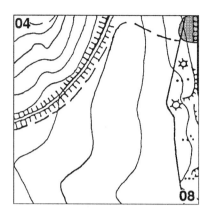

Fig. 56. Map of square 08–04 with the
location of the site

sea. He uncovered an east-west oriented structure composed of several rooms. Rectangular room no. 1 (4.75 m × 2.5 m) was located in the eastern part. It had walls made of herringbone and coursed patterns of stonework. In the north-western corner there was a 1.0 m × 1.25 m stone oven, and in the north-eastern one, a stone storage bin made of vertical limestone slabs and a clay floor. Fixed in the floor near the oven was a broken, round quern, and near the bin, a rectangular limestone slab. This room was adjoined to the west by Room 2 – a round tower with a diameter of 3.0 m. The stonework of the tower walls was also mixed. In the eastern part of the tower there was an oven analogous to the one found in Room 1. The walls of the tower were preserved to the height of 0.2–0.65 m. The tower had two construction phases.

The pottery remains consisted mainly of Saltovo-Majak amphora fragments as well as other vessels of that type. The whole complex can be dated to the late 8th century – the 870s. In the lower part of the occupation level, in the deposits in Room no. 2, fragments of amphorae dating to the 4th–3rd century B.C. were found.

40 m to the north of the investigated area remains of another complex, tentatively dated to the 8th–9th century, can be seen.

On the north-western edge of the settlement there are several barrows (see II.2.8.).

The artefacts are stored in the Kerč Museum.

KRUGLIKOVA 1975, p. 269, no. 171; ZIN'KO 1997b, pp. 40–41; ZIN'KO, PONOMAREV 1997.

II.1.24. THE SETTLEMENT OF GEROEVKA – 4
(08–04, SITE 5) [Fig. 56]

The site is located near a steep part of the seashore. It was discovered by I. Kruglikova in 1956 and dated, on the basis of the fragments of Thasian, Heraclean and Sinopian amphorae as well as fragments of roof tiles, to the Hellenistic period.

I. Kruglikova followed the occupation level connected with this settlement for a length of 300 m.

In 1989, due to the construction of holiday centre "Hellada" the area was investigated by V. Zin'ko. In sandy clay, visible along the abraded shore at the depth of 0.8–1.0 m from the modern topsoil a 0.3–04 m thick occupation level was visible. It was followed for a length of 150 m. The layer contained mainly fragments of Bosporan roof tiles and of amphorae dating to the 4th–3rd century B.C.

To the west pottery appears on the surface 200 m away from the shore of the Strait. The western part of the zone where the pottery appears is ploughed up. Fragments of pottery dating to the 8th–9th century can be mainly found. There are also concentrations of stones. On a dirt road between the holiday centre and the ploughed field a stamp on the neck of a Heraclean amphora dating to the 2nd–3rd quarter of the 4th century was found (see III.2.2.).

The site has not been excavated.

KRUGLIKOVA 1975, p. 269, no. 172.

II.1.25 THE SETTLEMENT OF GEROEVKA – 5
(10–03, SITE 2) [Fig. 57]

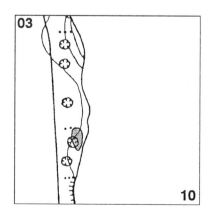

Fig. 57. Map of square 10–03 with the
location of the site

The site is located near a steep section of the shore of the Strait. It was discovered in 1956 by I. Kruglikova and dated, according to fragments of Heraclean and Sinopian amphorae, to the Hellenistic period. The author did not establish the area of the settlement and defined its function as that of a villa.

During the 1995 investigations, 15 m from the steep shore, a 40 m × 70 m pottery concentration was discovered. The majority of the settlement is covered with turf; in the western part the occupation level can be seen in a ploughed field, but not in the abraded part. To the north the settlement is delimited by a shallow gully. Fragments of Chian, Heraclean, Chersonesian, Sinopian, and other amphorae, dating to the 4th–3rd century B.C. were found as well as fragments of Bosporan tiles and a stamp on a handle of a Sinopian amphora. Moreover, fragments of amphorae from the first centuries A.D. have been collected.

The site has not been excavated.

KRUGLIKOVA 1975, pp. 269, no. 168.

II.1.26. THE SETTLEMENT OF GEROEVKA – 6
(07–04, SITE 2) [Fig. 58–64]

The site is located on the second terrace, 230 m to the west of the sea. It is visible over an area of more than 3 ha. To the north and south (for 250 m) it is delimited by shallow gullies, and to the west by the steep edge of the terrace (2 m high). The surface of the settlement is even; it inclines slightly to the west, the difference in levels being up to 4 m. The area is intensively cultivated.

In 1991 V. Zin'ko described the settlement and conducted excavations over a total area of 585.5 m². In a ploughed field 7 concentrations of stones were recorded, and 3 of them were excavated. The other 10 trial pits (5 m × 5 m each) were located along the edge of the terrace.

In trial pit no. 3 a pit burial, covered with a few unworked limestone rocks was found. The rectangular grave, 2.41 m × 1.03 m, and 0.75 m deep had an east-west orientation. The 1.70 m long skeleton was resting on its back, with the head to the east. The grave goods consisted of a knife, a dagger, and a plaque made of iron, and 40 rivets and a plaque made of bronze, as well as a bead made of grey glass paste, a whetstone, and a bone plaque with a diagonal hole. The burial is dated to the 8th–9th century.

Trial pit no. 7 revealed, at the depth of 1.2 m, the bottom part of a round storage pit with a diameter of 1.52 m, covered with washed out clay. The fill of the pit contained archaeological material dating to the 4th–3rd century B.C.: fragments of amphorae and of black-gloss cups, a stamp on a handle of a Sinopian amphora, and a small, polished jug made of grey clay.

Trench I had an area of 50 m². At a depth of 0.4–0.45 m the remains of a structure were uncovered, consisting of a 0.9 m wide stone wall and a pavement, adjoining it to the east. The pavement,

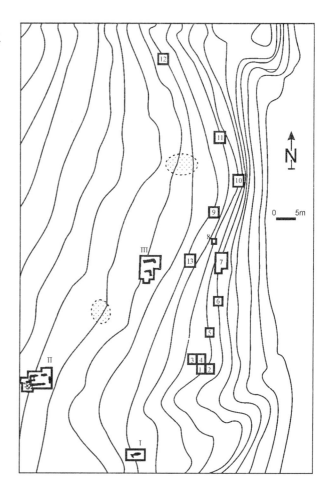

Fig. 59. Plan of trenches with remains of structures
(by V. Zin'ko)

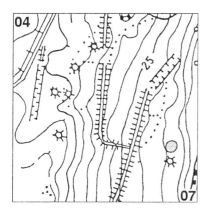

Fig. 58. Map of square 07–04 with the
location of the site

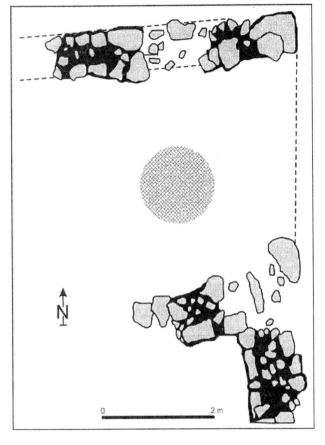

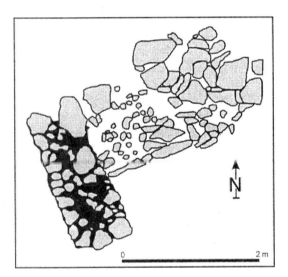

Fig. 60. Uncovered remains of structure (by V. Zin'ko)

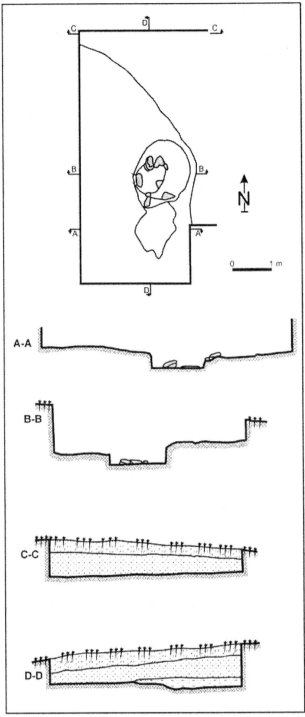

Fig. 61. Trial pit 7 – plan and sections (by V. Zin'ko)

5.4 m² of which has been preserved, was made of limestone rocks. Fragments of amphorae dating to the second half of the 8th century – the 9th century, fragments of Saltovo-Majak type vessels, 3 fragments of glazed ware made of white clay, and a quern were found.

Trench II occupied 115.5 m². At the depth of 0.3–0.4 m fragments of another rectangular (10.5 m × 5.8 m) structure (2), oriented according

to the four points of the compass, were uncovered. The external part of the western wall was adjoined by a semi-circular stone pavement. The wall, ca 1 m wide, was carefully constructed of irregularly sized stones. In the north-western corner remains of a stone oven (1.0 m × 1.2 m) were found. The upper layer contained fragments of amphorae dating to the 8th–9th century, a whole amphora from the 9th century with a graffito on its belly, Saltovo-Majak type

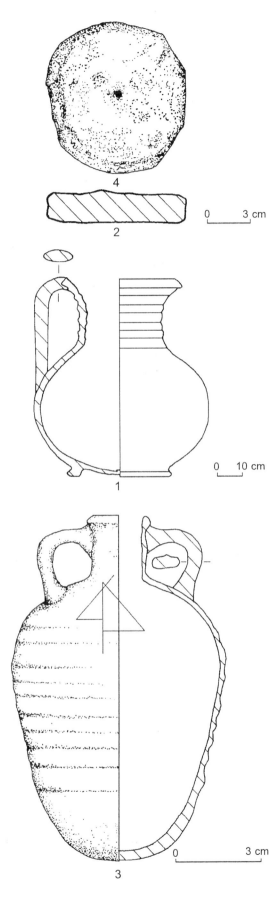

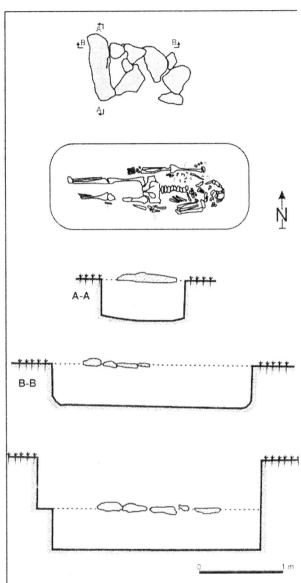

Fig. 63. Early Mediaeval burial from trial pit 1 – plan and sections of burial (by V. Zin'ko)

vessels, and a hand-thrown lamp. In the lower layers fragments of amphorae dating to the 4th century B.C. (Chian, Thasian, Heraclean) were unearthed.

Trench III occupied an area of 95 m^2. It revealed remains of a structure composed of two rooms, oriented according to the four quarters of the globe. In the centre there was a disturbed round hearth. The 1 m thick walls consisted of two faces and a fill of breakstone mixed with clay and soil. The structure is dated by fragments of the Saltovo-Majak type vessels to the second half of the 8th – the 9th century. Moreover, fragments of amphorae dating to the 4th–3rd century B.C., and one fragment of a Bosporan tile were found.

The artefacts from the excavations are stored in the Kerč Museum.

ZIN'KO 1994b, pp. 18–19; ZIN'KO 1997b, pp. 40–41.

Fig. 62. Selected artefacts from the settlement: 1 – jug of grey clay, the 4th–3rd century B.C.; 2 – ceramic plug for amphora; 3 – early Mediaeval amphora with graffito on belly; 4 – limestone quernstone (by V. Zin'ko)

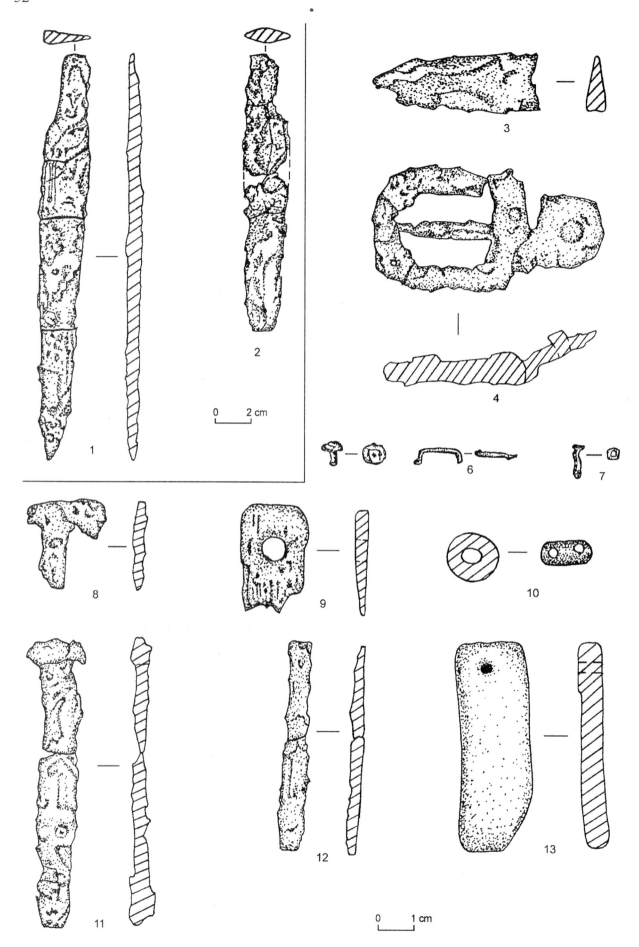

Fig. 64. Grave goods from trial pit 1: 1–4, 11, 12 – iron; 5–7 – bronze; 9 – bone; 10 – faience bead; 13 – stone pendant (by V. Zin'ko)

II.1.27. THE SETTLEMENT OF OGON'KI – 1
(10–10, SITE 1) [Fig. 65–66]

The site is located on the western edge of the modern village of Ogon'ki (formerly Ortel') on a promontory-like elevation, delimited on the east by a broad ravine and on the west by a gully. The southern part of the settlement has been flooded by Lake Tobečik. In 1964, D. Kirilin was able to see, under favourable weather conditions, a stone pavement and pottery concentrations at the bottom of the lake. Today pottery fragments are scattered over an area of ca 6ha.

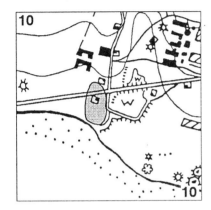

Fig. 65. Map of square 10–10 with the location of the site

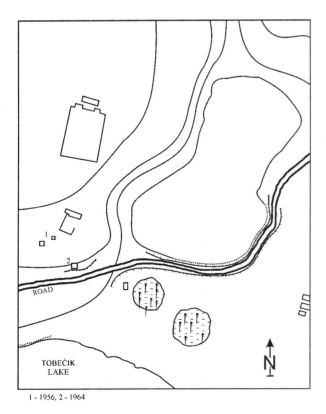

1 - 1956, 2 - 1964

Fig. 66. Location of trenches (after Kirilin Arch., 1964)

The settlement was discovered in 1956 by I. Kruglikova, who made two trial pits in its central part. In 1964–1965 D. Kirilin opened two trenches 29 m–32 m to the south of the trial pits of 1956. Altogether 200 m² were excavated.

Trench I, 10 m wide and 15 m long, was located at the highest point of the settlement. In its southeastern part two east-west oriented cist graves were uncovered. Grave no. 1 was 1.65 m long, grave no. 2 – 1.80 m. The skeletons had their heads pointing to the west and their arms crossed. Both burials are dated to the 10th–12th century. The occupation level was 4 m thick and consisted of several chronological strata: 1) the 1st–2nd century A.D., 2) the 3rd–2nd century B.C., 3) the 4th–3rd century B.C., each 1.35–1.4 m thick. In the last-mentioned stratum stone foundations of three rooms as well as the remains of three pavements located at different levels were uncovered. Underneath, at the depth of 3.6–4 m, one more, poorly visible stratum was distinguished, dating to the second half of the 5th – the 6th century B.C. by a few pottery fragments.

Trench II, 5 m × 5 m, was located to the south of Trench I, on the bank of the lake. Remains of a stone farm structure were uncovered, which had a floor laid out with stone slabs. The unearthed artefacts included fragments of Bosporan and Sinopian roof tiles, bronze coins (Bosporan and Amisan), fragments of amphorae and kitchen ware, as well as black-gloss vessels.

During I. Kruglikova's excavations archaeological material dating to the 1st–3rd century A.D. was also found, i.a., fragments of terra sigillata vessels, amphorae made of light-coloured clay and amphorae with horizontal ribbing.

During the 1995–1996 survey, besides pottery dating to the Hellenistic period, in the northern part of the settlement (09–10, site 2, in the area of 70 m × 40 m) a considerable amount of pottery dating to the 8th–9th century as well as further material from the late Middle Ages (also including some glazed) was collected.

The artefacts from the excavations are stored in the Kerč Museum.

KRUGLIKOVA, Arch. 1956a, d. 1251, 1.2; KIRILIN, Arch. 1964; KIRILIN 1966, pp. 16–18; KRUGLIKOVA 1975, pp. 94–95, 268, no. 163.

II.1.28. THE SETTLEMENT OF OGON'KI – 2
(09–10, SITE 1) [Photo 10, Fig. 67–68]

The site is located 0.8 km to the north of the village of Ogon'ki, on the edge of the steep eastern slope of a deep ravine with a stream at the bottom. At the side of the field there is an elevation in the shape of an open rectangle, probably the remains of walls.

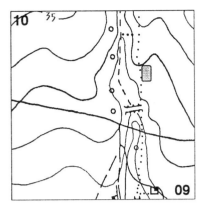

Fig. 67. Map of square 09–10 with the
location of the site

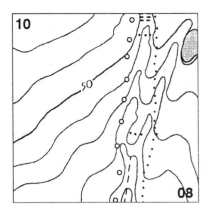

Fig. 69. Map of square 08–10 with the
location of the site

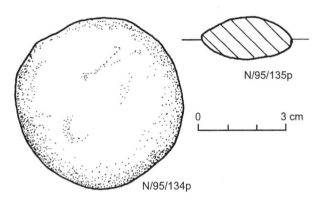

Fig. 68. Selected artefacts: N/95/135p – sling missile; N/95/134p
– amphora handle fragment, unidentified centre, first centuries A.D.

tury B.C., and a few fragments of amphorae and jugs from the 8th–9th century have been collected. There were also numerous concentrations of small stones.

The site has not been excavated.

ZIN'KO, Arch. 1995, 1. 32.

II.1.30. THE SETTLEMENT OF OGON'KI – 4 (07–08, SITE 1) [Fig. 70–73]

The site is located in a ploughed field, 400 m to the east of triangulation marker 81.8. A square elevation with sides ca 70 m long, with a depression in the middle where the yard probably was, has been recorded. From the northern, internal side it is adjoined by an ash-pit with a radius of 10–15 m. Farther to the

The eastern wall was 100 m long, the northern and southern ones, 50 m each. The majority of the settlement area was intensively ploughed up.

In the ploughed field, large concentrations of hand-thrown pottery characteristic of the 2nd millenium B.C. can be seen. Fragments of Hellenistic Bosporan tiles and fragments of amphorae from the 1st–3rd century A.D. have been found as well as 2 stone missiles for a sling. There are also concentrations of small stones. At the bottom of the ravine large limestone blocks, probably ploughed out from the field have been recorded.

The site has not been excavated.

ZIN'KO, Arch. 1995, 1.32; ZIN'KO 1996, p. 14.

II.1.29. THE SETTLEMENT OF OGON'KI – 3 (08–10, SITE 1) [Fig. 69]

The site is located 2 km to the north of the village of Ogon'ki, on the edge of a steep, eastern slope of a ravine. A 200 m × 100 m elevation oriented north-south and covered with steppe vegetation is visible. Fragments of hand-thrown pottery from the 2nd millenium B.C., amphorae dating to the 4th–3rd cen-

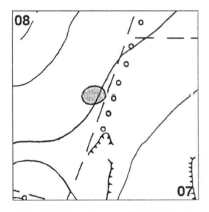

Fig. 70. Map of square 07–08 with the
location of the site

north, at the distance of ca 70 m, wall fragments are visible, which may be remains of a field enclosure. In the ploughed field many fragments of amphorae (Heraclean, Chian, Thasian, Sinopian, Chersonesian) dating to the 4th–3rd century B.C., black-gloss vessels and ones made of red clay, and Bosporan roof tiles have been found. There were also a few fragments of amphorae from the 1st–2nd century A.D.

The site has not been excavated.

ZIN'KO, Arch. 1995, 1. 32.

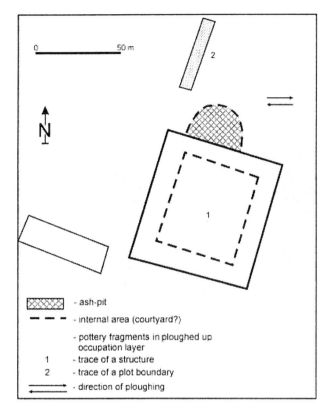

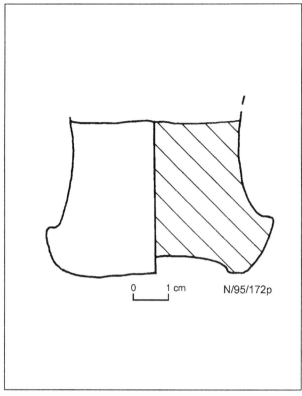

Fig. 71. Remains visible on surface (by I. Ačkinazi)

Fig. 72. Foot of Chersonesian amphora, N/95/172p
– the 4th century B.C. (by L. Berezovskaja)

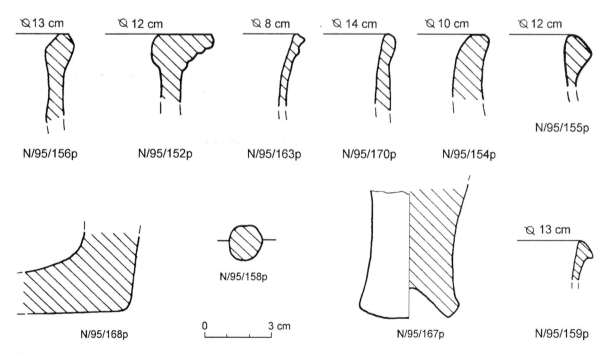

Fig. 73. Selected pottery fragments: N/95/156p – amphora rim fragment, the 3rd century B.C.; N/95/152p – rim fragment of Solokha I type amphora, the 1st half of the 4th century B.C.; N/95/163p – rim fragment of vessel, late Antiquity; N/95/170p – rim fragment of Chian amphora, the 4th century B.C.; N/95/159p – rim fragment of jug, Hellenistic period; N/95/154p – rim fragment of Heraclean amphora, the 4th century B.C.; N/95/155p – rim fragment of Thasian amphora, the 4th century B.C.; N/95/168p – fragment of Heraclean roof tile, Hellenistic period; N/95/158p – fragment of amphora handle, Hellenistic period; N/95/167p – foot of Heraclean amphora, the 4th century B.C.

II.1.31. THE SETTLEMENT OF OGON'KI – 5
(06–09, SITE 1) [Fig, 74]

The site is located 1 km to the north of triangulation marker 81.1, in a ploughed field. At an area of 300 m × 100 m, on a slight elevation, few fragments amphorae of (Thasian, Sinopian, Rhodian)

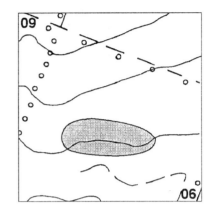

Fig. 74. Map of square 06–09 with the location of the site

dating to the 4th–3rd century B.C. were found. A few pottery fragments dating to the 8th–9th century, including an amphora fragment with fine zonal incisions, have been collected.

The site has not been excavated.

ZIN'KO, Arch. 1995, 1. 33.

II.1.32. THE SETTLEMENT OF OGON'KI – 6
(06–08, SITE 1) [Fig, 75]

The site is located 0.5 km to the north-east of triangulation marker 85.2, in a ploughed field. The settlement occupies an unploughed 150 m × 100 m elevation oriented to the north-south. Few fragments of amphorae dating to the 4th–3rd century

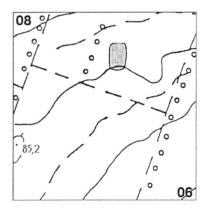

Fig. 75. Map of square 06–08 with the location of the site

B.C. (including Heraclean ones) and pottery fragments dating to the 8th–9th century have been found. Limestone rocks with traces of working have been recorded.

The site has not been excavated.

ZIN'KO, Arch. 1995, 1. 33.

II.1.33. THE SETTLEMENT OF OGON'KI – 7
(05–07, SITE 3) [Fig, 76]

The site is located 120 m to the north of a barrow with the triangulation point 97.9, on the eastern, gentle slope of an elevation. Pottery fragments are scattered over an area of more than 1 ha. The major part of the settlement is covered with turf, only its

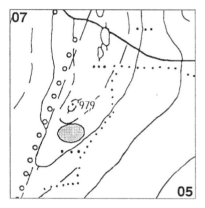

Fig. 76. Map of square 05–07 with the location of the site

eastern edges are ploughed up. Small fragments of amphorae (Chian, Heraclean, Thasian, Chersonesian) dating to the 4th–3rd century B.C. and vessels made of red clay have been collected. There was also a large number of amphora fragments dating to the 8th–9th century, as well as a fragment of a flint blade (see: III.1.7.).

The site has not been excavated.

ZIN'KO, A. 1995, 1. 33.

II.1.34. THE SETTLEMENT OF TOBEČIK – 1
(10–05, SITE 1) [Fig, 77–78]

The site is located near the south-eastern border of the village of Čeljadinovo in a depression cut by a stream. The surface of the site is covered with turf. An outline of a structure oriented according to the four points of the compass is clearly visible. The line of the north-west wall is marked on the surface by small elevations running for 60 m. The south-east wall is 22 m long, and in the western part of the settlement several medium-sized stones bearing traces of working can be seen. A few fragments of

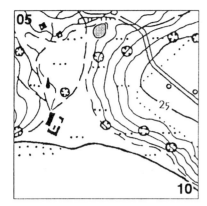

Fig. 77. Map of square 10–05 with the
location of the site

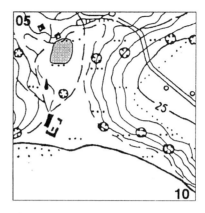

Fig. 79. Map of square 10–05 with the location
of the site

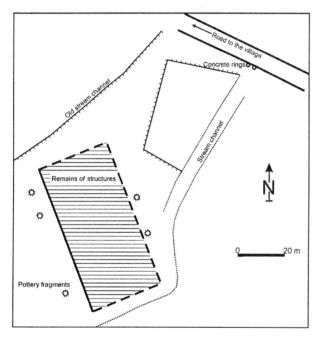

Fig. 78. The site – draft (by I. Ačkinazi)

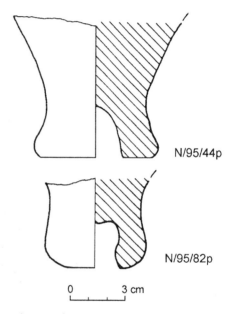

Fig. 80. Selected pottery fragments: N/95/44p – foot of amphora,
unidentified centre, the late 4th century B.C.; N/95/82p – foot
of amphora, unidentified centre, the 4th century B.C.

amphorae dating to the 4th–3rd century B.C. and to
the first centuries A.D. have been collected.

The site has not been excavated.

ZIN'KO, Arch. 1995, 1. 30.

II.1.35. THE SETTLEMENT OF TOBEČIK – 2
(10–05, SITE 3) [Fig. 79–80]

The site was discovered by I. Kruglikova in the
late 1950s. She recorded a small concentration
of Hellenistic pottery. The surface of the site is
overgrown with turf, which covers soil mixed
with ash. During the survey of 1995, from a
100 m × 100 m area located at the bottom of the
northern slope of a wide ravine, pottery fragments
including amphora fragments dating to the 4th–3rd
century B.C. (i.a., Heraclean and Chersonesian) and

a fragment of an unintelligible three-line Sinopian
stamp, have been collected.

The site has not been excavated.

KRUGLIKOVA 1975, p. 268, no. 160; ZIN'KO, Arch. 1995, 1. 30.

II.1.36. THE SETTLEMENT OF TOBEČIK – 3
(10–06, SITE 1) [Fig. 81–82]

The site is located near the south-western
border of the village of Čeljadinovo. The pottery is
scattered over an area of ca 500 m × 110 m. The
surface is overgrown with grass and weeds. Several
pits and stone concentrations are visible. During the
field survey amphora fragments including Mendean
(from the second half of the 5th century B.C), Chian
(from the late 5th – the 4th century B.C.), Solokha
I, Thasian, and Heraclean, have been collected as

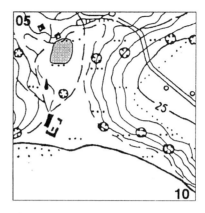

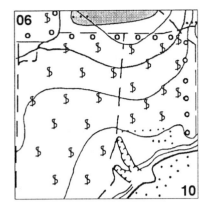

Fig. 81. Map of square 10-06 with the location
of the site

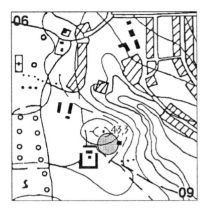

Fig. 83. Map of square 09–06 with the location
of the site

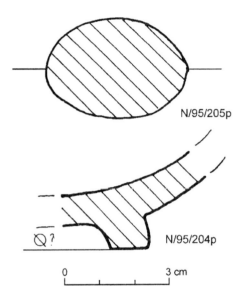

Fig. 82. Selected pottery fragments: N/95/205p – handle fragment
of Cnidian amphora, Hellenistic period; N/95/204p – bottom
fragment of vessel, the 13th–14th century

well as fragments of Bosporan roof tiles. To the
north the site is delimited by an ash-pit. On the
southern edge of the settlement a fragment of an
Attic marble relief (see III.4.3.) was discovered as
well as a few fragments of Mediaeval pottery and
a Tartar pipe (see III.5.3.).

The site has not been excavated.

ZIN'KO, Arch. 1995, l. 30.

II.1.37. THE SETTLEMENT OF TOBEČIK – 4
(09–06, SITE 5) [Fig. 83]

The site is located on the north-eastern and eastern slope of a hill which has triangulation marker
43.3 on its summit. In 1990, V. Zin'ko discovered a
scatter of pottery occupying the area of ca 1 ha and in

the north-eastern part he recorded two elevations:
both ash dumps. The surface of the settlement is covered with steppe grasses. During the survey of 1995,
pottery material, dating to the 1st–3rd century A.D.
and 8th–9th century, was collected.

The site has not been excavated.

ZIN'KO, Arch. 1995, l. 30.

II.1.38. THE SETTLEMENT OF TOBEČIK – 5
(09–06, SITE 6) [Photo 11, Fig. 84–85]

The site was discovered in the late 1950s by
I. Kruglikova, who recorded a small concentration of
Hellenistic pottery in this place. At the time of the
1995 survey the site was overgrown with grass and
weeds. From the area of ca 70 m × 60 m, pottery material was collected, composed mainly of amphora
fragments, i.a., Thasian, Sinopian, Chersonesian, and
Cnidian, dating to the 4th–3rd century B.C. and later,
Hellenistic examples.

The site has not been excavated.

KRUGLIKOVA 1975, p. 268, no. 161; ZIN'KO, Arch. 1995, l. 30.

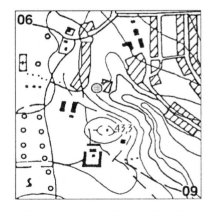

Fig. 84. Map of square 09–06 with the location
of the site

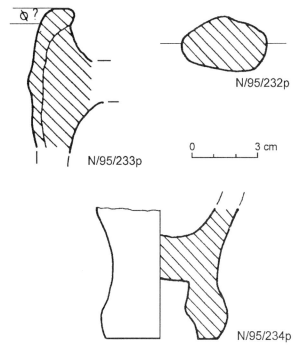

N/95/232p

N/95/233p

0   3 cm

N/95/234p

Fig. 85. Selected pottery fragments: N/95/233p – rim fragment of Thasian amphora, Hellenistic period; N/95/232p – handle fragment of Cnidian amphora, Hellenistic period; N/95/234p – foot of Chersonesian amphora, the second half of the 4th century B.C.

II.1.39. THE SETTLEMENT OF TOBEČIK – 6
(09–05, SITE 2) [Photo 12, Fig. 86–87]

The site is located to the east of the village of Čeljadinovo, on a plain gently sloping down east-wards, to the east of triangulation marker 54.5, on the eastern side of an asphalt road. The area of the settlement is ploughed intensively, due to which numerous concentrations of limestone rubble are clearly visible. From an area of ca 1 ha pottery was collected, mainly amphora fragments dating to the 4th–3rd century B.C.

The site has not been excavated.

ZIN'KO, Arch. 1995, 1. 31.

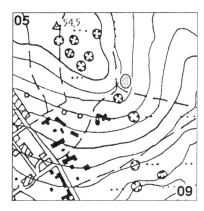

Fig. 86. Map of square 09–05 with the location of the site

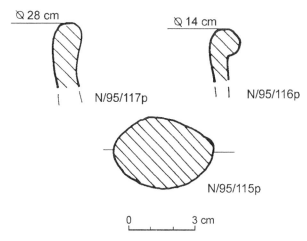

Q 28 cm

N/95/117p

Q 14 cm

N/95/116p

N/95/115p

0   3 cm

Fig. 87. Selected pottery fragments: N/95/117p – rim fragment of Thasian amphora, the 4th/3rd century B.C.; N/95/116p – rim of Chian amphora, the 4th century B.C.; N/95/115p – handle fragment of Chian amphora, Hellenistic period

II.1.40. THE SETTLEMENT OF TOBEČIK – 7
(08–05, SITE 1) [Fig. 88–89]

The site is located at the northern edge of the village of Čeljadinovo. Today, there are modern struc-tures and gardens in the area of the settlement. From

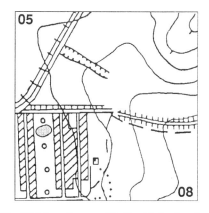

Fig. 88. Map of square 08–05 with the location of the site

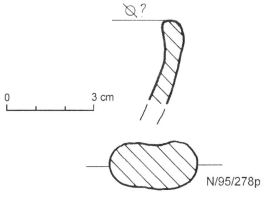

Q ?

0   3 cm

N/95/278p

Fig. 89. Selected pottery fragments: N/95/279p – rim fragment of vessel, the first centuries A.D.; N/95/278p – handle fragment, the 8th–9th century

an area of more than 0.5 ha outside the gardens, amphora fragments dating to the 4th–3rd century B.C as well as ones with fine, horizontal ribbing and hand thrown pottery of the Saltovo-Majak type, dating to the 8th–9th century, have been collected.

The site has not been excavated.

ZIN'KO, Arch. 1995, 1. 31.

II.1.41. THE SETTLEMENT OF TOBEČIK – 8
(10–06, SITE 2) [Fig. 90–93]

The site is located to the south of the village of Čeljadinovo, reaching the southernmost farm. The main part of the settlement is located in a ploughed field, the south-western part is occupied by a vineyard, while the north-eastern part is wasteland. The settlement was described in 1956 by I. Kruglikova, who recorded a small concentration of Hellenistic pottery.

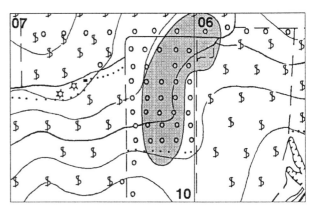

Fig. 90. Map of squares 10–06 and 10–07 with the location of the site

During the survey of 1995, a large amount of pottery dating to various periods, stone concentrations, and ashy soil, were found scattered at an area

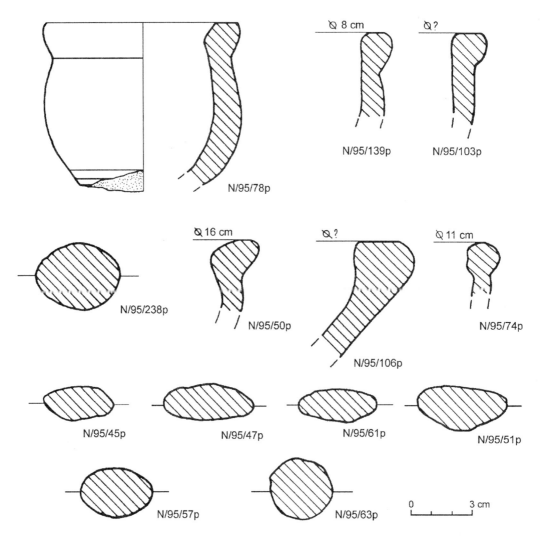

Fig. 91. Selected pottery fragments: fragments of amphora rims: N/95/78p – Chian, the 3rd quarter of the 5th century B.C.; N/95/139p – Thasian, the 4th century B.C.; N/95/103p – Chian, the 4th century B.C.; N/95/50p – Thasian, the 4th–3rd century B.C.; N/95/74p – Chian, the 4th–3rd century B.C.; N/95/106, fragment of mortarium, the 4th century B.C.; fragments of amphora handles: N/95/238p – Chian, the 1st half of the 4th century B.C.; N/95/45p – unidentified centre, Roman period; N/95/47p – Chersonesian, 4th–3rd century B.C.; N/95/61p – Rhodian, the 1st century B.C.; N/95/51p – Thasian, the 4th–3rd century B.C.; N/95/57p – Chian, Hellenistic period; N/95/63p – Colchian, the 1st–3rd century A.D.

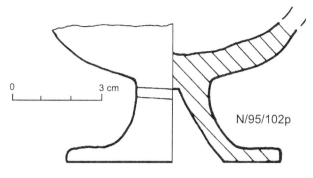

Fig. 92. Fragment of black-gloss kylix

of more than 15 ha. Fragments of amphorae dating from the late 6th – early 5th century B.C. to the 3rd century B.C, and of other vessels, including a fragment of a black-gloss kylix on a narrow foot, dating to ca 460 B.C., have been recorded. Moereover, amphora fragments dating to the first centuries of our era and others from the 8th–9th century have been discovered.

The site has not been excavated.

Kruglikova 1975, p. 268, no. 162; Nymphaion, Arch. 1995, p. 4; Zin'ko, Arch. 1995, 1. 31; Zin'ko 1996, p. 31.

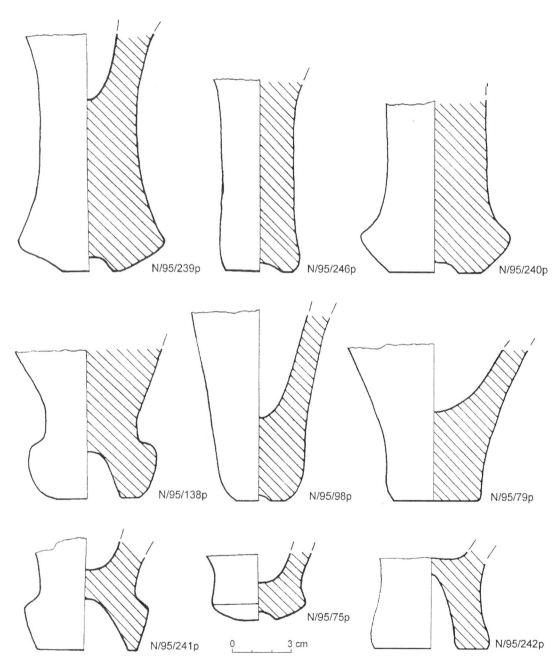

Fig. 93. Selected fragments of amphora feet: N/95/239p – Mendean, the 2nd half of the 5th century B.C.; N/95/46p – Heraclean, the 5th century B.C.; N/95/240p – Chersonesian, the 2nd half of the 4th century B.C.; N/95/138p – Solokha I, the 4th century B.C.; N/95/98p – Heraclean, the 4th century B.C.; N/95/79p – Chian, the 1st half of the 5th century B.C.; N/95/241p – Chersonesian, the 2nd half of the 4th century B.C.; N/95/75p – Rhodian, the 1st century B.C.; N/95/242p – Solokha, the mid–4th century B.C.

II.1.42. THE SETTLEMENT OF TOBEČIK – 9
(10–07, SITE 1) [Photo 13, 14, Fig. 94–106]

The site is located on a flat shore, 1 km to the south west of the village of Čeljadinovo. In 1995, in a ploughted field, four small elevations, each 30 m in diameter, were recorded. They are located in the corners of a quadrangular elevation with an area of ca 50 m × 50 m, oriented north-south (Fig. 95–97). The soil at the elevations is ashy and contains a large amount of pottery dating from the second half of the 5th century B.C. (Chian amphorae and fragments of black-gloss Attic wares) to the 4th–3rd century B.C. These are mainly fragments of amphorae, i.a., Hera-

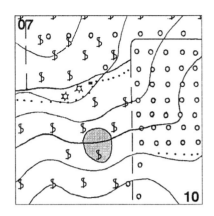

Fig. 94. Map of square 10–07 with the location of the site

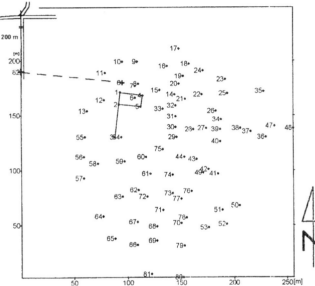

Fig. 95. Location of measurement points for contour line map with marked area of geophysical survey (by T. Nowicki)

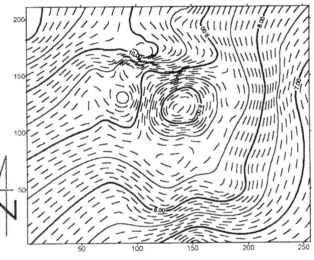

Fig. 96. Contour line map of site area with conventional ordinate (by T. Nowicki)

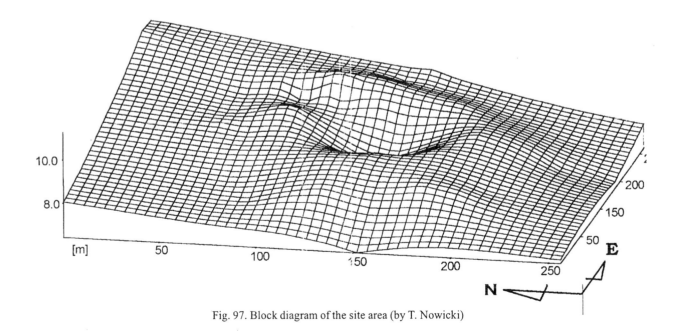

Fig. 97. Block diagram of the site area (by T. Nowicki)

clean, Thasian, Sinopian, Chersonesian, Mendean, and Bosporan examples. The few pottery remains from the 2nd century B.C. include a fragment of a terra sigillata bowl and a handle fragment of a Coan amphora, as well as fragments of pithoi. A small amount of pottery from the first centuries A.D. was also discovered as well as several fragments of granite querns and grinders. It is worth mentioning the following finds: some stamps (on fragments of Chian, Heraclean, and Sinopian amphorae: see III.2.3, 5, 6, 12.), several stone balls (one made of granite), and a spindle whorl of crystalline gypsum.

On the elevations there are numerous concentrations of small limestone rocks, and also among the some medium-sized stones (up to 0.4 m long) with traces of working.

In 1997, a geophysical survey by means of resistivity profiling with a twin-probe array was conducted in the north-western corner. The distance between probes was: AM = 1 m and BN = 5 m. It allowed the mesurement of resistivity changes in layers up to ca 1 m deep. The survey was based on a 1 m × 1 m grid. Moreover, a series of 14 soundings was carried out in an array in the central part of the investigated area (on a 30 m section) which allowed to determine the probable depth of the located structures. Altogether, an area of 40 m × 50 m (Fig. 95) was investigated. The results are presented in black-and-white contour maps with equal resistivity isolines (Fig. 98, 100) and three-dimensional model of resistivity distributions (Fig. 99). The resistivity ranged between 25 and 100 ohm. Resistivity between 25 and 45 ohm

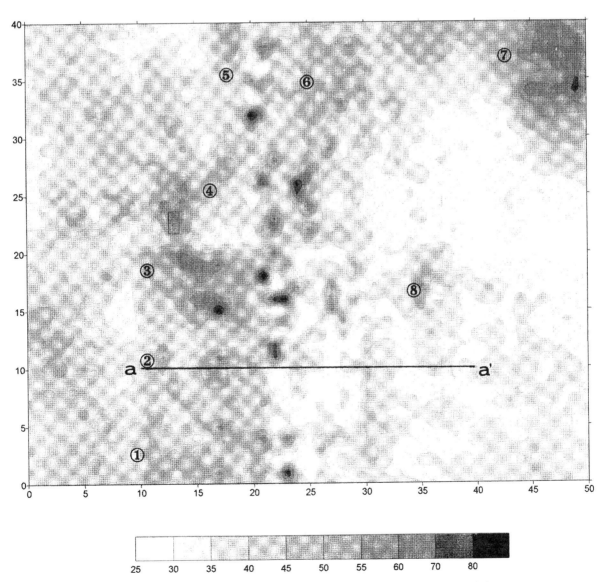

Fig. 98. Map of the distribution of apparent resistivity (by K. Misiewicz)

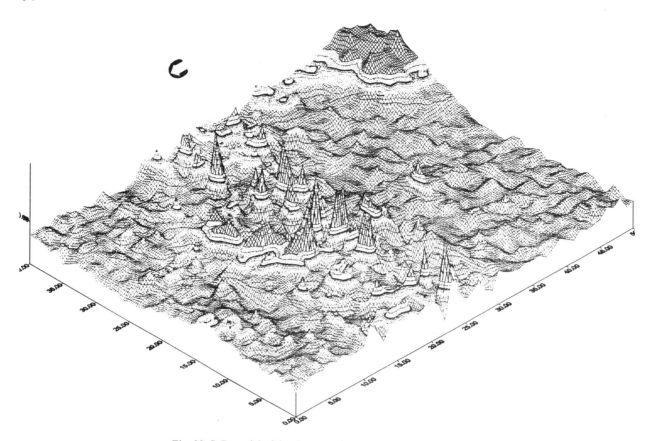

Fig. 99. S–D model of the changes of resistivity (by K. Misiewicz)

is characteristic for natural layers, i.e. the topsoil and the low-resistivity clay-loess layer in which the structures were embedded. The resistivity of these layers may vary, within the above-mentioned edges, in places where the topsoil is thicker, and the generally linear, east-west oriented arrangement of the disturbances in the top layers is caused by ploughing.

In such conditions archaeological remains cause high-resistivity anomalies up to 100–120%. These anomalies, visible in Fig. 98, are irregular, and they were recorded over the whole area of the survey. The scope of the anomalies, the lack of clear linear edges to the zones of higher resistivity, and the diversity of resistivity in these zones indicate that these anomalies are caused by the remains of walls and their foundations embedded in rubble. The array of geoelectrical soundings a–a' (Fig. 98) allowed us tentatively to determine the depth at which these structures were located. As can be seen from the printed isoline layout of vertical ground resistivity (Fig. 100) the discussed remains are represented by three groups of anomalies appearing at metres 1–7 (i.e. 11–17 in the grid), 22–24 (32–34), and 25–28 (35–37). The disturbances in the natural arrangement of strata,

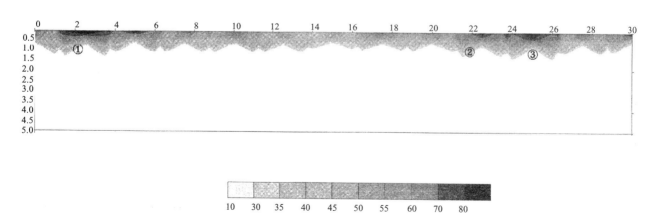

Fig. 100. Isolines of the vertical distribution of resistivity (by K. Misiewicz)

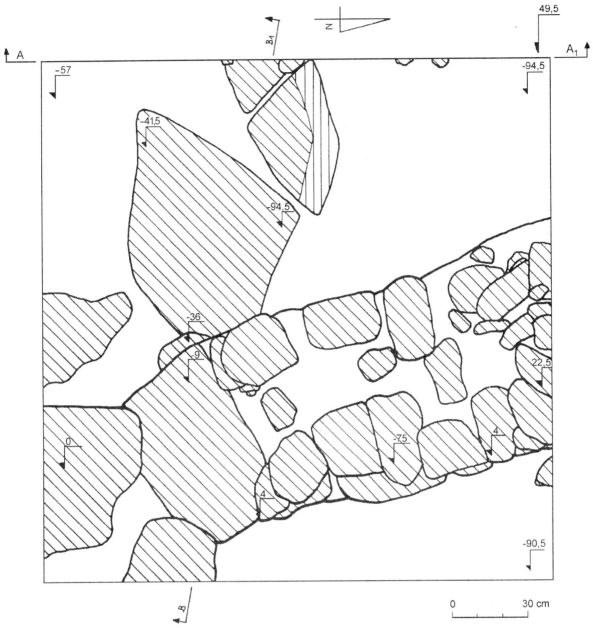

Fig. 101. Plan of trial pit

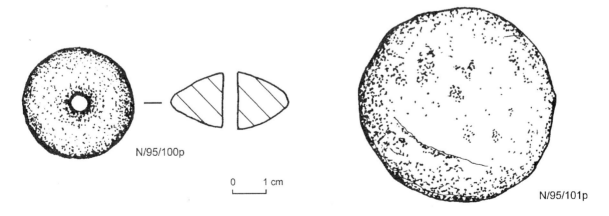

Fig. 102. Selected artefacts: N/95/100p – gypsum? whorl; N/95/101p – sling missile (by L. Berezovskaja)

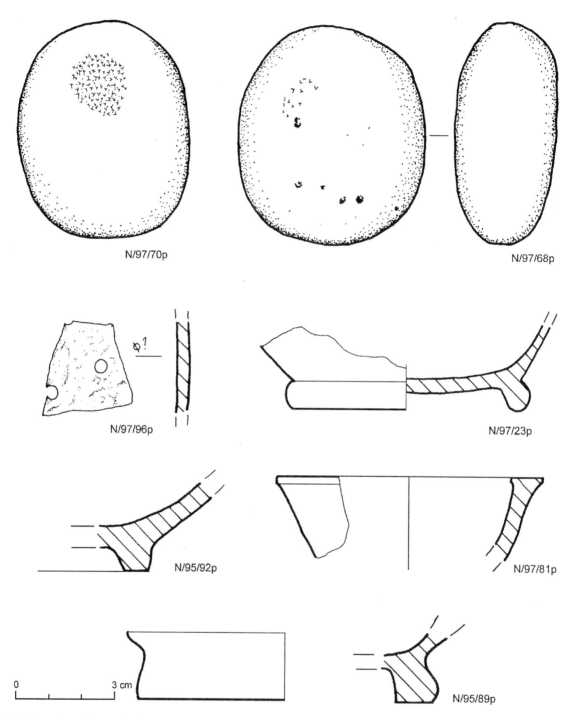

Fig. 103. Selected artefacts: N/95/70p – N/97/68p – sling missiles; N/97/96p – belly fragment of strainer: holes bored secondarily; N/97/23p – bottom fragment of jug, the 4th–3rd century B.C.; N/95/92p – bottom fragment of bowl, Hellenistic period; N/97/81p – rim fragment of bowl; N/95/89p – fragment of black-gloss bowl, import from Attica ?

visible in the increased resistivity values, appear directly under the surface, at a depth of 0.2–0.3 m and only in the case of the last-mentioned anomaly (metres 35–37), are they deeper than 1 m. In the other places they are either close to the surface (at a depth of 0.3 m) or slightly deeper (0.6–0.8 m). This arrangement may indicate that we are dealing with

a structure composed of one layer, most probably destroyed at one time and not, e.g. deserted. In the latter case the layer with the remains, formed over a longer period of time, would be considerably thicker than the registered disturbances indicate.

The above-presented data allowed to locate the places, where the probability of discovering compact

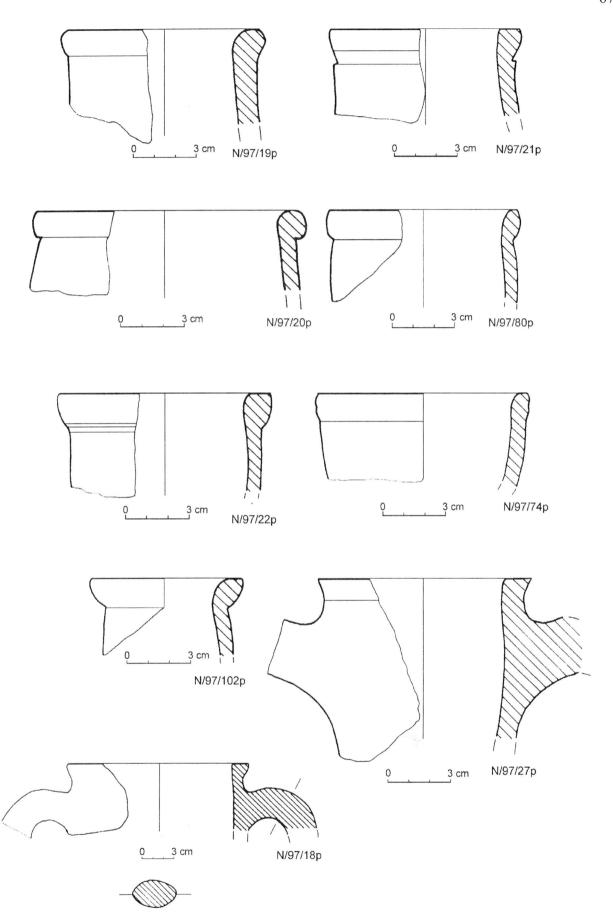

Fig. 104. Rim fragments of amphorae: N/97/19p – N/97/22p – N/97/18p – N/97/27p – Heraclean, the 4th–3rd century B.C., N/97/21p – unidentified centre, the 4th–3rd century B.C.; N/97/80p – unidentified centre; N/97/20p – Heraclean, the 5th century B.C.; N/97/74p – unidentified centre; N/97/102p – Heraclean.

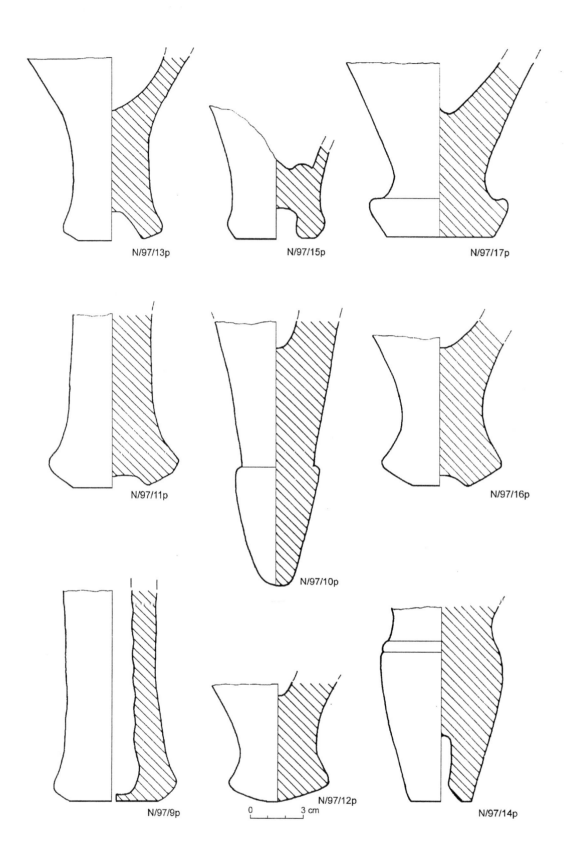

Fig. 105. Feet of amphorae: N/97/13p – Heraclean, the 4th–3rd century B.C.; N/97/15p – unidentified centre, the 4th–3rd century B.C.; N/97/17p – Bosporan, the 4th–3rd century B.C.; N/97/11p – Mendean, the 4th–3rd century B.C.; N/97/10p – Chian, the 4th–3rd century B.C.; N/97/12p, N/97/16p – Sinopan, the 4th–3rd century B.C.; N/97/9p – unidentified centre, the 4th–3rd century B.C.; N/96/14p – Chian, the 4th–3rd century B.C.

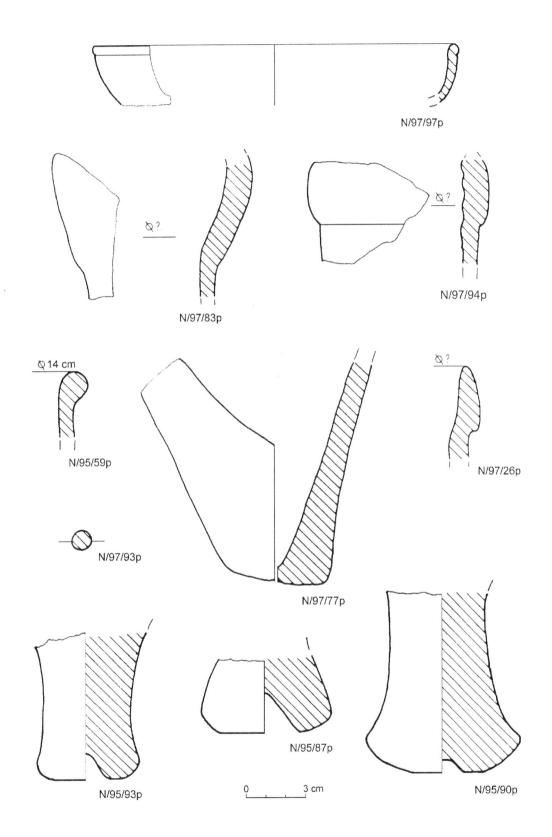

Fig. 106. Selected pottery fragments: N/97/97p – rim fragment of bowl, Attica, the 5th century B.C.?; N/97/83p – N/97/94p – neck fragments of Chian amphorae, the 5th century B.C.; N/97/93p – handle fragment of a kylix, Attica, the 5th century B.C.?; N/95/59p – rim fragment of Chian amphora, Hellenistic period; N/97/26p – rim fragment of Chian amphora, the 4th quarter of the 5th century B.C.; foot fragments of amphorae: N/97/77p – unidentified centre, later used as funnel; N/95/93p – Heraclean, the 4th century B.C.; N/95/90p – Mendean, the 4th century B.C.

structures such as walls or their foundations would be the greatest. Both the shape of the anomaly – best visible as three-dimensional model of resistivity distributions (Fig. 99) – and the dynamic of the changes within the zones of increased resistivity were taken into consideration. And thus in group 1 a narrow, linear anomaly with a preserved right angle was recorded. Group 2 consists of similar narrow anomalies arranged in semi-circles. In the 5 m × 10 m zone 3 of disturbances two clear structures can be distinguished at metre S (to the south) 17 – E (to the east) 15 and S12–16, E18–20. Zone 4 is a wide band of increased resistivity with an oblique, narrow linear anomaly oriented to the south-east. Groups 5 and 6 are clearly delimited to the north, east and south by linear anomalies with visible right angles. A small anomaly, 8, with two right angles preserved to the north-east and north-west, located at a certain distance from the above presented complex of disturbances, may indicate the remains of a single structure. Group 7 embraces a considerably different from the other ones resistivity increase up to 130–140 ohm. It is located in a depression and the reasons for such an arrangement of resistivities may be either anthropogenic or natural. In the former case it may be a paved yard, and in the latter case, natural rock outcrops. This zone was too wide, however, to allow us to determine its character by means of a small trial trench. Therefore, such a trench was made in another

area with similar anomalies. Zone 4 was chosen, where against a strongly disturbed (probably by rubble) background, a narrow, linear anomaly was distinguished. The 2 m × 2 m trench located at metres S12–13, E22–24 confirmed the existence of wall remains at a depth of 0.3 m below the modern ground surface. The upper parts of the wall were disturbed and the stones used in its construction lied both inside and outside it. The construction was clearly visible in deeper layers, i.e., below 0.5 m.

Thanks to the data obtained in the trial trench it was possible to state that the changes observed were caused by human agency. In the investigated part of the site it was thus possible to determine the ca 10 m wide remains of a complex of structures erected around a central yard. The northern and western part of the complex have been revealed and it seems that in the western part the structures were not so compact as in the northern part, and were composed of single buildings, such as the remains recorded by anomaly 8. It is, however, probable that this is due to the incomplete preservation of the structures.

It is possible that this is the settlement mentioned by V. Gajdukevič[2] as a "large fortified settlement" on the authority of K. Grinevič.

To the north-west of the settlement there is a pit and kurgan necropolis (see II.2.12.).

KRUGLIKOVA 1975, p. 268, no. 162; ZIN'KO, Arch. 1995, 1. 31; ZIN'KO 1996, p. 30; Nymphaion, Arch. 1997, pp. 4, 16.

II.2. NECROPOLISES (NOS. 1–16)

II.2.1. PIT AND KURGAN NECROPOLIS OF NYMPHAION (05–03, SITE 11) [Photo 15]

It surrounds the town towards the north-west, west, and south and occupies an area of ca 60 ha, embracing squares 04–03, 04; 05–02, 03; 06–03 (see map 2).

In the second half of the 19th century the necropolis was excavated by A. Ljucenko, N. Kondakov, and S. Verebrjusov, and in 1975–1976 and 1978 by N. Grač. In 1991 and 1993 rescue excavations were supervised by V. Zin'ko, and in 1994–1995, by A. Avetikov. Since 1995 the work has been conducted by S. Solov'ev.

The barrows are located to the south and northwest of the town. The southern group extends from the limits of the town of Nymphaion to the south and spreads over the heights of the hills along the shore of the Kerč Strait. The barrows, situated on rocky elevations, are large. The barrows belonging to the north-western group, scattered over the steppe alongside Lake Čurubaš, are considerably smaller. The majority of the barrows and part of the pit burials

were explored as early as the 19th century. On the basis of the 19th century materials (179 burial complexes), P.F. Silant'eva distinguished 8 burial types: urn burials, cremation burials at the site of cremation, cist graves, pit burials, pit burials covered with stone slabs, graves of dried mud brick, stone tombs, and catacombs. Another group is constituted by the burials of Scythian aristocracy (6 complexes) uncovered in barrows dating to the 5th – early 4th century B.C.

To the west of the town 27 burials from the first centuries A.D. were investigated by N. Grač. In the north-western part of the necropolis, a large completely plundered, complex of catacombs, dating to the 1st–3rd century A.D. was excavated. In the north-western side of a large, 200 m long mound, entrances to dromoi leading to 22 burial chambers were revealed. On the other side of the mound there were three tombs, and a further two, in a depression between the mounds. The catacombs were cut in

[2] GAJDUKEVIČ 1940, p. 317.

limestone rock. Each tomb consisted of a burial chamber with a rectangular or arched entrance and of a dromos with steps. The entrances were covered with large stone slabs. The tombs varied in their dimensions as well as in their construction and decoration. Two chambers were covered with stucco and painted. In some cases the walls had relief representations, e.g., the catacomb rediscovered by N. Grač, earlier excavated and published by M. Rostovtzeff.

In the pit necropolis N. Grač uncovered 250 burials. During the whole period of use of the necropolis, i.e., from the 6th century B.C. to the 4th century A.D., two types of burials co-existed: cremation and inhumation. In the inhumation burials the deceased was laid out straight, on his back, with the head oriented to the north-east. Burials of this type are dating to the 6th – early 5th century B.C. The bodies were placed in shallow graves hewn in the rock or bedrock. In the cremation burials the ashes were collected after the cremation and placed in urns. In the 5th–4th century B.C, besides the pit burials, there were tombs of dried mud bricks. The grave goods are richer. Two tombs, used repeatedly between the 3rd and 1st century B.C., were erected in the Hellenistic period.

The necropolis from the first centuries A.D. has three types of burials: tombs cut into the rock and covered with slabs, tombs of dried mud brick, and simple pit burials either covered with stone slabs or without them. Among the pit burials, one individual group can be distinguished, dated to the 3rd century A.D. by glass vessels and coins of Thothorses and Rhadamsadios found in them.

In the 1995 season, two plundered cist burials were discovered in square 04–04, site 4. They are, as far as it is known, the north-westernmost ones belonging to the pit necropolis of Nymphaion. During that season two monuments connected to the sepulchral architecture of Nymphaion were found (see III.4.4. and III.4.5.).

In 1994 geophysical research was carried out at the necropolis of Nymphaion in an area located to the west of the ancient town and to the north of the settlement of Èl'tigen Zapadnoe. The survey embraced an area of ca 1000 m² , partly disturbed by grave robbers. It demonstrated that in this location the ceiling of the bedrock lies close to the surface, and consequently the results of the survey proved to be of little use.

The finds from the 19th century excavations are stored in the Hermitage Museum in Saint Petersburg and in museums in Great Britain. Artefacts discovered by N. Grač are in the Hermitage and all the later finds are in the Kerč Museum.

SILANT'EVA 1959; M. VICKERS, *Scythian Treasures in Oxford*. Ashmolean Museum, Oxford 1979, p. 56, pl. 18; GRAČ 1989; Nymphaion, Arch. 1994, pp. 5, 17, fig. 3; ZIN'KO 1997c.

II.2.2. KURGAN NECROPOLIS OF ČELJADINOVO VOSTOČNOE (09–03, SITE 5) [Fig. 107–111]

The necropolis extends from north to south along the high, steep shore of the Kerč Strait, covering an area of 1000 m × 100 m. It is located at the north-western edge of the settlement of Geroevka – 1. In 1995, 21 barrows were recorded. Three of them (nos 6,7,8) have been partly destroyed by abrasion, and the majority are gradually disturbed by ploughing. In several mounds up to 2 m deep robbers' pits are visible. In the dumps of these pits fragments of amphorae dating to the 4th–3rd century B.C. and large amounts of limestone rubble of various sizes can be seen. In the south-western part of the mound of barrow no. 2 the robbers uncovered a large cist grave oriented east-west with walls made of large, well worked limestone slabs. A similar grave in a small barrow (no. 13) has also been plundered. The tallest barrow is 6 m high (triangulation marker 26.6), while the lowest is 0.7 m high.

In 1995 V. Zin'ko excavated barrow no. 16. The majority of the mound (preserved height 0.80 m) was disturbed by ploughing. In the central and southern part robbers' pits are visible. The mound, made of yellow-brown sandy-clayey soil with numerous lime intrusions, was disturbed in many places by pits and trenches, as well as by early Mediaeval ash-pits. In the layers from ancient times, numerous fragments of amphorae (Chian, Thasian, Heraclean, Sinopian) dating to the 4th century B.C. were found.

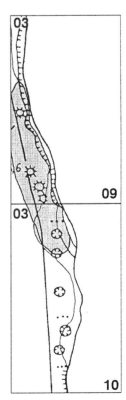

Fig. 107. Map of squares 09–03 and 10-03 with the location of the site

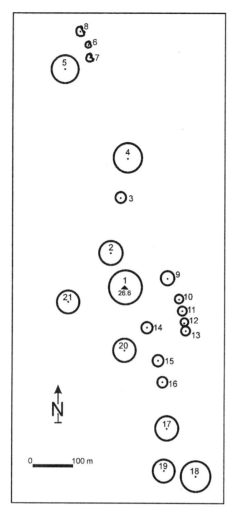

Fig. 108. Draft of distribution of barrows (by I. Ačkinazi)

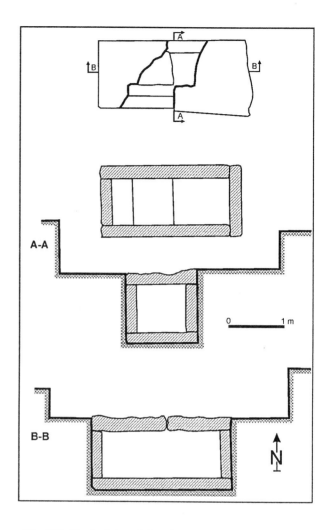

Fig. 109. Cist burial no. 1 from barrow no. 16 (by V. Zin'ko)

In the south-western part of the mound a Thasian amphora-handle with a poorly preserved two-line stamp (group I after Ju. Vinogradov[3]: the early 4th century B.C.) was discovered. Robbers' pits and early Mediaeval ash-pits had destroyed the main burials of the barrow. The first mound was raised over a large grave covered with a stone slab (similarly to barrows 2 and 13), lying in the south-eastern part of the barrow. The original mound was 8 m in diameter; the preserved height is 0.65 m.

The grave has an east-west orientation. It is constructed of carefully worked, rectangular limestone blocks resting on their longer sides. It is covered with two rectangular limestone slabs (1.35 m × 1.20 m large and 0.21–0.26 m thick). This cover was 0.65 m below the original ground level. Inside the grave was 2.01 m long and 0.80 m wide. Its height was 0.80 m. The floor was covered with carefully worked, large, rectangular limestone slabs. The fill contained sev-

eral human bones, pottery fragments, bronze and iron arrowheads, a fragment of an iron spearhead, a fragment of a sword (?), and of a knife. All the bones belonged to a 55–60 year old woman, 153 cm tall. The pottery from the fill consists of fragments of amphorae and vessels of the Saltovo-Majak type from the 8th–9th century and fragments of amphorae from the 4th century B.C., including some from Heraclea. The grave was robbed three times; twice in the Middle Ages, which is indicated by the pottery and two robbers' pits in the mound. The third robbers' pit was dug in modern times. Directly on the floor slabs there were fragments of two black-gloss lekythoi from the early 4th century B.C. and ca 40 arrowheads from the 4th century B.C. The burial is dated to the 4th century B.C.

0.85 m to the north of the north-western corner of the grave, at the then ground level a worked limestone slab was found, measuring 0.40 m × 0.36 m × × 0.18 m with a rectangular recess carved in the centre. This stone was used as a foundation stone for a funerary stele.

[3] Ju. VINOGRADOV, *Keramičeskie klejma iz ostrova Fassos*, Numismatika i Epigrafika 10, 1972, p. 20sq.

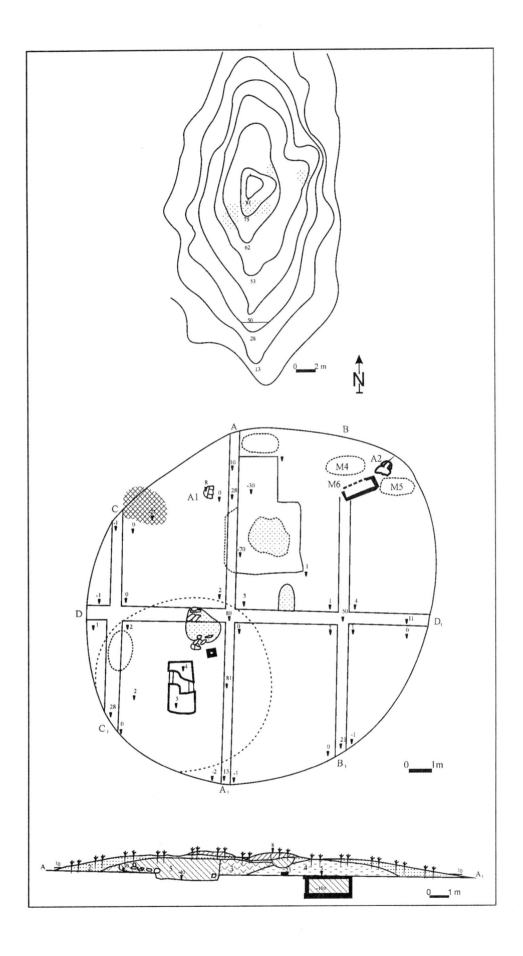

Fig. 110. Plan of excavations and section of barrow (by V. Zin'ko)

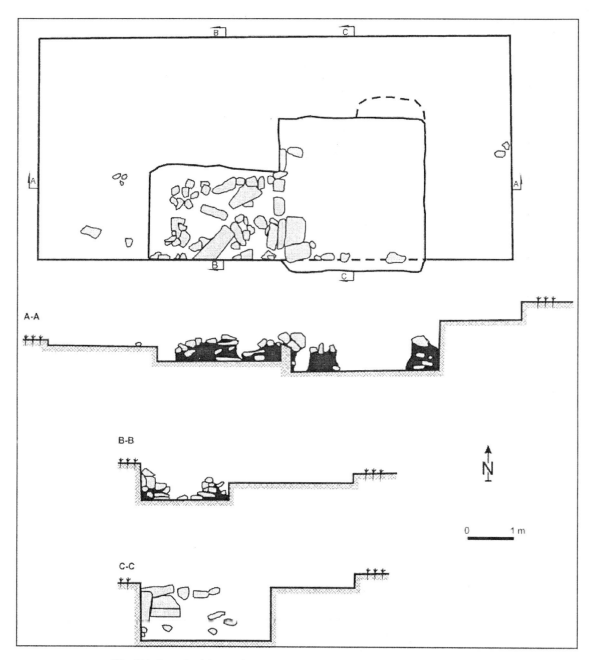

Fig. 111. Stone burial no. 1 from barrow no. 16. Plan and section (by V. Zin'ko)

To the north-west of the original mound there is a later stone tomb covered with a new mound with a diameter of 22–25 m. It was nearly completely destroyed in the early Middle Ages. Only the walls of the dromos and the south-western corner of the burial chamber (probably originally with dimensions of 2.5 m × 2.5 m) have been partly preserved. The walls of the chamber were made of limestone blocks, measuring 0.40 m × 0.40 m × 0.20 m. The burial chamber was approached from the west by a dromos made of unworked limestone blocks. The fill contained a large amount of pottery dating to the 8th–9th century and a fragment of a lekythos from the second half of the 4th century B.C. The tomb may probably be dated to

the second-half of the 4th century B.C. In the 8th–9th century the tomb was plundered and destroyed, and the site was used as a rubbish dump.

In the western part of barrow no. 16, to the north and south of the stone tomb two Sinopian amphorae containing burials were discovered. Burial A–1 was located 1.05 m to the south of the dromos wall, at a depth of 0.20 m below the then ground level. It consisted of the remains of a young man in an amphora from the second half of the 4th century – the early 3rd century B.C. with the neck and part of belly broken off. Burial A–2 was located 4.85 m to the north of the tomb. An amphora, analogous to that from burial A–1, rested on its side with the neck oriented to the north-west. Its bottom part was missing. Both burials should be dated to a period not before the second half of the 4th century B.C.

Pit burial M–1 was located in the southern part of barrow no. 16 and was a secondary burial. It was impossible to reconstruct the shape of the pit. Bone remains lay at a depth of 0.25 m from the then ground surface. The state of preservation of the bones was very bad. The deceased was placed on the back, with the head oriented to the west. In the scapula there was a strongly corroded trefoil-shaped arrowhead dating to the 4th–3rd century B.C.

Secondary burial M–2 was located in the central part of the barrow and had been completely destroyed by a modern robbers' pit. It was probably a burial of a child in a cist grave made of flat, unworked limestone slabs, with a floor constructed of small limestone rocks. The burial, of which only the south-eastern part was preserved, was oriented north-west to south-east. The inside width of the burial was 0.27 m. In the robbers' pit several fragments of pottery dating to the 8th–9th century were found, and hence the date of the burial is supposed to be the 8th–9th century.

Pit burial M–3 was in the western part of the barrow, 0.92 m to the west from the entrance to the dromos. It was impossible to reconstruct the shape of the burial. Bone remains were found at a depth of 0.65 m from the then ground level. Their state of preservation was very bad; the skull was missing. The deceased lay on the back, the head was oriented to the south, the right hand resting on the pelvis. There were no grave goods. The stratigraphy indicates the date of the burial to the 4th–3rd century B.C.

Pit burial M–4 was in the north-western part of the barrow, at a depth of 0.65 m from the then ground level. It was impossible to reconstruct the shape of the burial. The deceased rested on the back, the head was oriented to the south and turned towards the left shoulder, the cheekbones being oriented to the west. The left hand lay alongside the trunk, the right one, on the breast. To the right of the temple bone a fragment of an earring of copper wire was found. On the right arm there was a small piece of limestone. The burial may be dated to the 4th–3rd century B.C.

Pit burial M–5 was located near burial A–2, at a depth of 0.8 m from the then ground level. It was impossible to reconstruct the shape of the burial. The deceased rested on the back with the legs bent at the knee and turned to the left. The head was oriented to the south. The skull rested on the left shoulder. The left hand lay alongside the trunk, the right, on the breast. Of the grave goods a large belly fragment of a 4th–3rd century A.D. amphora was preserved, and the burial is to be dated to this period.

Pit burial M–6 was in a 1.42 m × 0.41 m pit with walls lined with 0.08–0.12 m thick dried mud-bricks. It was 0.69 m below the then ground level. The deceased rested on the back, with the head oriented to the north and the chin resting on the left shoulder. The legs were bent at the knee. In the fill a whole cup with a round bottom made of red clay and dating to the 4th century B.C. was found, and the burial is to be dated to this period.

Finds from the barrow are stored in the Kerč Museum.

Zin'ko, Arch. 1995, 1. 13–18; Zin'ko 1998.

II.2.3. PIT NECROPOLIS OF ČURUBAŠ
(02–09, SITE 9) [Photo 16, Fig. 112]

The necropolis is located to the west and south west from the settlement of Curubaš – 2. At an area of ca 2 ha, covered with steppe vegetation, rectangular depressions (2 m × 2.5 m) oriented east-west

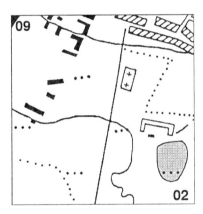

Fig. 112. Map of square 02–09 with the location of the site

can be seen. These depressions are arranged in clusters forming north-south oriented rows. At the western edge of the necropolis, near a dirt road, a rectangular, slightly worked 0.85 m tall limestone slab, perhaps a funerary stele, was found.

This necropolis is probably Mediaeval.

II.2.4. BARROWS NEAR THE SETTLEMENT
OF ČURUBAŠ – 3 (02–09, SITE 8) [Fig. 113]

These two barrows, covered with turf, are located near the south-western edge of the settlement of Čurubaš – 3 in a ploughed field. Barrow no. 1 has a diameter of ca 50 m and is preserved to a height of 1.7 m. At the top of the mound there is a round enclosure with a diameter of ca 6 m made up of slightly worked, vertically placed, large stones. Inside the enclosure a robbers' pit (?) with a stone slab at the bottom is visible. Barrow no. 2 has a diameter of

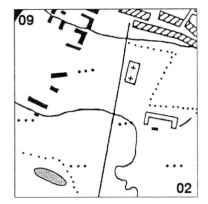

Fig. 113. Map of square 02–09 with the location
of the site

ca 30 m and is preserved to a height of 1m. At the top there is a round enclosure with a diameter of 9 m made up of large unworked limestone slabs. Inside the enclosure the walls of a stone structure resembling a cist are visible.

Date: probably ancient times.

II.2.5. BARROW NECROPOLIS OF ČURUBAŠ JUŽNOE (JUŽNO ČURUBAŠSKIJ) (04–06, SITE 5) [Fig. 114–119]

The necropolis is composed of 3 groups of barrows located to the north, east, and west of the settlement of Čurubaš Južnoe. All the mounds and elevations are covered with steppe vegetation and isolated blackthorn bushes.

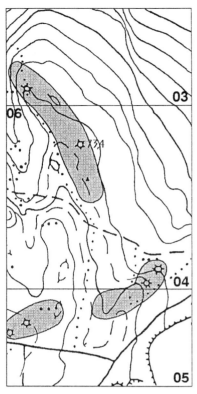

Fig. 114. Maps of squares 03–06, 04–06, and 05–06 with the locations of the sites (northern, southern, and western groups of barrows)

In 1996 with the help of an excavator, robbers dug up the central burials in three barrows of the eastern group, which were cleaned up later in the

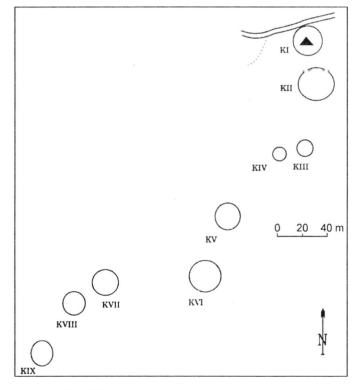

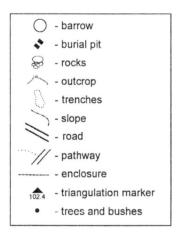

Fig. 115. Plan of southern group of barrows with key (the same for all maps by T. Nowicki)

Barrow	Diameter Ø NS [m]	Diameter Ø WE [m]	Height H rel. [m]	Stone covered	Stele	Pottery	Bones	Loose stones	Stone slabs	Burials	Plunderers' pits	Trenches from the 2nd World War	Preservation	Others
kI	21.5	25.5	0.80									•	Good	Triangulation marker undercut by road.
kII	27.5	31	0.50					•	•				Good	Asymmetrical. Four plunders pit.
kIII	13.0	10.0	0.65				•	•		•	•		Dug up	Three plunderers; pit grave with traces of cremation; fragment of scale armour and a spearhead.
kIV	10.0	12.0	0.40	•		•					•		Dug up	Broken tomb of stone slabs.
kV	21.5	20.8	1.50	•				•	•	•	•		Good	Asymmetrical. Entrance to burial chamber in a pit (three), upper part lintel visible.
kVI	22.5	25.8	1.93					•			•		Good	Two overgrown plunderers' pits.
kVII	20.0	19.5	1.10	•		•					•		Good	Circle of stones visible in pits. Three plunderers' pits.
kVIII	17.0	19.0	1.00	•		•					•	•	Disturbed	Many fragments of double circle of stones visible.
kIX	20.5	16.0	1.35	•							•		Good	Circles of stones visible in plunderers' pits. Two plunderers' pits.

Fig. 116. Tabular presentation of southern group of barrows (by T. Nowicki)

Barrow	Diameter Ø NS [m]	Diameter Ø WE [m]	Height H rel. [m]	Stone covered	Stele	Pottery	Bones	Loose stones	Stone slabs	Burials	Plunderers' pits	Trenches from the 2nd World War	Preservation	Others
kI	24.0	26.5	1.50	•				•				•	Disturbed	Remains of a triangulation marker; traces of trenches from the 2nd World War; double circle of stones partly visible
kII	18.0	17.0	0.50	•				•			•		Disturbed	Nearly entirely flattened down by ploughing. Three plunders pit.
kIII	19.0	25.0	1.40	•			•				•		Good	Asymmetrical.
kIV	24.0	20.5	0.75					•	•				Disturbed	Very much flattened down; limestone and stones slabs accumulated in one place – may have been gathered in the field.
kV	11.5	13.0	0.60						•				Good	Flat; three slabs symmetrically arranged.
kVI	14.0	15.0	0.30	•				•				•	Disturbed	Asymmetrical, with deposited stones.
kVII	24.0	19.5	1.00					•	•				Disturbed	Asymmetrical, with deposited stones.
kVIII	10.8	11.8	0.20	•		•		•	•				Dug up	Pottery visible in pits. Three plunders pit.
kIX	12.5	14	0.20					•			•		Disturbed	Not certainly a tumulus; covered with stones and overgrown with bushes – may be only an accumulation of stones from the field

Fig. 117. Tabular presentation of northern group of barrows (by T. Nowicki)

Barrow	Diameter Ø NS [m]	Diameter Ø WE [m]	Height H rel. [m]	Stone covered	Stele	Pottery	Bones	Loose stones	Stone slabs	Burials	Plunderers' pits	Trenches from the 2nd World War	Preservation	Others
kI	12.0	12.0	0.40					•					Disturbed	Flattened by ploughing.
kII	19.0	20.0	0.45	•				•	•				Disturbed	Hardly visible.
kIII	18.0	19.0	0.35			•		•	•		•		Disturbed	Considerably dug up. Five plunderers's pits.

Fig. 118. Tabular presentation of western group of barrows (by T. Nowicki)

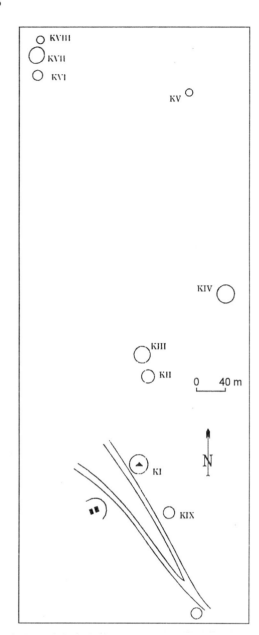

Fig. 119. Plan of northern group of barrows
(by T. Nowicki. Key, see fig. 115)

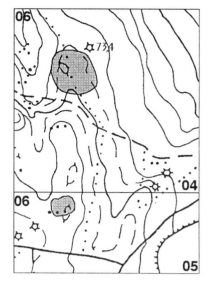

Fig. 120. Map of squares 04–06 and 05–06 with
the locations of the site (northern and southern part)

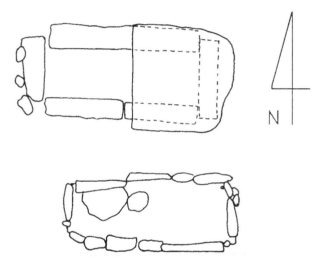

Fig. 121. Plans of plundered burials M–1 and M–2, scale 1 : 50
(by M. Nowakowska)

same year. The main burial in barrow 2 was a pit grave. Here, remains of iron scale armour and the shaft of an iron spear were collected. The burial dates to the 5th–4th century B.C. Barrow no. 5 contained a large cist grave, made of carefully worked limestone slabs. Also in barrow 4 part of a large cist grave from the 4th century B.C. is visible.

Date: probably the 5th–4th century B.C.

II.2.6. PIT NECROPOLIS OF ČURUBAŠ JUŽNOE
(JUŽNO ČURUBAŠSKIJ)
(04–06, SITE 6) [Photo 17, 18, Fig. 120–123]

The necropolis consists of two parts. The southern one is located 100 m to the south of the settlement of Čurubaš Južnoe on a small elevation and partly in a ploughed field. It occupies an area of more than 1 ha. I. Kruglikova opened trench VI upon the elevation and uncovered seven burial structures: six large cist graves and one pit burial. The pit burial and five cist graves are oriented south-east to north-west, and one cist grave is oriented south-west to north-east. In the last-mentioned burial two skeletons were found with their heads oriented to the south-west along with, i.a., 13 astragali, 3 vessels, and some beads. The burials are dated to the 4th century B.C.

In 1995–1996 the necropolis was intensively plundered. 6 other large cist graves made of carefully worked, rectangular limestone slabs and several pit burials were looted. In the plunderers' dumps large numbers of human bones and fragments of amphorae

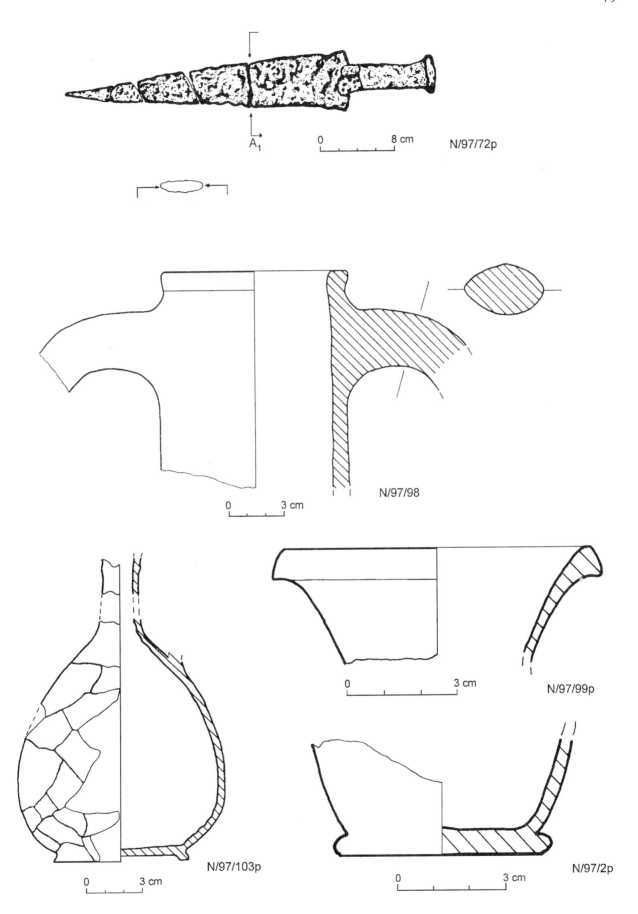

Fig. 122. Selected artefacts: N/97/72p – iron *akinakes*; N/97/98p – rim and handle of Heraclean amphora, the 4th century B.C.; N/97/99p – rim fragment of a jug; N/97/2p – bottom of lekythos, Pantikapaion, the 4th century B.C.; N/97/103p – jug, the 4th century B.C. (by L. Ponomarev)

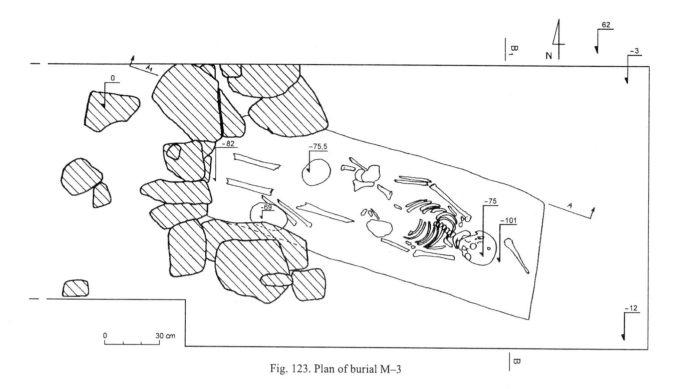

Fig. 123. Plan of burial M–3

dating to the 4th century B.C., including Heraclean, Thasian, and Chian, were found. Moreover, the stamped neck of a Heraclean amphora, dating to the 2nd–3rd quarter of the 4th century B.C (see III.2.1.) was collected. It is known that the robbers found several black-gloss kylikes.

In 1997 three burials disturbed by the robbers were excavated; two of them in the N part of the necropolis. Among the discovered artefacts were an *akinakes* dating to the early 4th century B.C. (from undisturbed grave no. 3 in part S), fragments of a lekythos also dating to the 4th century B.C. (grave no. 1, part N), numerous fragments of amphorae (i.a., a stamp on a handle of a Heraclean amphora, see III.2.4.), as well as fragments of broken luxury black-gloss table ware from the 4th century B.C.

KRUGLIKOVA, Arch. 1964; KRUGLIKOVA 1975, pp. 247–248; ZIN'KO 1986; Nymphaion, Arch. 1997, p. 4.

II.2.7. BARROWS NEAR THE SETTLEMENT OF GEROEVKA – 2 (08–04, SITE 7) [Fig. 124–126]

The barrows are located near the northern edge of the settlement of Geroevka – 2, on a high, steep shore of the Strait. To the north they are delimited by a deep gully, above which there was a tall mound, considerably disturbed during the second World War. In 1996, during earth-moving work, the upper part of the mound was destroyed and the southern part of the gully was cut to a depth of 5 m. In the trench, V. Zin'ko recorded mounds of two barrows with a diameter of up to 15 m and a height of up to 1.8 m,

made of sandy clayey bedrock. The mound was erected over a thin layer of topsoil, in which fragments of amphorae dating to the 4th–3rd century B.C. were discovered. No remains of grave structures were found. To the south there was a tall mound with a diameter of more than 30 m, and ca 5 m high overlooking the sea (until the earth-moving work commenced). In the eastern part of the mound the excavator disturbed the remains of a funerary meal. In this place an ashy spot with a diameter of more than 1 m was found, containing a large number of black-gloss pottery fragments (many of them burnt), part of which had been moved to the dump by the excavator. There were several types of vessels: fish-plates, kylikes, a painted askos, a ribbed lekythos, a salt-cellar, and several fragments of red-figure vessels.

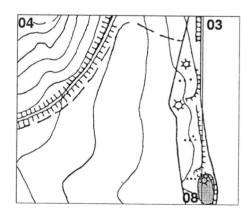

Fig. 124. Map of square 08–04 with the location of the site

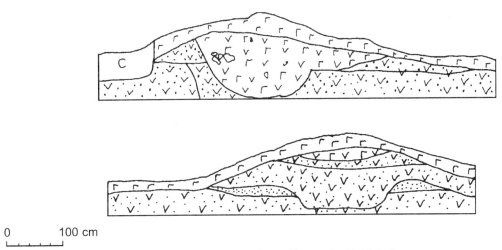

Fig. 125. Sections of barrow (by V. Zin'ko)

All these pottery fragments may be dated to the end of the 5th – the first half of the 4th century B.C. Fragments of Heraclean and Thasian amphorae dating to the 4th century B.C. were also collected from the dumps. In the western part of this barrow a stone structure from the 8th–9th century was uncovered (see II.1.22.: the settlement of Geroevka – 2).

In 1993, 100 m to the south of this barrow, another barrow (fig. 126) was excavated during archaeological work at the settlement of Geroevka 2. Its diameter was 15–19 m, and its height was up to 1m. Its eastern part was to some extent disturbed by abrasion. The barrow was erected in the early 4th century B.C. It contained four burials, three of which (nos. 2, 3, 4) date to the Antiquity and one (no. 1) to the Middle Ages.

Burials 3 and 4 were located in the central part of the mound and were destroyed in the Middle Ages. It was impossible to reconstruct their shape.

Burial no. 2, the main one in the barrow, was located in its northern part. After cremation, the remains were placed in an urn: a Chian ringed foot amphora from the first half of the 4th century B.C., dug vertically into the ground. A similar amphora lay nearby. Both of them were placed in a small depression made in the bedrock, and then covered with the mound.

The mound also contained a plundered Mediaeval burial. It was a cist grave made of very carefully worked stone slabs. Its length was 2.14 m and its width, 0.71 m. The deceased lay on the back, with the head oriented to the west. 0.7 m to the south of the burial traces of the funerary rite were discovered: 2 horse skulls and 5 cattle skulls. The burial is dated to the 8th–9th century.

The finds are stored in the Kerč Museum.

ZIN'KO 1994a, p. 125; ZIN'KO 1997a; ZIN'KO 1998.

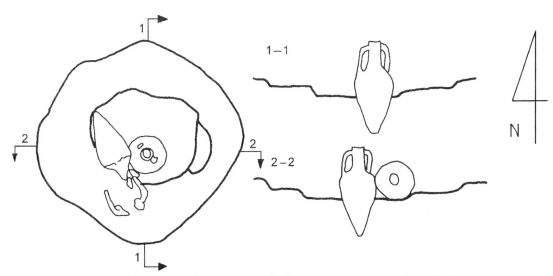

Fig. 126. Burial pit in barrow – burial 2; plan and section of burial pit (by V. Zin'ko)

II.2.8. BARROWS NEAR THE SETTLEMENT OF GEROEVKA – 3
(08–04, SITE 6) [Fig. 127]

These barrows are located near the western edge of the settlement of Geroevka – 3 and form a line running north to south. The barrows have been preserved to a height of 3 m and a diameter of 30–40 m.

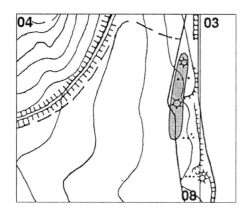

Fig. 127. Map of square 08–04 with the location of the site

The mounds are overgrown with grass. In many barrows there are grave robbers' pits with visible depths of more than 1m. In the dumps there are limestone rocks and fragments of Ancient amphorae.

Date: probably the 4th century B.C.

II.2.9. BARROWS NEAR THE SETTLEMENT OF OGON'KI – 6
(06–08, SITE 5) [Fig. 128]

Two mounds are located 120 m to the north of the settlement, in a ploughed field. Barrow no 1 has a diameter of 30 m and a preserved height of 0.3 m; barrow no 2 has a diameter of 25 m and a preserved height of 0.7 m.

Date: probably Ancient times.

ZIN'KO, Arch. 1995, 1. 33.

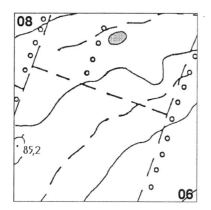

Fig. 128. Map of square 06–08 with the location of the site

II.2.10. KURGAN NECROPOLIS OF ORTEL'
(10–10, SITE 2, 3; 08–09, SITE 2)
[Fig. 129–134]

The necropolis is located to the north and north-east of the settlement of Ogon'ki – 1. It was described for the first time by I. Kruglikova in 1956. The barrows form several groups, each containing three or more mounds. The nearest group, composed of 3 barrows, is located to the north-east of the settlement on the slope of a gully joining a larger ravine. On barrow no. 1 there is a modern cemetery, on barrow no. 2 – a cemetery from the 19th century (10–10, site 2). Barrow no. 3, the smallest of the three, is located to the west of the other ones and in its centre a robbers' pit (?) is visible.

During the survey of 1996, in a ploughed field located to the west of the settlement, four small, ploughed up barrows (10–10, site 3) were recorded. Their diameters were between 10 m and 15 m and their preserved height, between 0.3 m and 0.5 m. On the mounds fragments of dried mud bricks, limestone rubble, and fragments of amphorae dating to the 4th–3rd century B.C. were found. During the survey of 1997 only three barrows were still visible.

The Trechbratnye barrows are located at the north-eastern edge of the necropolis (see II.2.13.).

KRUGLIKOVA, Arch. 1956a; KIRILIN, Arch. 1964; KIRILIN 1966, pp. 16–17.

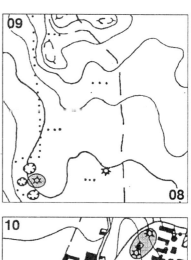

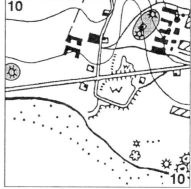

Fig. 129. Maps of squares 08–09 and 10–10 with locations of barrows

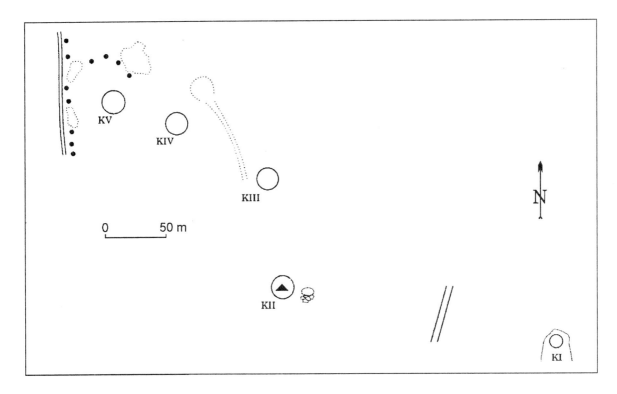

Fig. 130. Plan of the northern group of barrows (by T. Nowicki, Key, see fig. 115)

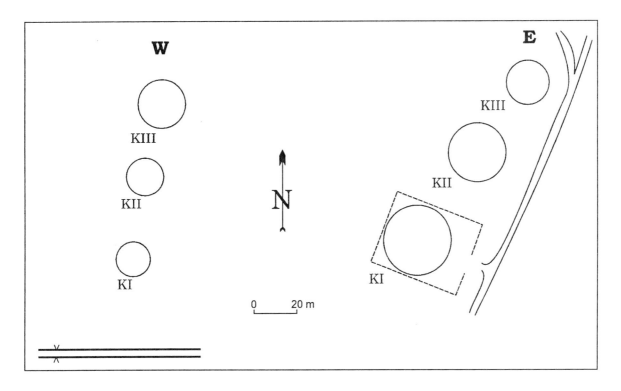

Fig. 131. Plans of eastern and western barrow groups (by T. Nowicki, Key, see fig. 115)

Barrow	Diameter Ø NS [m]	Diameter Ø WE [m]	Height H rel. [m]	Stone covered	Stele	Pottery	Bones	Loose stones	Stone slabs	Burials	Plunderers' pits	Trenches from the 2nd World War	Preservation	Others
kI	10.0	9.5	0.40										Good	Raised on a rock outcrop.
kII	19.0	21.0	1.30	•				•				•	Good	Disturbed triangulation marker.
kIII	15.0	15.0	0.70										Disturbed	Considerably flattened down by ploughing.
kIV	14.5	16.5	0.80					•					Disturbed	
kV	15.5	16.0	0.60					•				•	Disturbed	Deep pit in centre.

Fig. 132. Tabular presentation of northern group of barrows (by T. Nowicki)

Barrow	Diameter Ø NS [m]	Diameter Ø WE [m]	Height H rel. [m]	Stone covered	Stele	Pottery	Bones	Loose stones	Stone slabs	Burials	Plunderers' pits	Trenches from the 2nd World War	Preservation	Others
kI	15.0	13.0	0.30										Disturbed	Considerably ploughed, practically impossible to recognise.
kII	16.0	17.0	0.20										Disturbed	Considerably ploughed, practically impossible to recognise.
kIII	20.0	19.0	0.10										Disturbed	Considerably ploughed, practically impossible to recognise.

Fig. 133. Tabular presentation of western group of barrows (by T. Nowicki)

Barrow	Diameter Ø NS [m]	Diameter Ø WE [m]	Height H rel. [m]	Stone covered	Stele	Pottery	Bones	Loose stones	Stone slabs	Burials	Plunderers' pits	Trenches from the 2nd World War	Preservation	Others
kI	30.0	30.0	1.95							•			Good	Used as necropolis in modern times.
kII	27.0	23.0	1.40	•						•			Good	Used as necropolis in modern times.
kIII	19.0	20.0	0.70					•				•	Good	Small pit in central part.

Fig. 134. Tabular presentation of eastern group of barrows (by T. Nowicki)

II.2.11. KURGAN NECROPOLIS OF SKAL'NYJ
(04–07, SITE 6) [Fig. 135–137]

The necropolis is located on natural elevations, on the southern edge of the Curubaš Skal'ki range. 11 mounds with a preserved height between 1.1 m and 4 m have been recorded. The whole area of the necropolis is covered with steppe vegetation. In some of the mounds, structures made of unworked medium-sized limestone rocks have been preserved. On the mounds and in their vicinity fragments of amphorae dating to the 4th–3rd century B.C. were found. On many barrows trenches and traces of fortification works from the second World War are visible. These traces are particularly pronounced on the tallest barrow of the group surmounted by triangulation marker 102.4.

250 m to the east of the above-mentioned triangulation marker, in the steppe, a Scythian stone sculpture was discovered (see III.4.1.).

ZIN'KO, Arch. 1995, 1. 36; ZIN'KO 1996, p. 19.

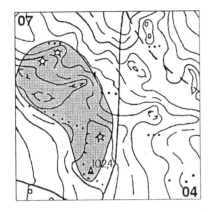

Fig. 135. Map of square 04–07 with the location of the site

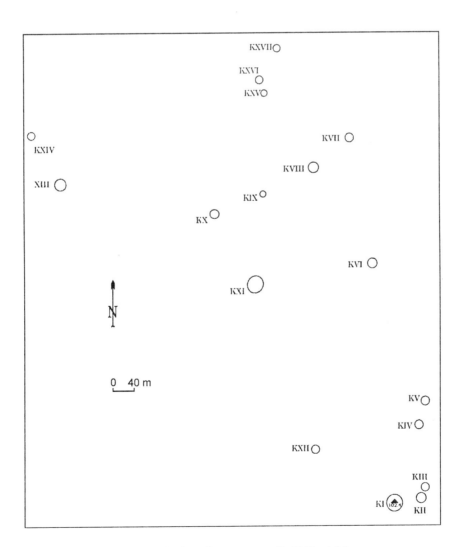

Fig. 136. Plan of barrow group (by T. Nowicki)

Barrow	Diameter Ø NS [m]	Ø WE [m]	Height H rel. [m]	Stone covered	Stele	Pottery	Bones	Stones	Stone slabs	Burials	Plunderers' pits	Trenches from the 2nd World War	Preservation	Others
kI	32.0	31.5	1.50									•	Good	Triangulation marker 102.4 m; numerous large trenches from the 2nd World War.
kII	17.0	22.0	0.30					•	•			•	Disturbed	Stone slab visible in a deep trench from the 2nd World War.
kIII	15.0	15.0	0.80	•				•				•	Disturbed	Large pit in the centre.
kIV	17.0	16.0	0.55	•				•			•		Disturbed	Very flat – ploughed up. Two plunderers pits.
kV	15.0	16.0	0.90	•								•	Good	Deep trench from the 2nd World War.
kVI	18.5	19.5	1.00	•		•		•				•	Disturbed	Asymmetrical; large pit; raised on a rock outcrop.
kVII	15.0	15.0	0.90					•	'			•	Good	Raised on a rock outcrop
kVIII	18.0	20.0	0.40									•	Disturbed	Large trenches from the 2nd World War.
kIX	13.0	14.0	0.80					•				•	Disturbed	Large trenches from the 2nd World War.
kX	15.5	15.5	1.00	•		•			•				Good	Large pit in the centre.
kXI	30.0	35.0	0.65	•				•			•		Disturbed	Large pit in the centre.
kXII	10.0	14.0	0.30		•			•	•				Disturbed	Very flat – ploughed up, overgrown.
kXIII	20.0	18.0	0.75	•								•	Good	Small pit in the centre.
kXIV	13.5	13.0	1.00	•				•	•		•	•	Good	Double circle of stones at the bottom.
kXV	12.0	12.0	1.30	•									Good	Raised on a rock outcrop.
kXVI	15.0	14.0	0.80	•									Good	Raised on a rock outcrop. small pit in the centre.
kXVII	14.0	14.0	0.65	•				•				•	Good	Raised on a rock outcrop. small pit in the centre.

Fig. 137. Table of barrow measurements (by T. Nowicki)

II.2.12. PIT AND KURGAN NECROPOLIS OF TOBEČIK
(10–07, SITE 4) [Fig. 138]

The necropolis is located in a belt of trees, 0.2 km to the north-west of the settlement of Tobečik – 9. On the western edge of the necropolis there are two barrows. On the barrow which lies more to the west, a triangulation marker 38.4 has been erected, and the mound is considerably disturbed by trenches from the second World War. On the second barrow

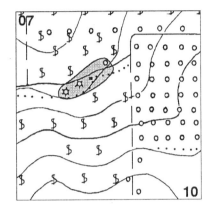

Fig. 138. Map of square 10–07 with the location of the site

traces of a modern store for chemical materials can be seen. It is possible that other elevations located nearby are also barrows but today on one of them there are ruins of a house, and on the other one, remains of vine posts. To the south of the barrows, in a belt of trees adjoining a dirt road, 8 large limestone slabs, probably covers of cist graves, are visible. Fragments of pottery dating to the 4th – 3rd century B.C. and 1st–3rd century A.D. have been collected from the surface.

The site has not been excavated.

ZIN'KO, Arch. 1995, 1. 31–32.

II.2.13. TRECHBRATNYE BARROWS
(09–08, SITE 1) [Fig. 139–145]

Three barrows are located in a field along a line running north to south. They may be considered to belong to the kurgan necropolis of Ortel'. The whole area was disturbed in the 1960s during works connected with the extraction of iron ore. The barrows had the following dimensions: no. 1 (the oldest) – height, 8.6 m, diameter, 45.6 m; no. 2 (the middle one) – height 6.7 m, diameter 42.5 m; no. 3 (the earliest) – height 4 m, diameter 25.5 m. The mounds were made of humus mixed with light-coloured clay. In 1965 the barrows were excavated by D. Kirilin. The mound of barrow 2 was further investigated by S. Bessonova in 1967.

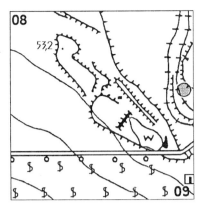

Fig. 139. Map of square 09–08 with the location of the site

Altogether six graves were discovered in the three barrows. In barrow no. 1 there were two tombs with a step roof, in barrow no. 2, one tomb and two cist graves of limestone blocks, and in barrow 3, one cist grave. On all the three mounds, on special clay platforms located in the vicinity of the graves, there lay horse skeletons. In barrows no. 2 and 3 these skeletons were partly disturbed by robbers. Only some of the components of the harness, decorated in Scythian style, were preserved, i.a., a fragment of a headdress in the form of a fantastic animal. Moreover, fragments of bronze *psalia* decorated with bulls' heads in a style known from the northern Caucasus were found. In the mound of barrow no. 2 bones of a horse and a dog were discovered.

Barrow no. 1 had a tomb located at a depth of 6.5 m from the top and 14.5 m to the south-west of the centre of the barrow, on the very edge of the mound. The tomb was cut into bedrock to a depth of 1.5 m. It consisted of one chamber with the following internal dimensions: length 3.2 m, width 1.78 m, height 2.75 m, and a short dromos, 0.85 m long, 1.15–1.35 m wide, and 1.70 m high. The chamber had walls made of limestone slabs without mortar and was covered with a step "ceiling" composed of 4 rows of limestone slabs. The entrance from the dromos to the chamber was closed with a stone slab. At the northern wall of the chamber there was a stone bed, 0.30 m high, 2.02 m long, and 0.74 m wide. On it lay the skeletons of two women with their heads oriented to the east. The first one was a poorly preserved skeleton probably of a girl (1.45 m tall) while the second one was of a middle-aged woman (1.75–1.80 m tall). At the head of the girl there was a clay vessel – an oinochoe. The other deceased had ornate clothes decorated with gold ornaments. On her head she had a gold kalathos with a veil decorated with 15 gold plaques bearing images of palmettes and a winged goddess, a tiara with representations of lions and panthers on the forehead, and gold earrings in the form of sphinxes.

Fig. 140. Drawing of relief found in mound of barrow 1
(after Bessonova, Kirilin 1977, p. 133, fig. 4)

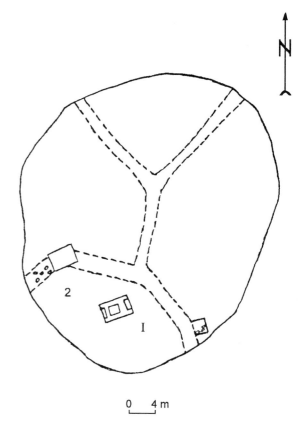

Fig. 141. Plan of barrow 1: 1, 2 – burials, 3 – place of finding
relicf (after Bessonova, Kirilin, 1977, p. 129, fig. 1)

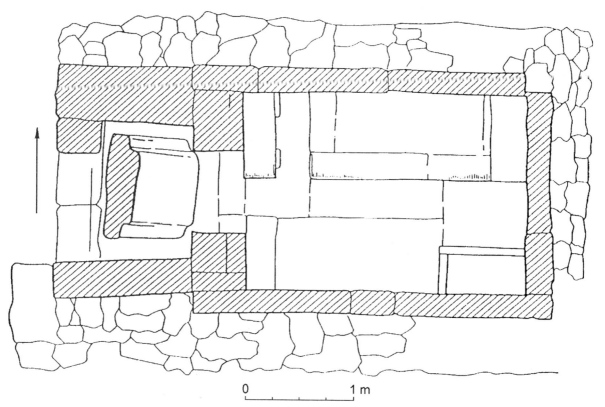

Fig. 142. Plan of barrow with a step vault in barrow 1 (after Kirilin 1968, p. 179, fig. 1)

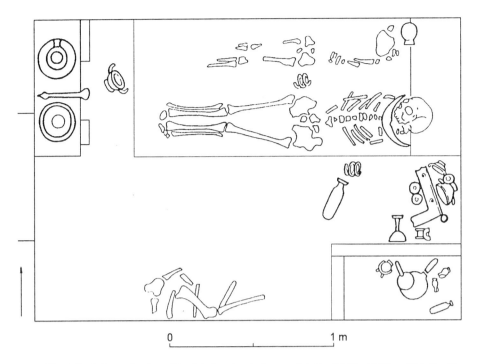

Fig. 143. Schematic plan of burial chamber in barrow 1 (after Kirilin 1968, p. 181, fig. 2)

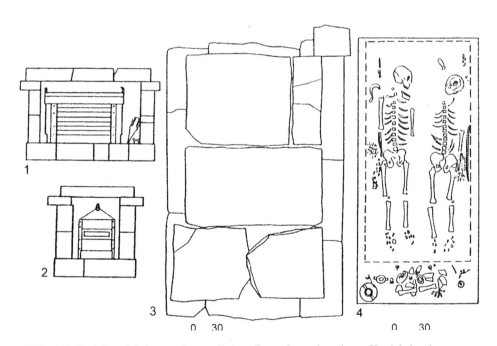

Fig. 144. Burial no. 3 in barrow 2, so-called medium, plan and sections of burial chamber:
1 – W–E section, 2 – N–S section, 3 – ceiling of burial, 4 – location of skeletons and grave goods
(after Bessonova 1973, p. 244, fig. 1)

On the breast there were gold beads, rings, and circular and triangular plaques. On the arms there were gold bracelets and a gold ring on the finger. At the feet there was a bronze coin of Pantikapaion dating to 330–315 B.C. Leather shoes were decorated with silver and gilded plaques with representations of sirens. Above the bed there was a canopy with gilded bronze sprigs of laurel. On the floor of the chamber there were, i.a.,

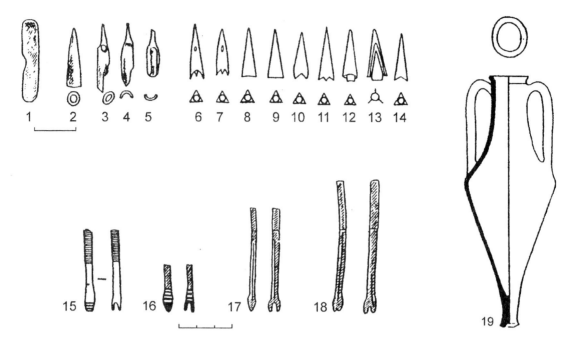

Fig. 145. Burial 3 in barrow 2 – grave goods: 1 – quiver fixture

a wooden box and pyxides, 3 black-gloss salt-cellars, a red-figure fishplate, 3 black-gloss kylikes, 3 lekythoi, 2 gilded bronze mirrors, a bone comb, beads, a red-figure Attic pelike, a Thasian amphora with a stamp of "Thasion Krinis"; on a wooden tray there probably would have lain some beef (for the bones were preserved) and an iron knife. 9 m to the east of the grave a large broken limestone relief was discovered with a representation of a woman wearing a kalathos, a quadriga and a rider. The relief was 2.5 m high, 1.6 m wide, 0.005–0.055 m deep, the slab was 0.255–0.275 m thick.

Tomb no. 2 was completely plundered. It is dated by a fragment of a stamp on a Sinopian amphora with the name of the "astinomos Zopirion".

In barrow no. 2 the stone tomb (no. 1) with a step cover, analogous to the tomb from barrow no. 1, was also completely plundered. In the south-western part of the barrow there was a burial (no. 2): a plundered cist grave with 6–7 skeletons. Burial no. 3 was a cist grave with a flat cover made of three stone slabs, walls of well fitted, massive (0.37–0.38 m thick) rectangular slabs, and a floor of 7 slabs. The dimensions of the cist were: 2.5 m (length), 1.25 m (width), 1.4 m (height). Inside there was a wooden sarcophagus with two skeletons lying on their backs with their heads oriented to the east. Skeleton no. 1 was that of a 35–45 year-old man, skeleton no. 2 was of a 30–40 year-old woman. The grave goods included: bronze arrowheads, a bronze ladle and a strigil, a bow, 2 alabastra, an amphora of the Murighol type,

a miniature net lekythos, a mirror, an amphoriskos with net decoration, wooden vessels. This burial is dated to the second half of the 4th century B.C.

Barrow no. 3 contained one completely plundered cist grave dated by bronze arrowheads and fragments of alabastra to the second half of the 4th century B.C.

The finds are stored in the Kerč Museum and in the Deržavnyj Muzej Koštovnostej in Kiev.

Kirilin 1966; Kirilin 1968; Bessonova 1971; Bessonova 1973; Bessonova, Kirilin 1977

II.2.14. KURGAN NECROPOLIS WITH TRIANGULATION MARKER 93.6 (05–12, SITE 4) [Fig. 146–147, 152]

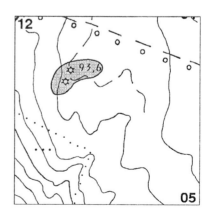

Fig. 146. Map of square 05–12 with the location of the site

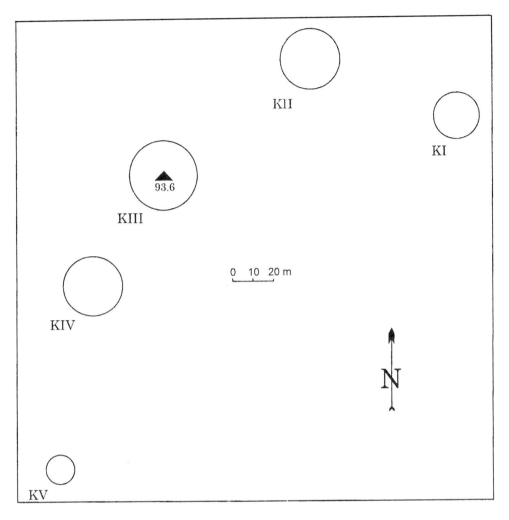

Fig. 147. Plan of group of barrows (by T. Nowicki)

The necropolis is located at the south-western edge of a large plateau-type elevation located near triangulation marker 93.6. The group consists of 5 barrows situated in a modern ploughed field. The tallest barrow, no. 3 (with the triangulation marker), has a diameter of 50 m and a preserved height of 1.8 m. The mound is overgrown with steppe grasses in which single stones, perhaps coming from the barrow, can be seen. In the western part of the mound a ring enclosure with a diameter of 8–9 m made of unworked limestones is visible. In this place a Scythian sculpture, made of one 1.75 m tall limestone block is located (see: III.4.2.). At the foot of the barrow there is probably one more such sculpture. Nearby, towards the south-west lies barrow no 4, on the mound of which, now overgrown with grass, single stones can be seen. The mound of barrow 5 is extensively ploughed up. To the north-east of barrow no. 3, in a ploughed field, there are barrows covered with limestone rubble, also extensively disturbed by ploughing.

II.2.15. KURGAN NECROPOLIS WITH TRIANGULATION MARKER 97.9 (05–07, SITE 6) [Fig. 148–149, 153]

The necropolis is composed of four barrows located along a north-south line. On barrow no. 4 there is a triangulation marker 97.9.

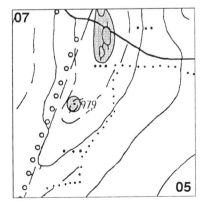

Fig. 148. Map of square 05–07 with the location of the site.

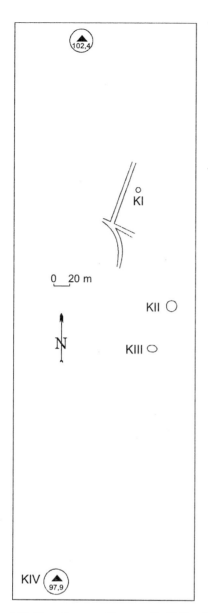

Fig. 149. Plan of group of barrows (by T. Nowicki)

II.2.16. KURGAN NECROPOLIS WITH TRIANGULATION MARKER 47.9
(04–04, SITE 3; 05–04, SITE 5)
[Fig. 150–151, 154]

The necropolis is composed of two groups of barrows. At the slope of the barrow with triangulation marker 47.9 a fragment of a pipeline was discovered (see II.4.10.).

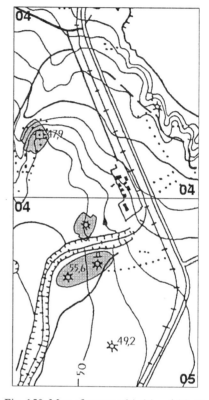

Fig. 150. Map of squares 04–04 and 05–04 with the location of the barrows

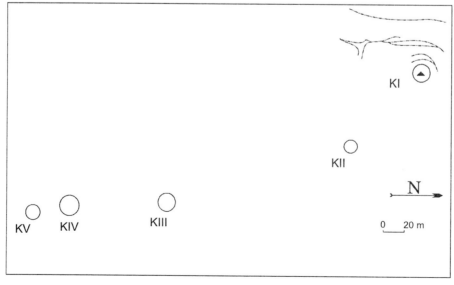

Fig. 151. Plan of group of barrows (by T. Nowicki)

Barrow	Diameter		Height	Stone covered	Stele	Pottery	Bones	Loose stones	Stone slabs	Burials	Plunderers' pits	Trenches from the 2nd World War	Preservation	Others
	Ø NS [m]	Ø WE [m]	H rel. [m]											
kI	22.0	23.0	0.20			•		•					Disturbed	Flattened by ploughing.
kII	30.0	31.0	0.30			•		•				•	Disturbed	Ploughed up.
kIII	35.0	34.0	1.55		•	•		•	•				Good	Triangulation marker 93.6 m. Two stele.
kIV	27.0	26.0	1.30	•	•			•	•		•		Good	Concentration of stones in one part.
kV	14.0	15.0	0.50						•		•		Disturbed	Slightly ploughed up.

Fig. 152. Table of barrow measurements (by T. Nowicki)

Barrow	Diameter		Height	Stone covered	Stele	Pottery	Bones	Loose stones	Stone slabs	Burials	Plunderers' pits	Trenches from the 2nd World War	Preservation	Others
	Ø NS [m]	Ø WE [m]	H rel. [m]											
kI	6.0	5.0	0.30					•	•				Disturbed	Has no clear features allowing to classify it as a barrow.
kII	15.0	16.0	0.40	•				•	•				Disturbed	Ploughed up.
kIII	9.0	13.0	1.10					•			•	•	Considerably disturbed	Dug up, large number of trenches from the 2nd World War.
kIV	32.0	30.0	2.50	•								•	Good	Pit in central part.

Fig. 153. Table of barrow measurements (by T. Nowicki)

Barrow	Diameter		Height	Stone covered	Stele	Pottery	Bones	Loose stones	Stone slabs	Burials	Plunderers' pits	Trenches from the 2nd World War	Preservation	Others
	Ø NS [m]	Ø WE [m]	H rel. [m]											
kI	20.0	18.0	2.50								•	•	Good	Numerous large pits, triangulation marker 47.9 m.
kII	16.0	15.0	1.70								•	•	Disturbed	A number of trenches from the 2nd World War.
kIII	18.0	19.0	2.10									•	Good	A number of trenches from the 2nd World War.
kIV	19.0	20.0	4.50									•	Good	Reconstructed in modern times – a monument.
kV	17.0	15.0	1.70									•	Disturbed	Trenches and pillbox from the 2nd World War.

Fig. 154. Table of barrow measurements (by T. Nowicki)

The majority of the plots were recorded by V. Zin'ko in the years preceding our joint project, or during the period of our cooperation but in months other than those in which we worked together (in spring or winter). Unfortunately, during our joint field surveys, especially in 1996–1997, the weather and vegetation conditions were very unfavourable for discovering the borders of the plots.

II.3.1. PLOTS NEAR THE SETTLEMENT OF ČURUBAŠ – 9
(03–07, SITE 4; 03–08, SITE 2)
[Photo 19, 20, Fig. 155–157]

They are located in the range Čurubaš Skal'ki, in a large valley oriented east-west and surrounded by rocky hills. In the western part of the valley there lies

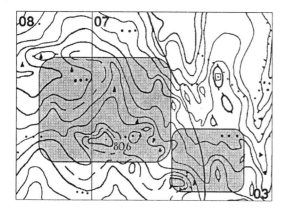

Fig. 155. Map of squares 03–07 and 03–07 with the location of site

the settlement of Čurubaš – 7, and in the eastern one, that of Čurubaš – 9. In 1856, Rjabov recorded the remains of plots visible in the area of Lake Čurubaš on a map (the exact location of the area he recorded is uncertain today). In 1938 V. Gajdukevič carried out a field survey in the area. In 1963 I. Kruglikova and B. Peters made a drawing of two adjoining plots surrounded by earthen embankments, located in the neighbourhood of the settlement of Čurubaš – 9. The eastern plot, rectangular in shape (a "country house" was located in its central part), had an area of 29.4 ha. Its longer sides, oriented almost exactly north-south, were ca 865 m long, and the shorter ones, 340 m. The southern part of the plot had an enclosure extending from the south-east to the north-west and reaching the elevation where the "country house" was located. The southern part of the plot had an area of ca 10 ha while the northern one, 19 ha. This plot was adjoined to the

Fig. 156. Plan of part of plot (after Kruglikova 1975, fig. 68)

west by another one, with an area of 35.4 ha. It was also divided into two parts: the southern one with an area of more than 12 ha and the northern one, with an area of ca 23.3 ha. At the eastern end of the enclosure crossing this plot there was a rocky hill on which, according to I. Kruglikova, another "country house" might have been located. The hill, however, has been completely destroyed by a quarry.

In 1995 elevations in the form of low north-south oriented earthen walls were recorded in the valley. At their foot they are ca 1.5 m wide, their preserved height is up to 0.2 m, and the distance between them is between 40 m and 50 m. In the northern part of the valley the remains of a structure with walls of limestone slabs resting on their longer sides can be seen. In the south-eastern part of the valley, on a rocky elevation, on flat parts of the rock, round depressions with a diameter of 0.5–0.8 m (press-beds?) were recorded. To the south the elevation is adjoined by another plot with remains of an enclosure in the form of earthen walls and stones. In many places the enclosures are composed of natural rock outcrops. All the plots are covered with turf.

Date: probably Ancient times.

GAJDUKEVIČ 1940, p. 317; KRUGLIKOVA 1975, p. 129, fig. 68, pp. 130–131; ZIN'KO, Arch. 1995, 1. 35, p. 25.

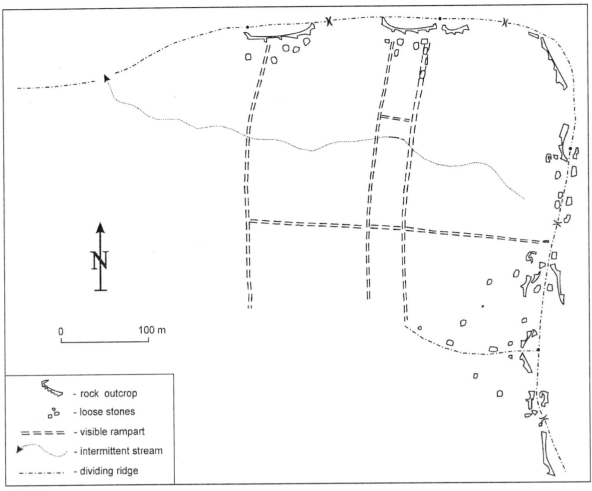

Fig. 157. Plan of part of plot (by T. Nowicki)

II.3.2. PLOT NEAR THE SETTLEMENT OF ČURUBAŠ CITADEL' (04–07, SITE 8) [Fig. 158]

It is located 100 m to the south of the settlement, between rocky elevations. Its north-south oriented sides are 200 m long; the shorter sides (oriented east-west) are 50 m long. The plot is covered with turf. At the northern, southern, and eastern boundaries of the plot, remains of enclosures are visible; to the west the plot is delimited by rock outcrops.

Date: probably Ancient times.

ZIN'KO, Arch. 1995, 1. 36; ZIN'KO 1996, p. 18.

II.3.3. PLOTS NEAR THE SETTLEMENT OF ČURUBAŠ JUŽNOE (JUŽNO ČURUBAŠSKOE) (04–06, SITE 4) [Photo 4, Fig. 159–160]

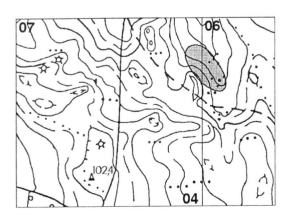

Fig. 158. Map of squares 04–07 and 04-06 with the location of the site

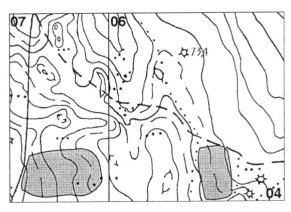

Fig. 159. Map of squares 04–06 and 04-07 with the location of the site

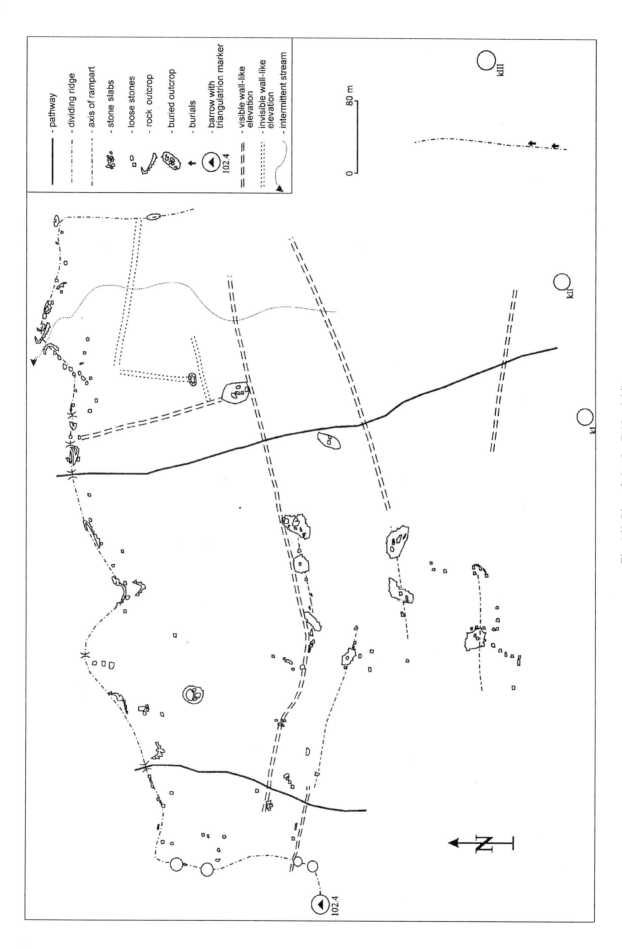

Fig. 160. Plan of plot (by T. Nowicki)

They are located to the east and west of the settlement. The eastern part was investigated in 1963–1964 by I. Kruglikova who made trial pits which allowed to delineate the probable boundaries of a plot adjoining a complex of three structures dating to the late 5th–6th century B.C. The distance between the northern and southern part of the enclosure was 115 m. The eastern and western boundaries were established by studying the location of ash pits and assuming a distance of ca 100 m between the sides (on the basis of knowledge of dimensions of plots at other "country houses"). I. Kruglikova observed a number of plots of this size in this very same place, having a surface area of little more than 1 ha.

During the survey of 1994 in a settlement located in a ploughed field and under turf on the eastern slope earthen wall-like elevations were recorded. Part of the enclosure made of stone and mud brick was probably discovered in trial pit no. 2.

The western complex is located between the barrow with triangulation marker 102.4 and the settlement. It is located in a valley surrounded at the north, west, and east by a rocky range, and open at the south. As a result the majority of the plots are situated on slopes with a southern inclination. In the valley, numerous rocky outcrops are visible (some with traces of cutting) and earthen wall-like elevations with various orientations, lengths and widths. These differences may have been caused by the fact that the plots were used in various periods. In flat parts or on slightly inclined slopes one can observe hollows without drainage outlets.

KRUGLIKOVA 1975, p. 93; ZIN'KO, Arch. 1994, 1. 20; SCHOLL, Arch. 1997.

II.3.4. PLOTS NEAR THE SETTLEMENT OF ČURUBAŠ MAJAK –1 (05–11, SITE 6) [Fig. 161]

They are located 600 m away from the settlement, on a ploughed field. Earthen elevations ca 2 m wide at their foot and with a preserved height of up to 0.3 m are oriented east-west. Three parallel lines of enclosures, 150 m long, 50–60 m away from each other, have been recorded.

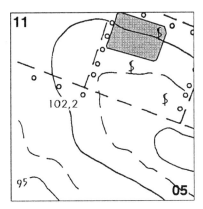

Fig. 161. Map of square 05–11 with the location of the site

II.3.5. PLOTS NEAR THE SETTLEMENT OF OGON'KI – 6 (06–07, SITE 4) [Fig. 162]

They are located 800 m to the east of the settlement. In a ploughed field two 0.3–04 m high elevations, 1.5–1.9 m wide at their base, oriented north-east – south-west, have been recorded. The distance between them is ca 40 m, and they are visible for a length of more than 150 m. Two surface structures, which may be interpreted as plots, are also visible in a satellite picture. Pottery fragments (amphorae from the 4th–3rd century B.C., including Chian, Heraclean, and Thasian ones) have been collected from the surface.

ZIN'KO, Arch. 1995, 1. 33, p. 16.

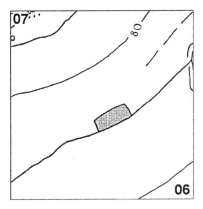

Fig. 162. Map of square 06–07 with the location of the site

98

II.4.1. WALL (07–09, SITE 4) [Fig. 163–170]

This wall was first mentioned in the second half of the 19th century by I. Beskrovnyj[4] without any particular location, as a wall which enclosed, i.a., the

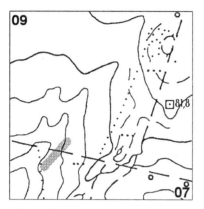

Fig. 163. Map of square 07–09 with the location of visible parts of wall

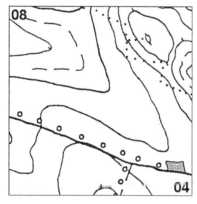

Fig. 164. Map of square 04–08 with the location of place where geophysical survey was conducted in order to find the supposed course of wall

lands belonging to Nymphaion,[5] to the west. Verification of this hypothesis in the field was one of the aims of our research. During the field survey several variants of the possible course of the wall were investigated. It was certain that it began near the settlement of Ogon'ki – 3 and ran to the north, along the eastern slope of a ravine, forming a curve bending to the east. In some parts of the hypothetical course of the wall, at elevations, there are several barrows. In the north the wall probably reached the rocky hills of the Čurubaš Skal'ki range.

---

[4] R.V. ŠMIDT, *K issledovaniju bosporskich oboronitel'nych valov*, SA 7, 1941, p. 274.

[5] SCHOLL 1981, pp. 344–348.

In 1995, near the settlement of Ogon'ki – 3, between two barrows, a fragment of the wall was recorded, more than 200 m long, up to 0.5 m high, and 2 m wide at its foot. In 1997 a series of 8 geo-electrical soundings were made in that place (carried out and described by K. Misiewicz). A high resistivity layer located directly under the surface was recorded. The absolute values of resistivity of this layer ranged between 1200 and 800 ohm with current probe spacing AB/2 = 14 m, i.e., at a depth of ca 5 m below the modern ground level. Such an image of resistivity clearly suggests that there is a rock outcrop in the investigated area. For that reason it was useless to apply geophysical methods to search for the wall.

The interpretation of satellite pictures allowed us to select several other places where the wall might run, which would be suitable for the application of geophysical methods. The area in square 04–08, where the supposed wall crossed a dirt road, seemed to be the most promising. To verify the assumed course of the wall geoelectrical soundings along 5 lines, each 30 m long, were made. The measurements made up a 2.5 m × 2.5 m grid. In this way a 10 m × 30 m surface was covered. The current probe spacing allowed us to distinguish layers at depths of between 0.15 m to 5 m below the modern ground level, in the area located between the road and the edges of ploughed fields. Such a location made trial pits possible. The lines of geoelectrical soundings were arranged so as to dissect the remains of the hypothetical wall and any structures possibly adjoining it (e.g. trenches), which allowed us to obtain clearly delineated, closed complexes of anomalies in places where the hypothetical remains were resting.

The ground resistivity survey provided an image of changes in its distribution within a range of 25–120 ohm, presented as black-and-white (Fig. 165) printouts of isolines of equal vertical resistivity. A horizontal layer with a resistance of 25–30 ohm at a depth of ca 2–2.5 m is evident in the printout. This layer constitutes the border between the natural stratigraphy and man-made changes. Changes in the resistivity of geological formations below this layer, which can be characterised as clays with an admixture of fen soils, are slight and result only from differences in humidity. Above this layer, the image of the geological structure reconstructed on the basis of resistivity changes is more complex. The registered differences in the resistivity of layers reaching 20–30 ohm are slight and may be caused by different humidity of the layers. On the basis of these soundings the black-and-white maps of resistivity

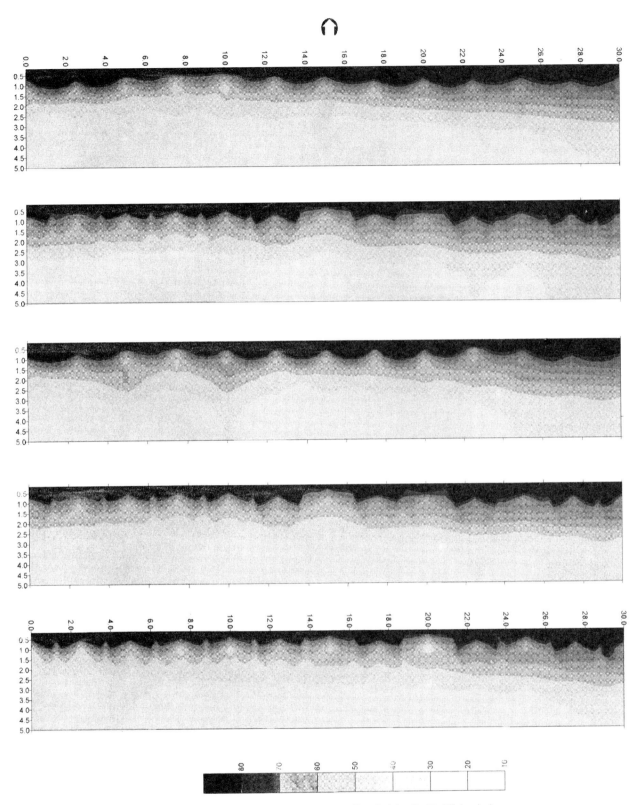

Fig. 165. Maps of vertical distribution of soil resistivity (by K. Misiewicz)

distribution changes were made for various levels of prospection, obtained by increasing the distance between the electrodes (Figs 166, 167, 168). The maps did not reveal dynamic changes of resistivity different from its surroundings such as would have been caused by a trench filling or a stone construc- tion of a wall. It has been found that at no level of prospection narrow, anomalous structures are distinguished, as ought to have happened if there were remains of any structures in the investigated area. Moreover, the image of resistivity distribution on the maps made for prospection levels below 2 m

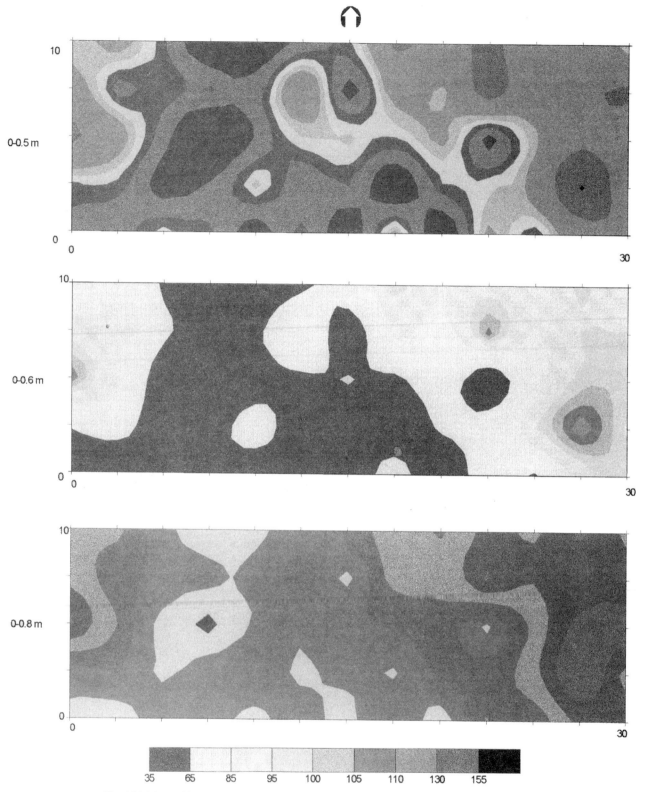

Fig. 166. Maps of isolines of vertical distribution of resistivity, depth 0.5–0.8 m (by K. Misiewicz)

suggests that in the investigated area only an undisturbed, natural, arrangement of layers was found. To find the reason for the lack of uniformity in resistivity distribution a precise analysis of phenomena appearing in layers above the assumed bedrock (Fig. 168) was conducted. It was assumed that due to heavy dis-

turbance of the remains being searched for only indirect traces of their existence would be found in the form of small changes in layers close to the surface. These may have been caused by, e.g., faster drying of the soil in the places where the natural stratification has been disturbed. Precise plotting of vertical resis-

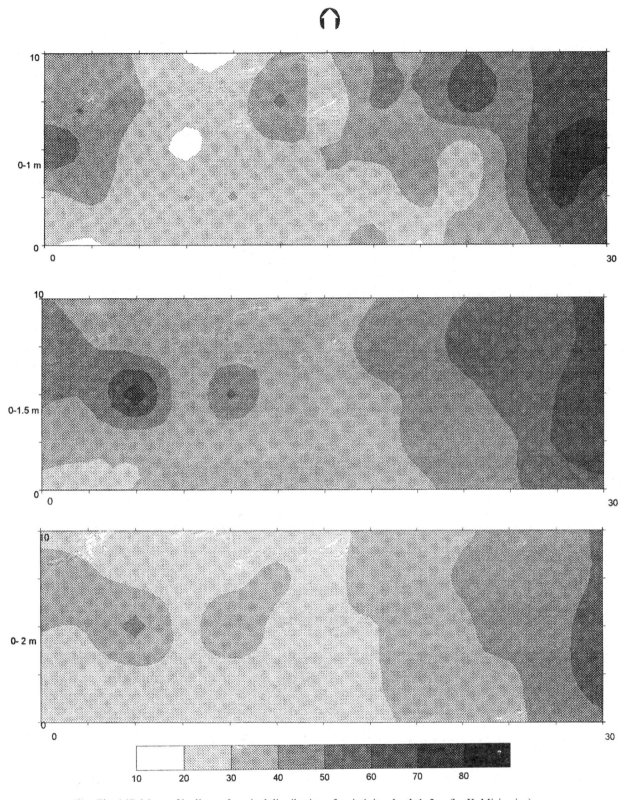

Fig. 167. Maps of isolines of vertical distribution of resistivity, depth 1–2 m (by K. Misiewicz)

tivity distribution for the different pseudo-sections allowed to distinguish the above-described changes, which were particularly visible in pseudo-section 3 (Fig. 169) and 4 (Fig. 170). They are located at metres 14–16, 19–21, and 24–26. In all cases they consisted of a lowering in the thickness of the high-resis-

tivity layer lying close to the surface. A trial pit was made at line 4 at metres 19–21 where the registered changes in the surface layers are also perceptible at greater depth. In a 1 m × 2 m trench dug to a depth of 1 m below the modern ground level only natural stratification without any traces of sequences

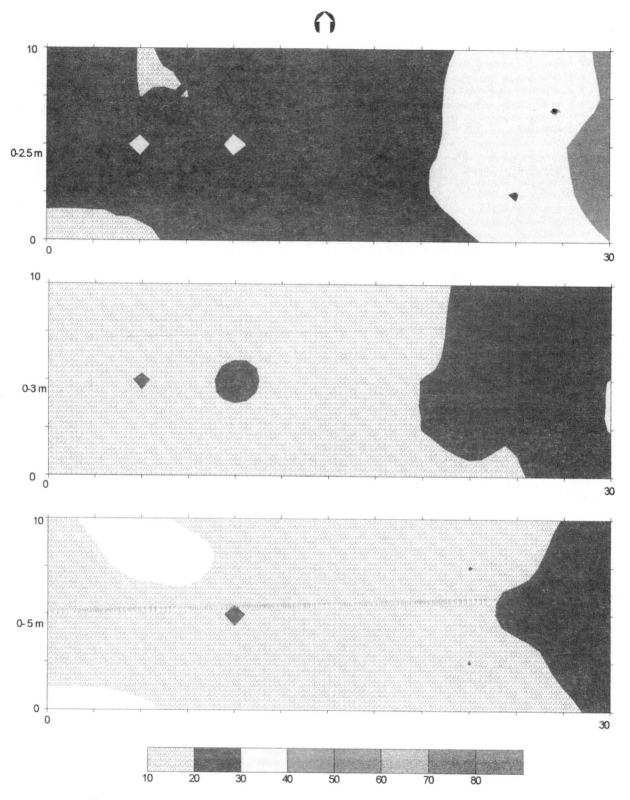

Fig. 168. Maps of isolines of vertical distribution of resistivity, depth 2.5–5 m (by K. Misiewicz)

deposited by human agency was discovered. The changes observed in the maps of isolines were due to the process of erosion. In those places lying close to the surface where disturbances in the layer of topsoil had occurred, the thickness of the soil was greater where it filled natural depressions in the bedrock.

This produced an image similar to that obtained from man-made trenches.

On slopes the loess soil is washed down during heavy rains and produces loess diluvia in depressions. The results of such processes were visible in the profile of the trial trench. In the upper part of

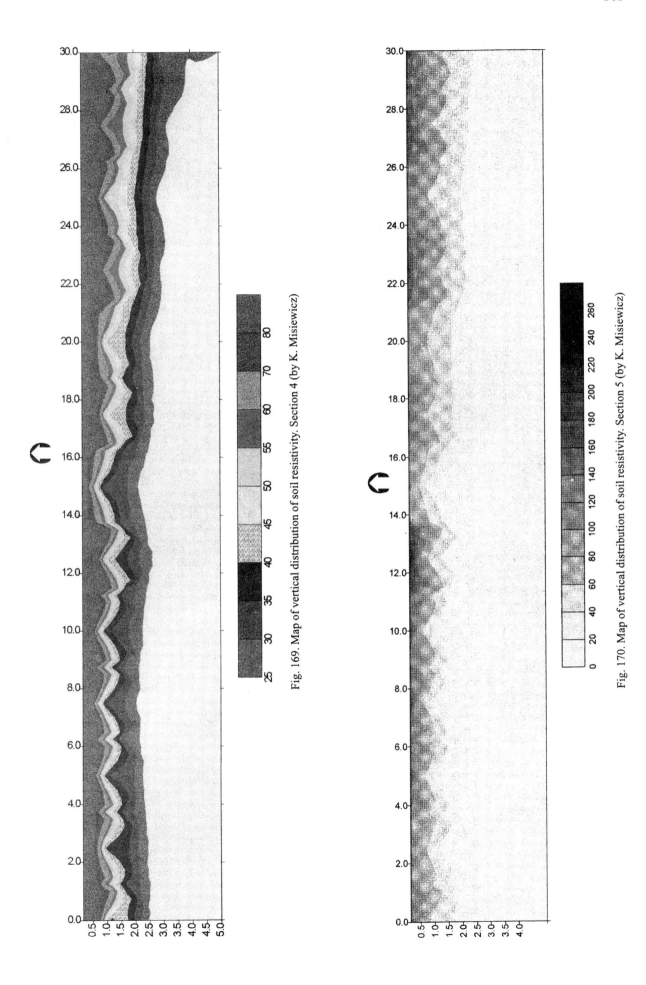

Fig. 169. Map of vertical distribution of soil resistivity. Section 4 (by K. Misiewicz)

Fig. 170. Map of vertical distribution of soil resistivity. Section 5 (by K. Misiewicz)

the profile, from the bottom of the topsoil layer to a depth of ca 0.8 m there lies a layer of soil (most probably) composed of mineral and organic particles washed down from the slope. Underneath there is a 20 cm thick layer of brown soil, probably once cultivated, resting on the lower part of a soil profile consisting of carbonate concretions produced by water migration and the washing out of carbonates from the upper parts of the profile.

The information gathered by means of geophysical survey completed by that obtained from the trial pit allows us to state that no clear traces of remains of defense structures have been found in the investigated area. Even the small changes in the resistivity of surface layers are of natural origin.

Nymphaion, Arch. 1995, p. 3; SCHOLL, Arch. 1996; Nymphaion, Arch. 1997, p. 4; SCHOLL, Arch. 1997.

☆ ☆ ☆

Overland pathways were traced by various means. Some of them could be reproduced by analysing the lay of the land. Another method consisted in recording settlement traces on a satellite map. Moreover, a topographical map with all settlements and barrows (often raised along pathways) could be used for finding all the suitable overland links.

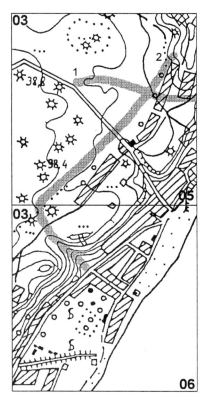

Fig. 171. Map of squares 05–03 and 06–03 with the presumed course of Ancient pathways

II.4.2. PATHWAY NO. 1
(05–03, SITE 9) [Photo D, Fig. 171–173]

It was discovered by N. Grač. According to her oral information it began at the western gate of Nymphaion and ran westwards across the pit and kurgan necropolis of Nymphaion. In that place it can be traced for ca 0.5 km in the form of a long, narrow depression with an east-west orientation. In its lower part it is from 6 m to 8 m wide. Its further course is impossible to follow because of the disturbances caused by an iron ore strip mine.

Nymphaion, Arch. 1995, p. 4; SCHOLL, ZIN'KO 1997, p. 64.

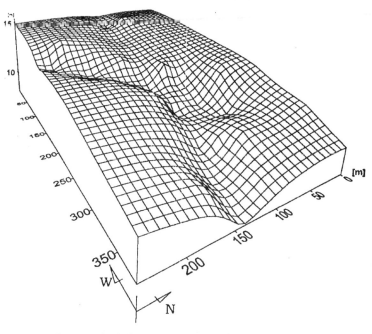

Fig. 172. Block diagram: crossroads of pathways 1 and 2
(by T. Nowicki)

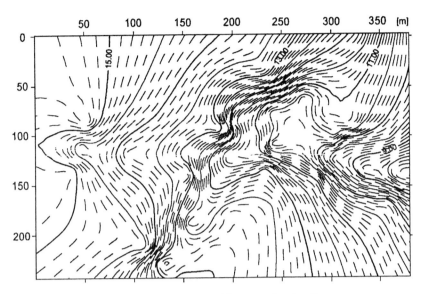

Fig. 173. Contour line map with conventional ordinate:
crossroads of pathways 1 and 2 (by T. Nowicki)

II.4.3. PATHWAY NO. 2
(05–03, SITE 9) [Photo 21, Fig. 171–173]

This pathway ran from north to south and is clearly visible at the crossroads formed with pathway no. 1 in the area of the settlement of Èl'tigen Zapadnoe. It is preserved in the form of a shallow depression with gentle slopes. Farther on it ran to the south-west along the southern part of the barrows of the necropolis of Nymphaion, located on the edge of the second terrace. After passing the second lighthouse, the pathway descended to the sea shore along a gentle slope in a natural pass across the hill range, which is probably the only one in the vicinity.

The existence of a pathway in this place was confirmed during the field survey of 1995, when recording the early Mediaeval settlement. The further course of the pathway may be followed by studying the arrangement of barrows along the shore, which make up a line leading directly to Lake Tobečik. The whole pathway is more than 6 km long.

of pottery dating from the 4th–3rd century B.C. to the 8th–9th century for more than 1 km (10–04, site 1, 2, 3, 4; 10–05, site 4). The pathway is also clearly visible in satellite pictures.

Today there is an asphalt road running in its immediate vicinity.

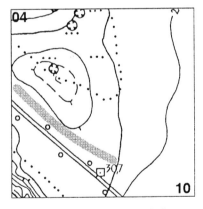

Fig. 174. Map of square 10–04 with the presumed course of pathway

II.4.4. PATHWAY NO. 3
(10–04, SITE 5) [Fig. 174]

It began at the south-eastern boundaries of the chora and ran to the north-west on an elevation alongside Lake Tobečik. In the latter place the existence of the pathway is confirmed by stray finds

II.4.5. PATHWAY NO. 4
(04–12, SITE 8) [Fig. 175]

Its course was followed from the south-western corner of a large elevation. In this part there is only a natural depression, leading towards a plateau. It contained single pottery fragments dating to the first

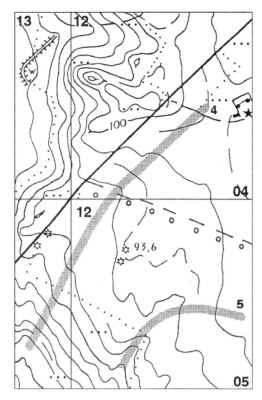

Fig. 175. Map of squares 04–12 and 05–12 with
the presumed courses of pathways

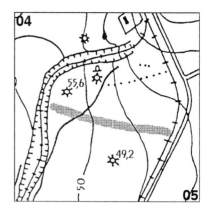

Fig. 176. Map of square 05–04 with the presumed
course of pathway

B.C. to the first centuries A.D. (05–04, sites 1, 2, 3, 4). The eastern and western parts of the pathway were disturbed by an iron ore strip mine.

II.4.8. QUARRY NO. 1
(03–08, SITE 4) [Fig. 177]

At the rocky elevations in the north-western part of the Čurubaš Skal'ki range traces of old quarrying and fragments of large limestone blocks were discovered. Quarrying traces are visible in the form of vertical, oval depressions, 0.03–0.04 m

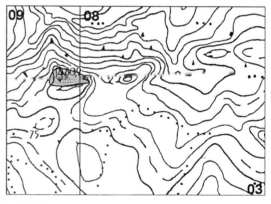

Fig. 177. Map of squares 03–08 and 03–09 with the location
of the site

wide and 0.80 m long. Similar traces can be seen near the Scythian stone sculpture no. 1 found close to the kurgan necropolis of Skal'nyj (see III.4.1.).

II.4.9. QUARRY NO. 2
(05–03, SITE 13) [Fig. 178]

It is located in the north-eastern part of the necropolis of Nymphaion. Outcrops of limestone can be found there at a depth of 0.8–1.2 m. During excava-

centuries A.D. (06–13, site 1). Then the pathway runs to the north-east, towards the settlements of Čurubaš Majak – 1 and 2. This section is confirmed by single finds of pottery dating from the 4th–3rd century B.C. to the first centuries A.D. (05–13, sites 1, 2). To the east and west the pathway is adjoined by barrows. Near the settlement of Čurubaš Majak – 1, at its western boundaries, there is a clearly visible, 200 m long depression with a north-east orientation. Then the pathway ran to the north east, towards the settlement of Čurubaš – 3. Altoghether the pathway was followed along 3 km.

Today there is a dirt road running parallelly to the ancient pathway, at a distance of 0.2–0.3 km.

II.4.6. PATHWAY NO. 5
(05–12, SITE 10)[Fig. 175]

It began at the south-western edge of a low elevation and, after reaching a plateau, ran to the east. The course of this pathway is confirmed along ca 3 km by fragments of pottery dating to the 4th–3rd century B.C. and 8th–9th century (05–12, sites 1, 5, 7, 9).

II.4.7. PATHWAY NO. 6
(05–04, SITE 6) [Fig. 176]

It was followed along ca 1 km on the basis of pottery fragments found in a line running from east to west, and was confirmed by a satellite picture. Pottery fragments were dating from the 4th–3rd century

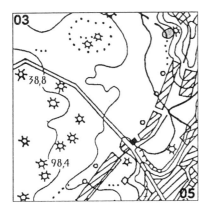

Fig. 178. Map of square 05–03 with the location
of the site

tions carried out by N. Grač, traces of cuttings for
limestone blocks were discovered in the virgin rock.

☆   ☆   ☆

II.4.10. PIPELINE (04–04, SITE 5)
[Photo 22–26, Fig. 179–185]

During the field survey of 1995, on the western
slope of the hill with triangulation marker 47.9 a flat
limestone slab was recorded, which was interpreted
as the entrance to the dromos of a barrow. In 1997,
after heavy rains, part of the slope was eroded. In

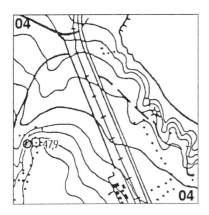

Fig. 179. Map of square 04–04 with the location
of the site

the profile a fragment of a stone wall could be seen.
When cleared it proved to be a part of a shaft with
stone walls, ending in a stone tank to which ceramic
pipes ran from two sides. The shaft had dimensions
of 1.10 m × 0.72 m and a depth of 2 m and its walls
were made of broken stones fixed with a mortar of
silt, clay, soil and broken shells (maltha). The wall
of the shaft adjoining the slope was sagging under
the pressure of the soil. The tank had a diamond-

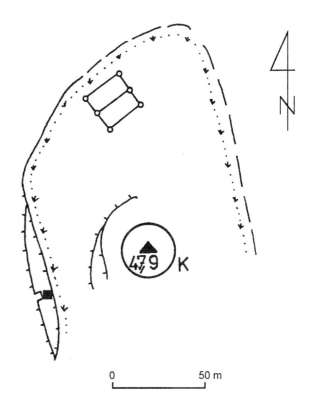

Fig. 180. Plan of location of pipeline in trench
and the area of geophysical survey

shaped bottom and was hewn from one limestone
block. The dimensions of its upper surface were
0.72 m × 0.72 m along the outside and 0.52 m × 0.52 m
on the inside, and it was 0.12 m deep. At the bottom
the tank measured 0.40 m × 0.37 m on the inside.
Originally, the tank was covered with a limestone
slab, a fragment of which was found in situ in
the south-western corner. To follow the course of
the ceramic pipes a trial trench was dug 0.30 m to
the north of the shaft. It revealed that the ceramic
pipes had a casing made of stones fixed in a similar
way to those in the shaft, making up a stone tunnel
0.85 m wide and 0.45 m high. Altogether 2 pipes
were uncovered, each 0.944 m long with 0.03 m
thick walls and with an internal diameter of 0.1 m.
The pipes are made of dark-orange clay with limestone, sand, and broken pottery inclusions; colour
rubs off the outer surface of the pipes. They had
simple sliding joints and lime mortar was used for
fixing them. At the outlet of one of the pipes a significant carbonate precipitation was discovered
(trace amounts of it were also found on the inside).
Near the shaft and in the trial pit a few fragments of
pottery, including Heraclean and Chian amphorae
from the 4th century B.C. were collected.

The microgeological profile of the slope revealed
the effects of loess sedimentation in the water environment, probably in the form of a lake filled with
salty water, which explains the fact of the numerous

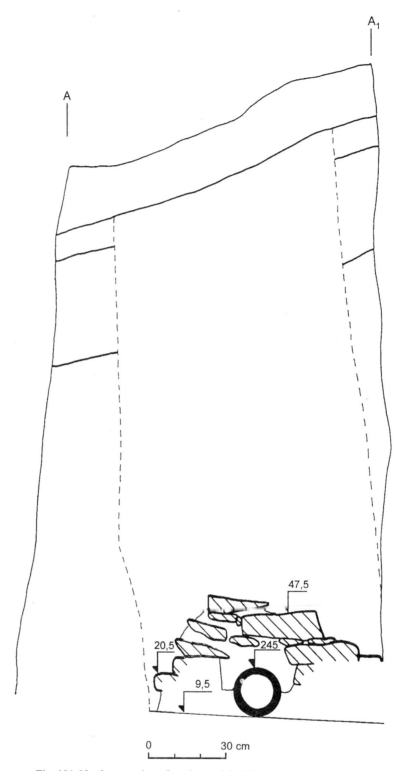

Fig. 181. Northern section of northern trial pit (by M. Nowakowska)

gypsum precipitations. Due to the admixture of silty minerals the loess can have vertical walls.

The discovered structure is probably part of a water conduit: a sump ending with a sediment trap.

An attempt was made at tracing the further course of the pipeline by means of geophysical methods.

Due to the considerable depth at which the remains were lying the system of measuring of Average Gradient with potential probe spacing $MN = 1$ m and current probe spacing $AB = 20$ m, was arranged perpendicularly to the supposed course of the structure. The measurements were made in a 1 m grid.

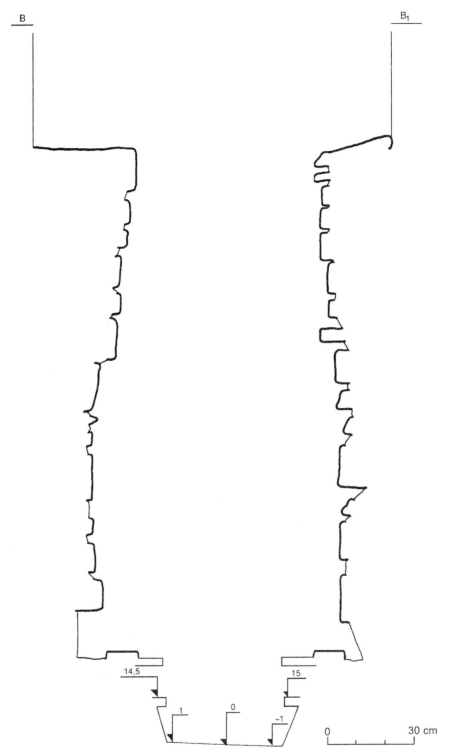

Fig. 182. Section of gully (by M. Nowakowska)

The survey was carried out over an area between two depressions (Fig. 180) which might have been interpeted as traces of sediment traps similar to the one discovered with the fragment of a pipeline. Altogether the survey embraced an area of ca 2500 m². Resistivity ranging between 20 and 500 ohm was recorded. Such considerable differences indicated that lithological changes in the medium were mainly being recorded, and any effects caused by human agency were only of secondary importance. Linear anomalies on the east-west axis are visible on the map and it is possible to interpret

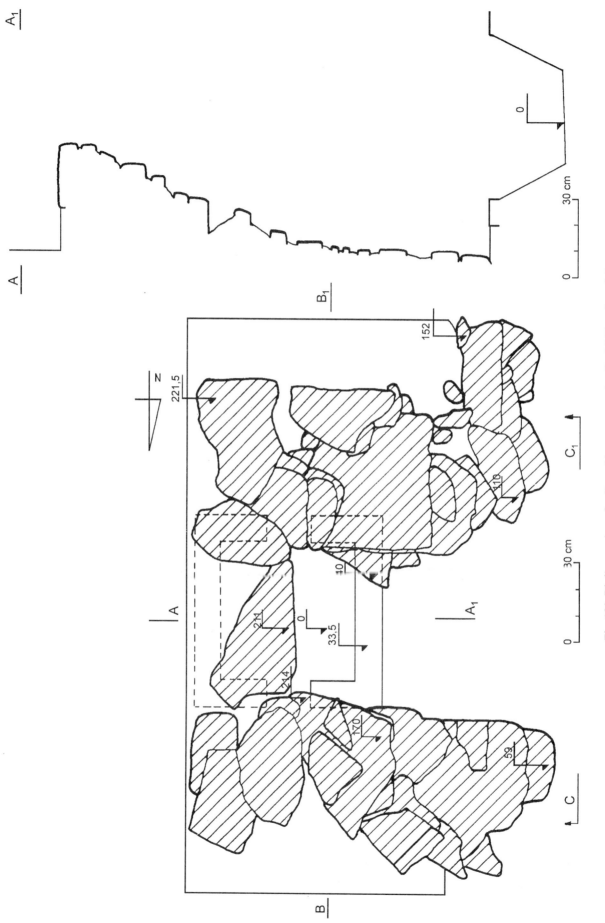

Fig. 183. Bird's eye view of gully and its eastern section (by M. Nowakowska)

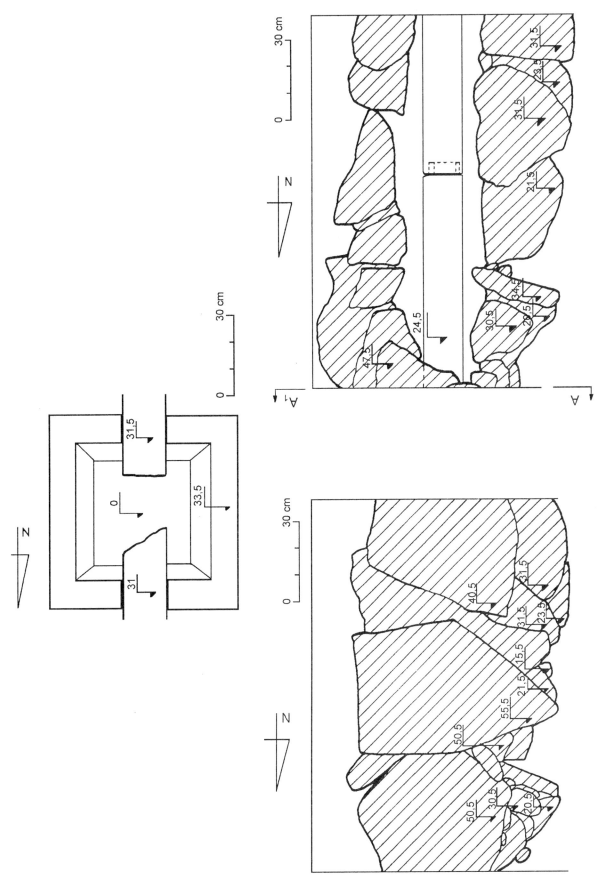

Fig. 184. Gully and the course of pipeline in northern trial pit (by M. Nowakowska)

112

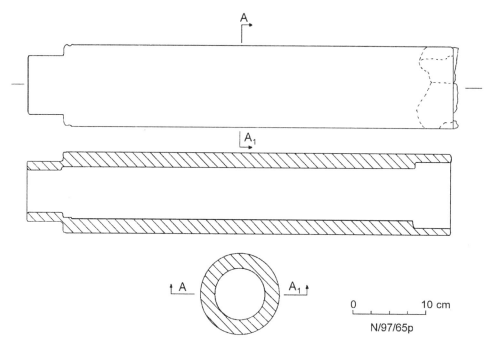

Fig. 185. Ceramic pipe (by R. Karasiewicz-Szczypiorski)

them univocally. They register the so-called slope-effect, i.e., linear anomalies perpendicular to the line of measurements, and represent the oblique edge of a ploughed field. No disturbances which could be connected with the remains of a waterpipe have been recorded.

Nymphaion, Arch. 1997, p. 4; SCHOLL, Arch. 1997.

II.5. STRUCTURES DISCOVERED UNDER WATER (NOS. 1–5)

II.5.1. SITE OF A SHIPWRECK
(09–03, SITE 6) [Fig. 186]

Located near the settlement of Geroevka – 1, at a depth of 3.6 m, it was discovered in 1990 by V. Zin'ko and A. Šamraj. It consists of the remains of a wooden ship, nearly completely covered with sand. Bronze and copper rivets and nails from the part of

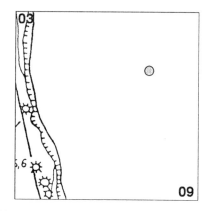

Fig. 186. Map of square 09–03 with the location of the site

the vessel completely destroyed by the sea can be seen in the sand. The difficult hydrological conditions in place during the period when our investigations were carried out allowed only to make a side drawing of the elements protruding from the sand. Several clamping rings, nails and rivets were collected as examples. The total length of the visible part of the ship is ca 40 m.

The catastrophe probably took place in the 17th –18th century.

ZIN'KO, Arch. 1990, 1. 73.

II.5.2. SETTLEMENT NO. 1
(06–02, SITE 2) [Photo 27, Fig. 187–188]

It is located 300–500 m away from the shore, opposite the First Geroevskaja lighthouse. In 1990, two amphorae lying next to one another and dating to the 9th century A.D. were accidentally discovered (06–02, site 1). One of them, 0.42 m tall with graffito on the belly – two Greek letters „H", was sent to the Kerč Museum. In 1990, the place where the amphorae were discovered was investigated by V. Zin'ko and A. Šamraj, and then again in 1994, in cooperation with

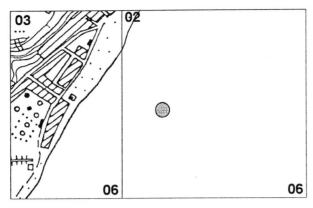

Fig. 187. Map of squares 06–02 and 06–03 with the location of the site

The archaeological material and the way it is distributed indicate that we are dealing with a monumental stone structure, which had been situated on the sea shore and then, due to changes in the shoreline, was covered with the sea.

The finds are stored in the Kerč Museum.

ZIN'KO, Arch. 1990, 1. 72–73; Nymphaion, Arch. 1994, pp. 8, 19, fig. 6; ZIN'KO, Arch. 1994, 1. 22–23; KARASIEWICZ-SZCZYPIORSKI 1995, p. 546.

II.5.3. SETTLEMENT NO. 2
(06–03, SITE 6) [Fig. 189–190]

In 1977, at the request of N. Grač, a group of divers from KIAM under the guidance of V. Lavruchin, studied the remains of a structure which was called a "country house". The remains consisted of walls made of large limestone blocks lying on the sea bed up

a group of divers from Poland. On the sandy sea bed a field of limestone rocks of an area of 0.4 ha was discovered. 40 per cent of the stones bears traces of working and some of them are 0.8 m × 0.4 m × 0.2 m slabs. The majority of them rests on hard sand and between the stones loose sand silts 0.10 m thick are visible. Among the stones there is a layer of maritime flora and crustacea. This layer contains pottery fragments destroyed by sea water. They include parts of amphorae dating to the 4th–3rd century B.C. (including a Chian peculiar ringed foot one), handles of amphorae from the 1st–2nd century A.D., as well as fragments of Bosporan roof tiles which exceed in number any other kind of ceramic. In the place of the greatest concentration of roof tiles part of a limestone vessel with two handles was found. In 1990 a stone altar was collected from the settlement.

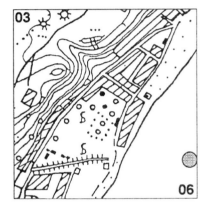

Fig. 189. Map of square 06–03 with the location of the site

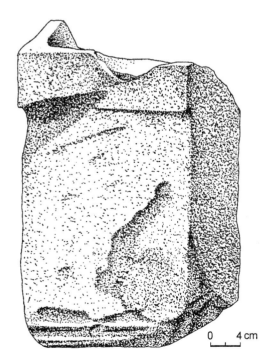

Fig. 188. Stone altar (by V. Zin'ko)

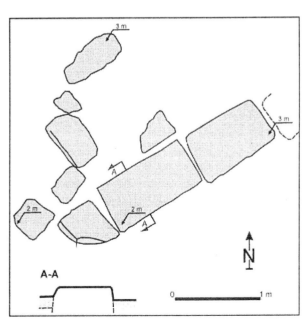

Fig. 190. Plan of underwater stone structure (after Lavruchin, Arch., 1977)

114

to 20 m away from the shore. In 1982 the plan of this structure was drawn by V. Golenko, a scientific consultant of the Bosporan Underwater-Archaeological Expedition. The preserved remains consist of a wall fragment parallel to the shore. The structures were placed on the sea bed at a depth of between 1 m and 3 m and probably ran deeper under a layer of sand.

In 1990, V. Zin'ko and A. Šamraj carried out an investigation of the site. A field of large limestone blocks with single ashlars visible, extending from the north to the west at an area of ca 0.5 ha, was recorded. Among the stones belly fragments of amphorae and two fragments of Bosporan roof tiles were discovered. The pottery material is dated to the 4th–3rd century B.C.

LAVRUCHIN, Arch. 1977, opis' 3, ed. chran. no. 739, 45s; ZIN'KO, Arch. 1990, opis' 2; ed. chran. no. 1075, l. 73.

II.5.4. SETTLEMENT NO. 3
(07–03, SITE 1) [Fig. 191]

It is located to the south of settlement no 2, at a depth of between 3 m and 3.5 m. It was discovered in 1990 by V. Zin'ko and A. Šamraj. A field of large limestone blocks, oriented north-south, which also

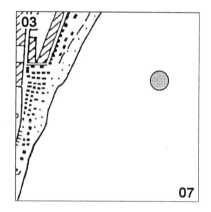

Fig. 191. Map of square 07–03 with the location of the site

included ashlars, was recorded over an area of ca 0.4 ha. Among the stones, a nearly complete Bosporan roof tile as well as fragments of pottery dating to the 4th–3rd century B.C. were collected.

ZIN'KO, Arch. 1990, opis'2, ed. chran. no. 1075, l. 73.

II.5.5. ANCHORAGE
(06–02, SITE 3) [Fig. 192]

It is located at a depth of 6–6.5 m to the east of settlement no. 1. It was discovered by V. Zin'ko and A. Šamraj in 1990. Additional survey was carried

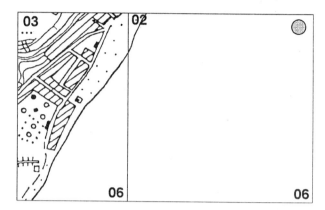

Fig. 192. Map of squares 06–02 and 06–03 with the location of the site

out in 1994 in cooperation with divers from Poland. 15 anchor stones buried in sand at a depth of 0.14–0.25 m were discovered. At the whole area of the anchorage diorite cobbles, not found locally, are distributed. Three kinds of anchors were distinguished: 1 – stones with one depression, 2 – stones with several rounded depressions, 3 – stones with a surrounding groove for attaching the rope.

At the anchorage, pottery fragments were frequently discovered. It should be stressed that Mediaeval fragments are located in the upper layers of soil while the Ancient ones can be found at the same level as the anchors.

In the place of the greatest concentration of archaeological material, remains of four carefully worked wooden posts with a diameter of 0.08 m, driven into the ground and extending above it to 0.10 m, were discovered. Some of the posts were longer than the other ones and had well-preserved parts below ground.

The archaeological material and stratigraphy allow to assume that this was an anchorage for light vessels, used for a long period of time, including Antiquity (anchors and amphora fragments dating to the 4th–3rd century A.D., including Heraclean and Chian ones). In later times this place was used for setting up nets.

The finds are stored in the Kerč Museum.

ZIN'KO, Arch. 1990, opis'2, ed. chran. no. 1075, l. 72; ZIN'KO, Arch. 1994, l. 23–24.

III. SPECIAL FINDS

III.1. LITHIC ARTEFACTS

BY MARCIN BEDNARZ (INSTITUTE OF ARCHAEOLOGY, WARSAW UNIVERSITY)
[Fig. 193–194]

The lithic inventory is rather scant and does not contain any elements providing precise dating of the discovered sites. It is composed of 10 flint and 1 stone artefacts. The artefacts were studied on the basis of photographs and drawings.

III.1.1. N/95/344p
(02–08, SITE 1)

A flint chip with retouches on the ventral face, near the bulp. It does not seem to be connected with the Mediaeval pottery appearing at that site.

III.1.2. N/95/254p
(03–09, SITE 1)

A small flake with a preserved fragment of cortex and multidirectional negatives of previous blows, and several irregular, probably spontaneous retouches on the ventral face.

III.1.3. N/95/255p
(03–09, SITE 1)

A fragment of an end-scraper made on a flake with traces of splinting on ventral and dorsal faces. Probably the flake was first splintered off and then the splintered piece served as a blank for the end-scraper.

III.1.4. N/95/256p
(03–09, SITE 1)

A hammer with very clear traces of bruising, probably made of a flint pebble quite regular in shape. It can not be excluded that the round shape is the final (intended?) effect of the bruising. Then its function would be difficult to define: we may be dealing here with a weapon designed for hurling (bolas, sling missile, etc.); other interpretations are also possible.

III.1.5. N/95/246p
(03–09, SITE 1)

A fragment (head) of a polished battle-axe made of crystalline rock. The axe broke in the most vulnerable place: near the aperture. In the photograph a negative of a flake knapped off the head is visible. It also seems possible (although without any certainty) that the "protrusions" left on both sides of the aperture might have been polished through use (after the tool had been broken).

Artefacts III.1.2–4. are the so-called ubiquitous forms, thus it is not possible to attach them to any particular culture. Artefact III.1.5. is a standard piece of equipment of Neolithic and early Bronze Age steppe groups. It can thus be linked to the pottery of the Sroubnaya culture discovered at that site.

III.1.6. N/97/63p
(04–04, SITE 6)

A fragment of a blade retouched in the proximal part so as to form a kind of a "bec". It is broken and damaged in such a way that it resembles a burin on a broken blade with burin spalls on the ventral face of the blade. This form, an isolated find, may come from the Neolithic.

III.1.7. N/95/257p
(05–07, SITE 3)

A proximal fragment of a blade with traces of micro-retouching sponateous or caused by use. It does not seem to be connected with the pottery found at the site.

III.1.8. N/96/25p
(05–11, SITE 4)

A small flake with probably spontaneous micro-retouching. Nearby, several similar flakes were found.

116

III.1.9. N/96/39p (07–10, SITE 1)

A central fragment of a rather regular bladelet with traces of retouching on one edge. It may be connected with fragments of hand-made pottery found at that site.

III.1.10. N/96/38p (08–10, SITE 2)

Probably a fragment of a quite massive flake (the drawing does not allow one to state this with certainty), broken along its axis, forming a flat, relatively thick plate with high sides (a kind of a natural back on the whole circumference of the tool). On the sides there are traces of rather irregular retouching. The tool might have served as a strike-a-light. Links with the pottery dating to the 2nd millenium B.C. found at that site are as probable as those with other periods.

III.1.11. N/97/64p (09–04, SITE 5)

A central part of a subcortical blade with traces of (probably spontaneous) retouching. Links with the pottery dating to the 2nd millenium B.C. are as probable as in the case of the artefact described above.

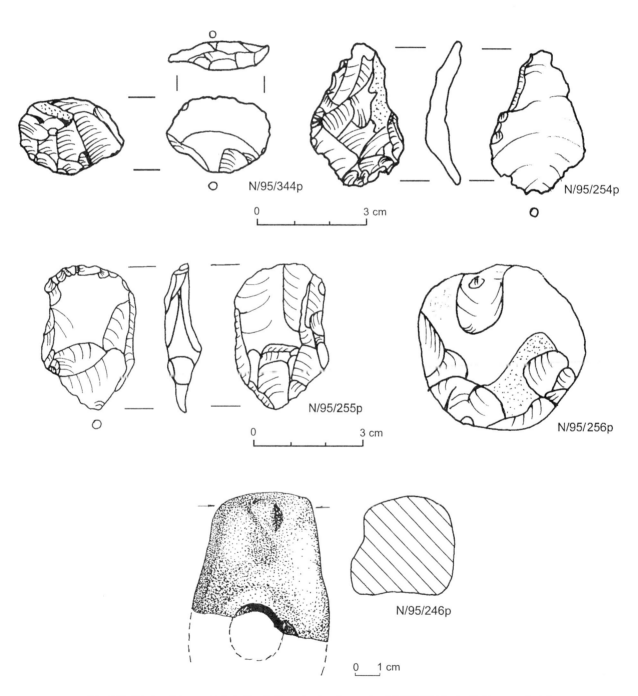

N/95/344p

0   3 cm

N/95/254p

N/95/255p

0   3 cm

N/95/256p

N/95/246p

0   1 cm

Fig. 193. Flint and stone artefacts (by R. Karasiewicz-Szczypiorski, N/95/246p, by L. Berezovskaja)

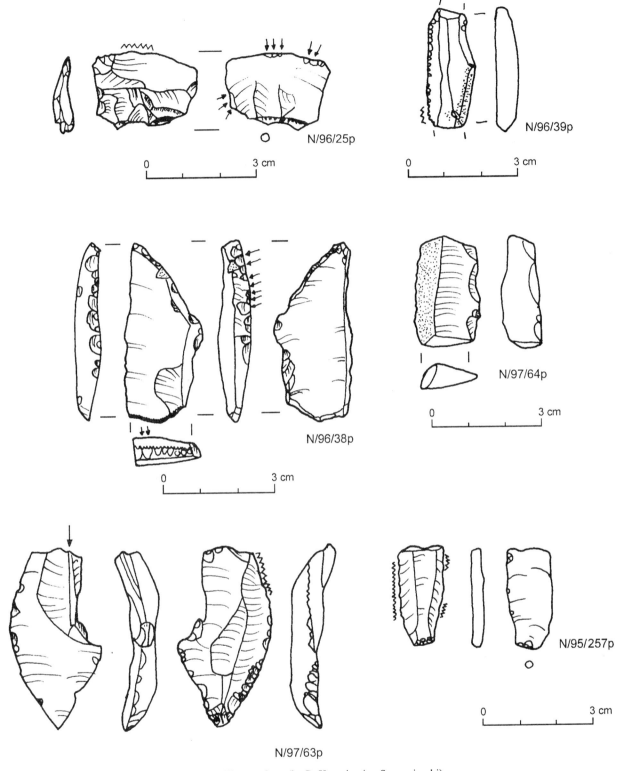

Fig. 194. Flint artefacts (by R. Karasiewicz-Szczypiorski)

To sum up it should be stated that apart from the fragment of the battle–axe, all the other forms are ubiquitous and existed during the whole prehistoric period. Any links with the pottery dating to about the 2nd millenium B.C. (mainly of the Sroubnaya culture) which appear at the same sites quite frequently remain only hypothetical as the material has been collected from the surface. For that reason the majority of traces of retouching have been considered as most probably spontaneous.

III. 2. CERAMIC STAMPS

BY NIKOLAJ F. FEDOSEEV (ARCHAEOLOGICAL MUSEUM IN KERČ)

[Photo 28–42]

The presented selection of pottery stamps from field survey at the area of Nymphaion chora consists of 16 items: 10 coming from common research and 6 discovered at another time (Nos. 1, 2, 4, 6,9, 10). The material is too scarce to draw any far-reaching conclusions. It is however possible to state the quantitative domination of stamps from Pontic Heraclea and Sinope, dating to the 2nd half of the 4th century B.C.[1] and the presence of Chian stamps, perhaps coming from the 5th century B.C.

Neither the stamps from the town of Nymphaion nor those from earlier excavations from the area of the chora (e.g., the settlement Geroevka – 1) have been studied in detail or the catalogue of stamps presented as Appendix in I. Kruglikova's doctoral dissertation[2] has been published. Only recently a publication of stamps from excavations in the settlement Geroevka – 2 has been issued.[3]

CATALOGUE OF STAMPS

HERACLEA

No	Field Reg. / year of finding	Place of finding	Legend	Analogues and remarks
1	1995	04–06, site 6. Pit necropolis Čurubaš Južnoe	Δαμόφων ἐπὶ Σκύϑα	IOSPE III, no. 396
2	1996	07–04, site 2. Settlement Geroevka – 4	Μῦος → caduceus ἐπὶ Σκύϑα	new-made join
3	N/97/66p	10–07, site 1. Settlement Tobečik – 9	......ιδ (?) [ἐπὶ φ]ιλίνου	name in first line illegible; official, Filinos, known in IOSPE III, no. 448
4	1997	04–06, site 6. Pit necropolis Čurubaš Južnoe	Διονύσιο (–) → mace .... ?	
5	N/97/69p	10–07, site 1. Settlement Tobečik – 9	Σκύϑας ....?	inverse stamp (?), name in second line illegible

CHIOS

6	N/95/83p	10–07, site 1. Settlement Tobečik – 9	Impressed circle	
7	N/97/102p	05–03, site 7. Settlement Èl'tigen Zapadnoe	?	stamp on a neck of typical Chian swollen neck amphora

[1] N. F. FEDOSEEV, Chronologija sinopskich magistratskich klejm, in: Problemy skifo – sarmatskoj archeologii Severnogo Pričernomor'ja. II. Tezisy dokladov konferencii. Zaporož'e, 1994, pp. 188–190. See also: E.M. PRIDIK, Inventarnyj katalog klejm na amfornych ručkach i gorlyškach i na čerepicach Èrmitažnogo sobranija, Petersburg 1917 (= Pridik 1917), p. 191; I.T. KRUGLIKOVA, Ju.G. VINOGRADOV, Klejma Sinopy na amforach iz poselenija Andreevka Južnaja, KSIA 133, 1973 (= Kruglikova, Vinogradov 1973), pp. 44–53; V. I. CECHMISTRENKO, Zametki o sinopskich klejmach (III–V), SA 1, 1967 (=Cechmistrenko 1967), pp. 256–261; M. COJA, Les centres de production d'amphores timbrées identifiées à Istros, Bulletin de Correspondance Hellénique, Suppl. XIII, 1986 (= Coja 1986), pp. 417–450; Inscriptiones antiquae orae septentrionalis Ponti Euxini (=IOSPE), III [manuscript].

[2] I.T. KRUGLIKOVA, Sel'skoe chozjajstvo Bospora. Rukopis' doktorskoj dissertacii, Moskwa 1974, in: Archiv IA RAN. R–2. No. 2133, 2134.

[3] FEDOSEEV, ZIN'KO, 1998.

continue CATALOGUE OF STAMPS

SINOPE

8	N/96/26p	04–12, site 1. Settlement Čurubaš Majak – 2	Αἰσ[χίνου] [ἀστυνόμου] ← mace ....?	potter's name illegible
9	1997	as above	[Ἀττάλου ἀσ]τυ– [νομοῦντος] → Apollo's head [Πύθης]	there are 8 unpublished analogues known to author
10	1991	07–04, site 2. Settlement Geroevka – 6.	Βόρυος ἀσ– τυνομοῦντο– ς Δημητρίου	IOSPE III, nos. 1836 – 1839
11	N/97/71p	04–12, site 1. Settlement Čurubaš Majak – 2	Βόρυος → head ἀστυνόμου Φιλοκράτου	IOSPE III, nos. 1868, 1927 – 1951, 8623; Pridik 1917, p. 87, no. 520
12	N/97/58p	10–07, site 1. Settlement Tobečik – 9	Διονυσίου ↓ bunch, ἀστυνο( ) wreath [Ἡρα]κλεί (δης)	new-made join
13	N/96/27p	04–12, site 1. Settlement Čurubaš Majak – 2.	Ἐπιέπλου ἀστυνο( ) ↓ shell Πρυτάνι(ος)	IOSPE III, nos. 3133–3135; Pridik 1917, p. 89, no. 557; Coja 1986, p. 433, no. 71
14	N/96/28p	as above	Καλλίστρατο(ς) ἀστυνο( ) ↑ flower Ποσειδω(νίου)	IOSPE III, no. 4802; Kruglikova, Vinogradov 1973, p. 51, no. 26
15	N/97/57p	as above	Ποσιδείου του Ἡφαστο(δώρου) ↓ mace ἀστυνόμου	IOSPE III, nos. 6792 – 6797; Cechmistrenko 1967, p. 77, fig. 7.4
16	N/97/60p	04–12, site 1. Settlement Čurubaš Majak – 2	.... ↓ bunch	inscription obliterated; emblem may indicate that official's name is, perhaps, Mnesikles

III.3. ROCK ANALYSIS

BY MAURIZIO MAZZUCHELLI (UNIVERSITY OF MODENA)

Two rock samples were investigated by means of petrographical analysis. Both fragments are not indigenous to the investigated area. They were found at the north-eastern edge of the area. Fragments of marbles with traces of working were found on the slope.

III.3.1. WHITE SAMPLE
(04–03, SITE 1)

It is a piece of metamorphic, holocrystalline, medium-grained rock composed mainly of calcite and, to a small degree, of epidotes. The investigated microsection also contained a very small crystal of mica. It has a grainy, isotropic and compact texture. Calcite crystals have partly irregular, rounded, and sometimes denticulated rims. Twin polysynthetic forms are frequent. The investigated rock can be classified as marble.

III.3.2. PINK SAMPLE
(04–03, SITE 2)

It is a piece of sedimentary, carbonate, microcrystalline rock. Fragments of fossils such as algae, echinoderms, foraminifers, and elognated agglutinants are recognizable. The investigated rock may be defined as limestone which was deposited in an environment connected with the presence of Mesozoic carbonate platforms.

SCHOLL, ZIN'KO 1997, p. 64.

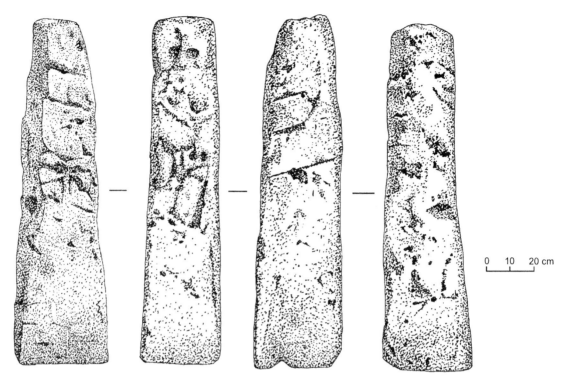

Fig. 195. Stone statue no. 1 (by L. Berezovskaja)

III.4. SCULPTURES (NOS. 1–5)
BY ELENA ZIN'KO (ARCHAEOLOGICAL MUSEUM IN KERČ)
[Photo G, H, 43, Fig. 195–197]

III.4.1. SCYTHIAN STONE STATUE NO. 1
(04–07, SITE 5) [Fig. 195]

It was found 250 m to the east of the barrow with triangulation marker 102.4, belonging to the kurgan necropolis of Skal'nyj. The 1.4 m tall statue was cut from one limestone block. A 0.22 m high head and shoulders are distinguished. The facial features, arms, and attributes are marked by deep contour and flat relief. On the right side a double edged axe is represented, and on the left side, a bow in a 0.26 m long quiver. In the frontal part, to the right, a 0.18 m long rhyton can be seen. All the edges have been worked.

On the basis of the state of preservation of the stone, the statue stood dug into the ground to a depth of 0.45 m, facing the west, towards the steppes, for a considerable length of time.

All the above-mentioned elements, their iconography and location are, characteristic of early Scythian statues dating to the 6th–5th century B.C.[4]

KARASIEWICZ-SZCZYPIORSKI 1996, p. 465; SCHOLL, ZIN'KO 1997, p. 63.

III.4.2. SCYTHIAN STONE STATUE NO. 2
(05–12, SITE 2) [Photo G, H]

It was found on the western side of the top of the barrow with triangulation marker 93.6, partly buried in the ground, leaning towards the north, facing the west. The 1.75 m × 0.55 m statue was cut in one cylindrical piece of limestone. The head and shoulders are delineated to a height of 0.40 m. The statue may be classified as an anthropomorphic stele with the characteristic form of an elongated rectangle, geometric in style and with unworked edges. It should be stressed that the statue is still located at the top of the barrow in the same place and position as when discovered.

The statue can be dated to the 6th–5th century B.C.[5]

Nymphaion, Arch. 1996, p. 5; SCHOLL, Arch. 1996; SCHOLL, ZIN'KO 1997, p. 63.

---

[4] Cf. V.S. OL'CHOVSKIJ, G.L. EVDOKIMOV, *Skifskie izvajanija VII–III vv. do n. è.*, Moskva 1994, pp. 67–73.

---

[5] Cf. OL'CHOVSKIJ, EVDOKIMOV, op. cit., p. 48.

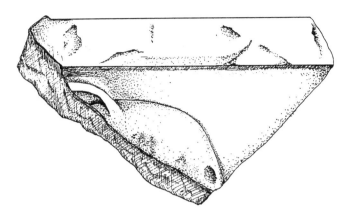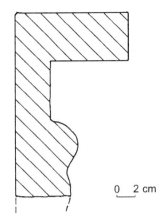

Fig. 196. Fragment of marble relief (by L. Berezovskaja)

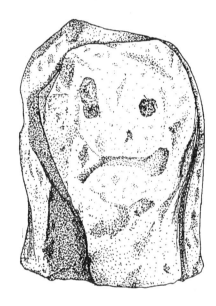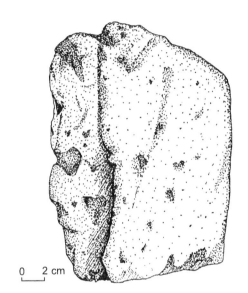

Fig. 197. Head (by L. Berezovskaja)

III.4.3. FRAGMENT OF A MARBLE RELIEF
(10–06, SITE 3) [Fig. 196]

It was found in a ploughed field on the eastern edge of the settlement of Tobečik – 3. The preserved fragment is made of white Attic marble with the following dimensions: height, 0.19 m, greatest width, 0.33 m; depth, from 0.08 m to 0.03 m. The representation is separated from the edges of the relief by a wide border (height up to 0.08 m, width 0.05 m), beneath which the head and part of the ear of an animal, perhaps a panther, can be seen. The relief details are exceptionally finely worked.

On the basis of style this fragment can be dated to the 5th–4th century B.C.[6]

KARASIEWICZ-SZCZYPIORSKI 1996, p. 465; SCHOLL, ZIN'KO 1997, p. 64.

---

[6] Cf. K.P. JOHANSEN, *The attic grave – reliefs of the Classical period*, Copenhagen 1951, p. 117.

III.4.4. FRAGMENT OF A STELE – SEMI-FIGURE
(06–03, SITE 1) [Fig. 197]

It was found in a ploughed field near the second lighthouse of Èl'tigen. It is a strongly weathered fragment of a 0.23 m high limestone head and neck, covered with a veil. The fragment is considerably damaged both by its secondary use as a construction stone and by ploughing. Despite that the folds of the veil, facial features and chin are clearly visible.

It is a fragment of a stele popular in the Bosporan area in the first centuries A.D.[7]

KARASIEWICZ-SZCZYPIORSKI 1996, p. 465; SCHOLL, ZIN'KO 1997, p. 64.

---

[7] A.P. IVANOVA, *Skul'ptura i živopis' Bospora*, Kiev 1961, pp. 90–97, figs. 36–40.

III.4.5. ANTROPOMORPHIC STELE
(05–03, SITE 8) [Photo 43]

It was found near a modern dump pit at the area of the pit and kurgan necropolis of Nymphaion, to the west of the village of Èl'tigen. It is made of one, well worked, rectangular, limestone block with the following preserved dimensions: height, 0.85 m, greatest width, 0.48 m. The head is missing (it has been broken off). The neck is well polished and rounded. In the bottom part of the stele there is a special projection for fixing it in an upright position. The projection is 0.18 m high and 0.27 m wide.

The stele represents a type different from the semi-figure described above, but one which was still widely popular in the Bosporan area in the first centuries A.D.[8]

SCHOLL, ZIN'KO 1997, p. 63.

III. 5. CLAY TOBACCO PIPES (NOS. 1–3)[*]
BY KATARZYNA MEYZA (MUSEUM OF HISTORY OF WARSAW) [Photo 44–45]

III.5.1. N/95/197p (05–08, SITE 2)

L / Length	–
Hp / Height preserved	– 0, 041 m
W / Width	– 0, 028 m

Brown clay. Rim and shank end missing. Small pipe, richly decorated flat bottom of the bowl with central band of rouletting and double zigzag lines on its sides, ending in small simple flowers. Bowl shallow, around lower end band of disks with impressed rosettes. Scraps of upper bowl suggest vertical bands. Probably 18th century.

III.5.2. N/95/179p (07–09, SITE 1)

L	–
Hp	– 0, 041 m
W	– 0, 02 m

Light brown clean clay. Rim missing, shank end chipped. Small pipe, simple ring with single molding on inner end. Single line and one line of rouletting at shank end. On inner molding single line of rouletting and double line. Otherwise nonexistent keel marked by double lines and rouletting the right one snapping to left at bowl front. Early 18th century.

A similar pipe has been found in later 17th century context with a coin of 1664 at the Royal Castle in Warsaw.[9] Another close counterpart was found at Hlincea (Jassy voivodship, Moldova) and was dated 17th / 18th centuries.[10] They should belong to Hayes' Sarachane types XXIV and VI, dating to the early 18th century.[11]

III.5.3. N/95/203p (10–06, SITE 1)

L	–
Hp	– 0, 049 m
W	– 0, 027 m

Dark gray clay with brown slip. Rim and most of bowl missing. Probably lily – shaped pipe. Outlined keel, shank flaring to flat end. Three lines of rouletting around shank, two of them unfinished in the middle. 19th to 20th century. A similar pipe was found in a stratified level at the Agora of Athens.[12] Lily – shaped pipes correspond to Sarachane type VIII dated to late 19th century.[13]

---

[8] Cf. A.P. IVANOVA, *Bosporskie antropomorfnye nadgrobija*, SA 13, 1950, pp. 242–243.

[9] K. MEYZA, *Fajki gliniane z XVII i pierwszej połowy XVIII w. z badań archeologicznych Zamku Królewskiego i Starego Miasta w Warszawie*, Almanach Muzealny, Warszawa 1997, pp. 31–44, Tabl. II/1.

[10] N. ZAHARIA, M. PETRESCU-DIMBOVITA, Em. ZAHARIA, *Asezari din Moldova. De paleolitic pina in secolul al XVIII – lea*, Bucuresti 1970, p. 196, Pl. CLXXV / 13.

[11] J.W. HAYES, *Excavations at Sarachane in Istanbul*, vol. 2, *Pottery*, Princeton 1992, p. 393.

[12] R.C.W. ROBINSON, *Tobacco Pipes of Corinth and of the Agora of Athens*, Hesperia 54, 1985, p. 200, Pl. 64, catalogue nos. A 37, C 119.

[13] J.W. HAYES, *Turkish Clay Pipes: A Provisional Typology*, in: *The Archaeology of the Clay Tobacco Pipe*, BAR S92, London 1980, p. 7.

[*] *Translated by K. Meyza*

CONCLUSIONS

In its present form the Archaeological Map of Nymphaion represents only a certain stage of research on the subject of those rural areas which constitute the supposed chora of the Ancient town of Nymphaion. It should be followed up by recording in detail all the sites on the official land usage maps in order to ensure their full protection. As far as it is possible, the particularly interesting sites should be excavated after a detailed field survey in cooperation with a geophysicist and a topographer. These sites include, principally, the settlement of Tobečik – 9 and the continually disturbed barrows. Of course, for specialists studying prehistoric cultures or the Middle Ages, other sites will be more interesting. It should not be forgotten that field surveys should be verified as often as possible, especially in places particularly threatened by human acitvity, both as regards agriculture and construction. The necessity of carrying out such work is particularly well illustrated by the settlement of Čurubaš Nižnoe (04–04, site 1). In 1995 only one fragment of Ancient pottery was found there. In 1997, after deep ploughing, an archaeological site, probably connected with a fragment of an Ancient water pipe uncovered above it (04–04, site 5), was discovered.

The concrete results of our works are, i.a., the considerable increase of the number of known Ancient and Mediaeval settlements, verification of the number of barrows, recording of plots on topographical maps, locating previously unknown settlements from the 2nd millenium B.C., and the precise delineation of the extent of Mediaeval settlement along the Kerč Strait (see Map 3).

Our research provided more data serving to verify the hypothesis about the existence of a wall forming the western boundary of the Nymphaion chora.

We also hope that our records of remains of the 19th–20th century cemeteries will help to save them, or, at least, inspire the interest of historians and ethnographers.

Altogether 232 charts of archaeological sites were made at which, i.a., 65 settlements (41 Ancient ones), 24 necropolises (15 Ancient ones), 6 pathways, 5 areas with traces of plots were recorded. All these sites, found in the investigated area, have different functions, occupy different areas, and are dated to different periods.

Obviously, it is difficult to provide an exact date when a pathway was made, yet it seems that they appeared in Ancient times and were also used in the Middle Ages. The formation and utilisation of plots should also be linked with the Antiquity, yet it can not be excluded that they also existed in the Mediaeval period.

The photographic documentation (more than 1200 photographs of the area and artefacts) may provide a basis for further studies of this area not only for archaeologists but also specialists from other disciplines.

It was also our aim to provide evidence for the debate over the location of the harbour of the town of Nymphaion, whether it lay to the north or the east. The survey of pits dug in the northern part of the village of Èl'tigen (below the preserved part of the Ancient town) yielded layers of soil sometimes with remains of occupation debris alternating with sand layers down to a depth of more than 1.5 m. A comparison of this depth with that of the Ancient layer at the site Èl'tigen Muzej (06–03, site 2) seems to indicate that at least part of the area located to the north of the town was land in Ancient times. Of course, the harbour could have been located more to the north or north-east. Also the excavations conducted by V. Zin'ko in 1995 below the eastern slope of Nymphaion revealed an occupation layer reaching a depth of more than 3 m, covered with a layer of sand.

The discovery of settlements with Ancient material far into the sea (200–300 m) also seems to be helpful in establishing the Ancient shoreline in the vicinity of Nymphaion. This issue is studied by L. Ménanteau, who also utilised our conclusions about the pathway network. It has also proved that the extent of some of the settlements may be established on the basis of satellite pictures (e.g., the settlement of Tobečik – 9).

Finally, the geophysical survey also brought positive results, yet the geological structure of the discussed area requires trial excavations to be made at each investigated site for the purpose of verification.

ABBREVIATIONS

Arch.	– Archives
AIK	– Archeologičeskie Issledovanija v Krymu, Simferopol'
AN	– Akademija Nauk
BAC	– Bosporskij Archeologičeskij Centr Goskomiteta po ochrane i ispol'zovaniju pamjatnikov istorii i kul'tury, Kerč
BS	– Bosporskij Sbornik, Moskva
Goskomitet	– Gosudarstvennyj komitet po ochrane i ispol'zovaniju pamjatnikov istorii i kul'tury, Simferopol'
IA	– Institut Archeologii
IAE PAN	– Instytut Archeologii i Etnologii Polskiej Akademii Nauk, Warszawa
IA UW	– Instytut Archeologii Uniwersytetu Warszawskiego
IIMK	– Institut Istorii Materjal'noj Kul'tury
KF IA NANU	– Krymskij Filial IA NANU
KIAM	– Kerčenskij Istoriko – Archeologičeskij Muzej
KIKZ	– Kerčenskij Istoriko – Kul'turnyj Zapovednik
KO IV NANU	– Krymskoe otdelenie instituta vostokovedenija NANU
KPAÈ KIKZ	– Kompleksnaja Postajannodejstvujuščaja Archeologičeskaja Èkspedicija KIKZ
KSIA	– Kratkie soobščenija o dokladach i polevych issledovanijach IA AN SSSR, Moskva
KSIIMK	– Kratkie soobščenija o dokladach i polevych issledovanijach IIMK AN SSSR, Moskva
KwHKM	– Kwartalnik Historii Kultury Materialnej, Warszawa
MAIET	– Materialy po archeologii, istorii i ètnografii Tavrii, Simferopol'
MIA	– Materialy i issledovanija po archeologii SSSR, Moskva
NANU	– Nacional'naja Akademija Nauk Ukrainy
Nymphaion	– Nymphaion. Historia i struktura polis greckiej. Sprawozdanie z prac w ... roku. IAE PAN, Warszawa
RAN	– Rossijskaja Akademija Nauk
SA	– Sovetskaja Archeologija, Moskva
SBIAUW	– Sprawozdania z badań IAUW w roku akademickim ..., Warszawa
SGE	– Soobščenija Gosudarstvennogo Èrmitaža, Saint Petersburg (formerly Leningrad)
StArch.	– Studia Archeologiczne, Warszawa
VDI	– Vestnik Drevnej Istorii, Moskva

ARCHIVES

KIRILIN, Arch. 1964 – D.S. KIRILIN, Otčet o razvedočnych rabotach Antičnoj ekspedicii Kerčenskogo istoriko – archeologičeskogo muzeja v 1964 g. u derevni Ogon'ki, in: Archiv KIKZ

KRUGLIKOVA, Arch. 1956a – I.T. KRUGLIKOVA, Otčet o rabote Vostočno – Krymskogo otrjada ekspedicii IIMK AN SSSR v 1956 g., in: Archiv IA RAN, R – 1, d. 1251, l. 2

KRUGLIKOVA, Arch. 1956b – I. T. KRUGLIKOVA, Otčet o rabote Vostočno – Krymskogo otrjada ekspedicii IIMK AN SSSR v 1956 g., in: Archiv IA NANU, no. 1956/16, p. 7

KRUGLIKOVA, Arch. 1964 – I.T. KRUGLIKOVA, Otčet o rabotach Vostočno – Krymskogo otrjada ekspedicii IA AN SSSR v 1964 g., in: Archiv IA AN SSSR, R – 1, d. 2998, l. 32

LAVRUCHIN, Arch. 1977 – V.N. LAVRUCHIN, Rabočij žurnal poiskovoj gruppy podvodnych rabot KIAM za 1977 g., in: Archiv KIKZ, opis' 3, ed. chran. no. 739, 45 s

Nymphaion, Arch. 1993 – Nymphaion 1993. Aleksandra WĄSOWICZ and Tomasz HERBICH, 1994

Nymphaion, Arch. 1994 – Nymphaion 1994. Aleksandra WĄSOWICZ and Tomasz HERBICH, collaboration: Krzysztof DOMŻALSKI, Robert HOROSZ, Walery KASPAROW, Małgorzata MYCKE-DOMINKO, Ewa PILICH, Tomasz SCHOLL and Viktor ZIN'KO, 1995

Nymphaion, Arch. 1995 – Nymphaion 1995. Aleksandra WĄSOWICZ and Krzysztof DOMŻALSKI, collaboration:

Joanna GROSZKOWSKA, Radosław KARASIEWICZ-SZCZYPIORSKI, Krzysztof NAWOTKA and Tomasz SCHOLL, 1996

Nymphaion, Arch. 1996 – Nymphaion 1996. Aleksandra WĄSOWICZ and Krzysztof DOMŻALSKI, 1997

Nymphaion, Arch. 1997 – Nymphaion 1997. Aleksandra WĄSOWICZ and Krzysztof DOMŻALSKI, 1998

SCHOLL, Arch. 1993 – T. SCHOLL, Badania archeologiczne na Krymie, in: SBIAUW 1992/1993, 1993, p. 18

SCHOLL, Arch. 1994 – T. SCHOLL, Drugi sezon badań Nymphaionu, in: SBIAUW 1993/1994, 1994, p. 44

SCHOLL, Arch. 1996 – T. SCHOLL, collaboration R. KARASIEWICZ- SZCZYPIORSKI, Nymphaion 1996 – kolejny sezon badań, in: SBIAUW 1995/96, 1996, p. 51

SCHOLL, Arch. 1997 – T. SCHOLL, collaboration R. KARASIEWICZ- SZCZYPIORSKI, Nymphaion 1997, in: SBIAUW 1996/1997, 1997, p. 34

ZIN'KO, Arch. 1990 – V. N. ZIN'KO, Otčet o rabote KPAČ KIKZ v 1990 g., in: Archiv IA NANU, l. 73

ZIN'KO, Arch. 1994 – V.N. ZIN'KO, Otčet o rabote Bosporskoj ochranno – archeologičeskoj ekspedicii v 1994 g., in: Archiv KF IA NANU, l. 19 – 24

ZIN'KO, Arch. 1995 – V.N. ZIN'KO, Otčet o rabote Bosporskoj ochranno – archeologičeskoj ekspedicii v 1995 g., in: Archiv KF IA NANU, l. 13 –18, 30 – 36

BIBLIOGRAPHY

BESSONOVA S.S
1971 *Rekonstrukcija derevjannogo sarkofaga iz Trechbratnego kurgana*, SA 1971, 4, pp. 215 – 221.
1973 *Pogrebenie IV v. do n. è. iz Trechbratnego kurgana*, in: *Skifskie drevnosti*, Kiev 1973, pp. 243–252.

BESSONOVA S.S., KIRILIN D.S.
1977 *Nadgrobnyj rel'ef iz Trechbratnego kurgana*, in: *Skify i Sarmaty*, Kiev 1977, pp. 128–139.

CHUDJAK M.M.
1962 *Iz istorii Nimfeja VI–III vekov do n.è.*, Leningrad 1962.

FEDOSEEV N.F., ZIN'KO V.N.
1998 *Ceramic stamps from the rural settlement of Geroevka –2 (The chora of Nymphaion)*, Archeologia 48, 1997 (1998), pp. 55–60.

GADLO A.V.
1968 *Rannesrednevekovoe selišče na beregu Kerčenskogo proliva (po materialam raskopok 1963 g.)*, KSIA 113, 1968, pp. 78–84.

GAJDUKEVIČ V.F.
1940 *Raskopki Mirmekija i Tiritaki: archeologičeskie razvedki na Kerčenskom poluostrove v 1937–39 gg.*, VDI 1940, 3–4, pp. 314–317.

GORONČAROVSKIJ V.A.
1991 *Novye dannye dlja izučenija bosporskoj chory v VI–II vv. do n.è.*, in: *Drevnee Pričernomor'e*, Odessa 1991, pp. 23–24.
1993 *O polevych issledovanijach Iluratskogo otrjada Bosporskoj èkspedicii IIMK RAN*, in: *Archeologični doslidžennja v Ukraini 1991 roku*, Luc'k 1993, pp. 22–23.

GRAČ N.L.
1989 *Nimfejskaja archeologičeskaja èkspedicija (osnovnye itogi issledovanij za 1973–1987 gg.)*, in: *Itogi rabot archeologičeskich èkspedicii Gosudarstvennogo Èrmitaža*, Leningrad 1989, pp. 61–79.

KARASIEWICZ-SZCZYPIORSKI R.
1995 *II Konferencja „Nymphaion, historia i struktura polis greckiej", Igołomia, 4–5 maja 1995 r.*, KwHKM 43, 1995, 4, pp. 545–550.
1996 *„Nymphaion: historia i struktura polis greckiej" III konferencja IAE PAN, Igołomia, 8–11 maja 1996*, KwHKM 44, 1996, 4, pp. 463–466.

KIRILIN D.S.
1966 *Archeologičeskie issledovanija Ortel'skoj èkspedicii Kerčenskogo muzeja v 1965 g. (rajon Tobečikskogo ozera)*, in: Plenum IA AN SSSR 1966 g. Tezisy dokladov sekcii antičnoj archeologii, Moskva 1966, pp.16–18.
1968 *Trechbratnye kurgany v rajone Tobečikskogo ozera*, in: *Antičnaja istorija i kul'tura Sredizemnomor'ja i Pričernomor'ja*, Leningrad 1968, pp. 178–188.
1980 *Unikal'nye nachodki mestnoj bosporskoj skul'ptury*, in: Tezisy dokladov Vsesojuznoj naučnoj konferencii „Problemy antičnoj istorii i klassičeskoj filologii", Char'kov 1980, pp. 19–21.

KRUGLIKOVA I.T.
1960 *Raboty vostočno-krymskogo otrjada Pričernomorskoj èkspedicii v 1957 g.*, KSIIMK 78, 1960, pp. 64–73.
1975 *Sel'skoe chozjajstvo Bospora*, Moskva 1975.

SAVOSTINA E.A.
1995 *Tema nadgrobnoj stely iz Trechbratnego kurgana v kontekste antičnogo mifa*, in: Istoriko-archeologičeskij al'manach, 1, Armavir–Moskva 1995, pp. 110–119.

SCHOLL T.
1981 *Fortyfikacje państwa bosforskiego od IV w. p.n.e. do połowy I w. p.n.e.*, in: St. Arch. 1, 1981, pp. 319–353.

SCHOLL T., ZIN'KO V.
1997 *Archeologiczna mapa Nymphaion*, KwHKM 45, 1997, 1, pp. 61–65.

SILANT'EVA P.F.
1959 *Nekropol' Nimfeja*, MIA 69, 1959, pp. 5–107.

SKUDNOVA V.M.
1964 *Raskopki Nimfeja 1960 g.*, SGE 25, 1964, pp. 59–62.

SOLOV'EV S.L., ZIN'KO V.N.
1995 *Research on the chora of Nymphaion. Study problems*, Archeologia 45, 1994 (1995), pp. 73–78.

STĘPNIEWSKI J.
1994 *Nymphaion. Struktura i historia polis greckiej. Konferencja IAE PAN, Warszawa, 4 grudnia 1993 r.*, KwHKM 42, 1994, 2, pp. 275–278.

ZIN'KO V.N.
1986 *Silski mogil'niki Schidnogo ta Pivnično-Zachidnogo Krymu V–III st. do n.è.*, Archeologija 56, 1986, pp. 24–32.
1994a *Ochrannye archeologičeskie issledovanija v g. Kerči*, in: AIK 1993, 1994, pp. 124–129.
1994b *Rannesrednevekovye žilišČno-chozjajstvennye kompleksy na poselenijach Geroevka – 2 i Geroevka – 6*, in: *Vizantija i narody Pričernomor'ja i Sredizemnomor'ja v rannee srednevekov'e (IV–IX vv.)*. Tezisy dokladov, Simferopol' 1994, pp. 18–20.
1996 *Nekotorye itogi izučenija sel'skoj okrugi antičnogo Nimfeja*, in: MAIET 5, 1996, pp. 12–20.
1997a *Geroevka – 2. A rural settlement in the chora of Nymphaion (Ancient period)*, Archeologia 47, 1996 (1997), pp. 85–94.
1997b *Novye rannesrednevekovye pamjatniki Vostočnogo Kryma*, in: Meždunarodnaja konferencija „Vizantija i Krym", Sevastopol', 6–11.06.1997 g. Tezisy dokladov, Simferopol' 1997, pp. 40–41.
1997c *Ochrannye issledovanija Nimfejskogo nekropolja*, in: Bachčisarajskij istoriko-archeologičeskij sbornik, 1, Simferopol' 1997, pp. 67–75.
1997d *Ochrannye archeologičeskie issledovanija na chore Nimfeja*, in: AIK 1994, 1997, pp. 110–124.
1998 *Pogrebal'nye kompleksy s chory Nimfeja*, in: MAIET 6, 1998, pp. 173–185.

ZIN'KO V.N., PONOMAREV L.JU.
1997 *Keramika saltovo-majackogo tipa s rannesrednevekovych pamjatnikov v okrestnostjach Nimfeja*, in: Meždunarodnaja..., op. cit., pp. 42–43.

ZIN'KO V.N., SOLOV'EV S.L.
1994 *Raskopki na poselenii Geroevka –2 v 1992 godu*, BS 4, 1994, pp. 159–163.

АРХЕОЛОГИЧЕСКАЯ КАРТА НИМФЕЯ

Совместый польско–русско–украинский научный проект „Нимфей – история и структура греческого полиса" (1993–1997 гг.) был создан в 1993 г. благодаря усилиям Элеоноры В. Яковенко и Александры Вонсович (научный руководитель проекта с польской стороны). Одной из основных задач проекта было создание подробной археологической карты памятников, расположенных в окрестностях древнегреческого города Нимфея. Этот город на протяжении нескольких столетий является одним из важнейших центров Боспорского государства.

В течении более полутора столетий Керченский полуостров являлся полигоном на котором формировалась и развивалась русская античная археология. Все это время на повестке дня стояла задача сплошного обследования территории полуострова – в античную эпоху Европейского Боспора. Впервые археологические памятники близ деревни Эльтиген описывает в начале 19 века П. Дибрюкс. Однако вплоть до 50-х гг. нашего столетия, изучение археологических памятников сельской округи Нимфея носили безсистемный характер. Лищь благодаря исследованиям И.Т. Кругликовой были развернуты планомерные археологические изыскания на сельской территории Европейского Боспора. В ходе разносторонних маршрутных разведок была составлена археологическая карта-схема окрестностей Нимфея, обнаружено более десятка поселений античной эпохи. На трех поселениях: Героевка – 1, Чурубашское, Южно-Чурубашское, – И.Т. Кругликова провела стационарные раскопки. В 1991 г. к комплексному исследованию Нимфейской хоры приступила Боспорская охранно-археологическая экспедиция под руководством В.Н. Зинько.

В основу совместных работ по созданию археологической карты были положены методологические разработки как польских архелогов (AZP), так и бывшей советской археологической школы, имеющей большой опыт в проведении комплексных исследований всех видов археологических памятников на сельских территориях античных государств Северного Причерноморья. Территория проведения разведок была разбита на сеть километровых квадратов (масштаб рабочих карт 1 : 10 000). В каждом квадрате визуальные сплошные пешие разведки проводили смешанные польско-украинские группы археологов, состоящие из 6–7 специалистов. Данные по каждому выявленному артефакту фиксировались в карточках разработанных польской стороной. Атрибутация и датировка артефактов производилась украинскими археологами. Затем данные вводились в компьютер. В работах принимали также участие польские геофзики, географы, геологи. В результате было изучено около 70 кв. км окрестней Нимфея.

В первой части книги представлен полный каталог артефактов, выявленных в каждом километровом квадрате. Вторая часть – описание в алфавитном порядке различных категорий памятников: поселений, курганных и грунтовых некрополей, наделов, вала, дорог, каменоломен, водопровода, подводных объектов, – большая часть которых впервые широко вводится в научный оборот. Третья часть книги состоит из описаний обнаруженных при разведках отдельных категорий находок: кремневных отщепов, керамических клейм, каменных изваяний, керамических трубок, выполненных благодаря помощи польских и украинских ученых.

В целом книга явилась результатом совместной пятилетней работы авторов и состоялась лишь благодаря участию многих специалистов и в первую очередь археологов Крыма и Польши.

A. Nymphaion, view of the territory of Ancient town as seen from the sea. II.1.1.
B. Nymphaion chora, the south-eastern part; view from the sea on the cliff of Kerč Strait. II.1.1.

C. Čurubaš Majak – 3. South-east view. II.1.15.
D. View of pathway no. 1. II.4.2.
E. Geroevka – 2. II.1.22. Attic kylix with figural scenes

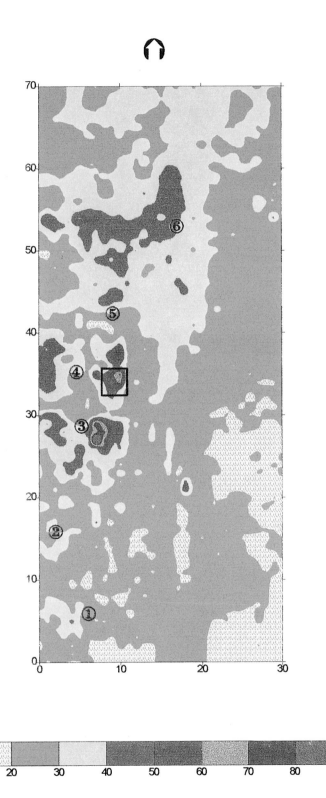

F. Map of resistivity changes made on the basis of geophysical survey of part of the site Èltigen Zapadnoe. II.1.20

G–H. Stone statue. III.4.2.

1. Nymphaion. West view of the area of Ancient town. II. 1. 1.
2. Čurubaš – 8. South view. II. 1. 9.
3. Čurubaš Citadel'. West view. II. 1. 11.

4. Čurubaš Južnoe. Plots. II. 3. 3.
5. Čurubaš Nižnoe – 2. South view. II.1.17.
6. Èltigen Zapadnoe. Trial trench. II. 1. 20.

7. Geroevka – 1. North view. II. 1. 21.
8. Geroevka – 2. II. 1. 22. Attic kylix with figural scenes
9. Geroevka – 2. II. 1. 22. Painted Ionian amphora

10. Ogon'ki – 2. South-west view. II. 1. 28.
11. Tobečik – 5. North-west view. II. 1. 38.
12. Tobečik – 6. Overall view. II. 1. 39.

13. Tobečik – 9. Area embraced by geophysical survey. II. 1. 42.
14. Tobečik – 9. Trial trench. II. 1. 42.
15. Necropolis of Nymphaion and view of the town. II. 2. 1.

16. Čurubaš – 2. Remains of stonework in one of barrows. II. 2. 3.
17. Čurubaš Južnoe. Robbers' pits. II. 2. 6.

18. Čurubaš Južnoe. Grave no. 3 uncovered during survey. II. 2. 6.
19. Čurubaš Skal'ki. Plot limits. II. 3. 1.

20. Čurubaš Skal'ki. Plot limits. II. 3. 1.
21. Pathway no. 2. II. 4. 3.

22–24. Pipeline. II. 4. 10.: 22 – overall view; 23 – view from the west; 24 – interior of gully

25–26. Pipeline. II. 4. 10.: 25 – stoning of ceramic pipe; 26 – ceramic pipe inside stoning
27. Amphora raised from the bed of Kerč Strait. II. 5. 2.

28 – stamp, cat no. 1

30 – stamp, cat no. 3

29 – stamp, cat no. 2

31 – stamp, cat no. 4

32 – stamp, cat no. 5

28-42 Ceramic stamps gathered during field survey. III. 2.

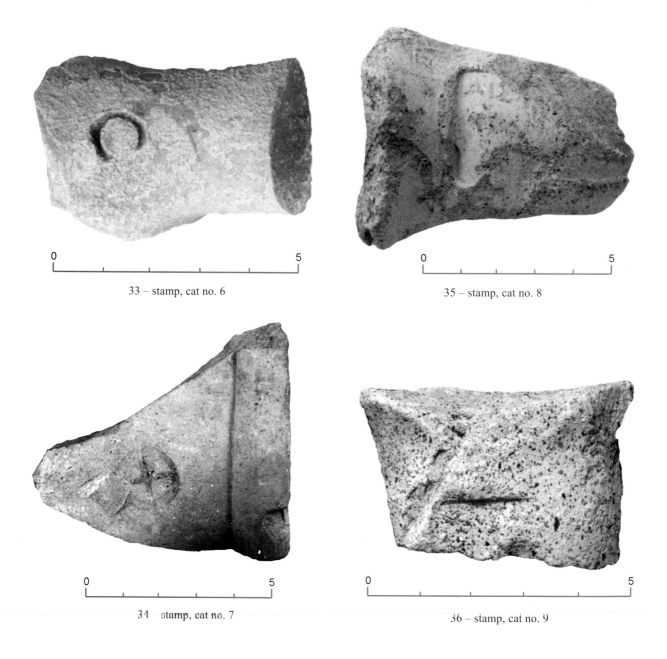

0   5

33 – stamp, cat no. 6

0   5

35 – stamp, cat no. 8

0   5

34 – stamp, cat no. 7

0   5

36 – stamp, cat no. 9

0   5

37 – stamp, cat no. 10

38 – stamp, cat no. 11

40 – stamp, cat no. 13

39 – stamp, cat no. 12

41 – stamp, cat no. 14

42 – stamp, cat no. 16

43. Antropomorphic stele. III. 4. 5.
44. Fragments of ceramic pipe heads. Front view. III. 5.
45. Fragments of ceramic pipe heads. Back view. III. 5.

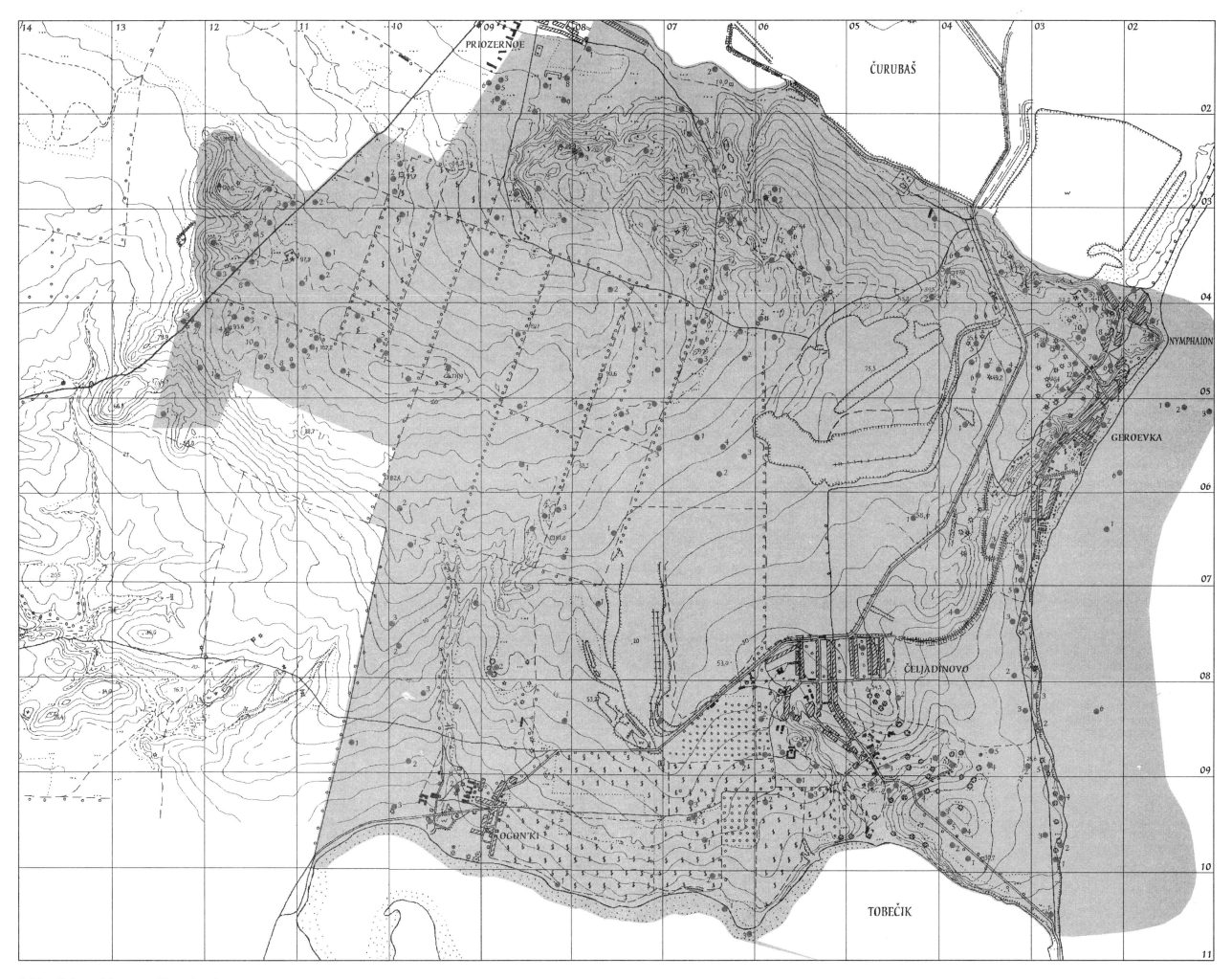

1. Map of sites and the extent of investigated area.

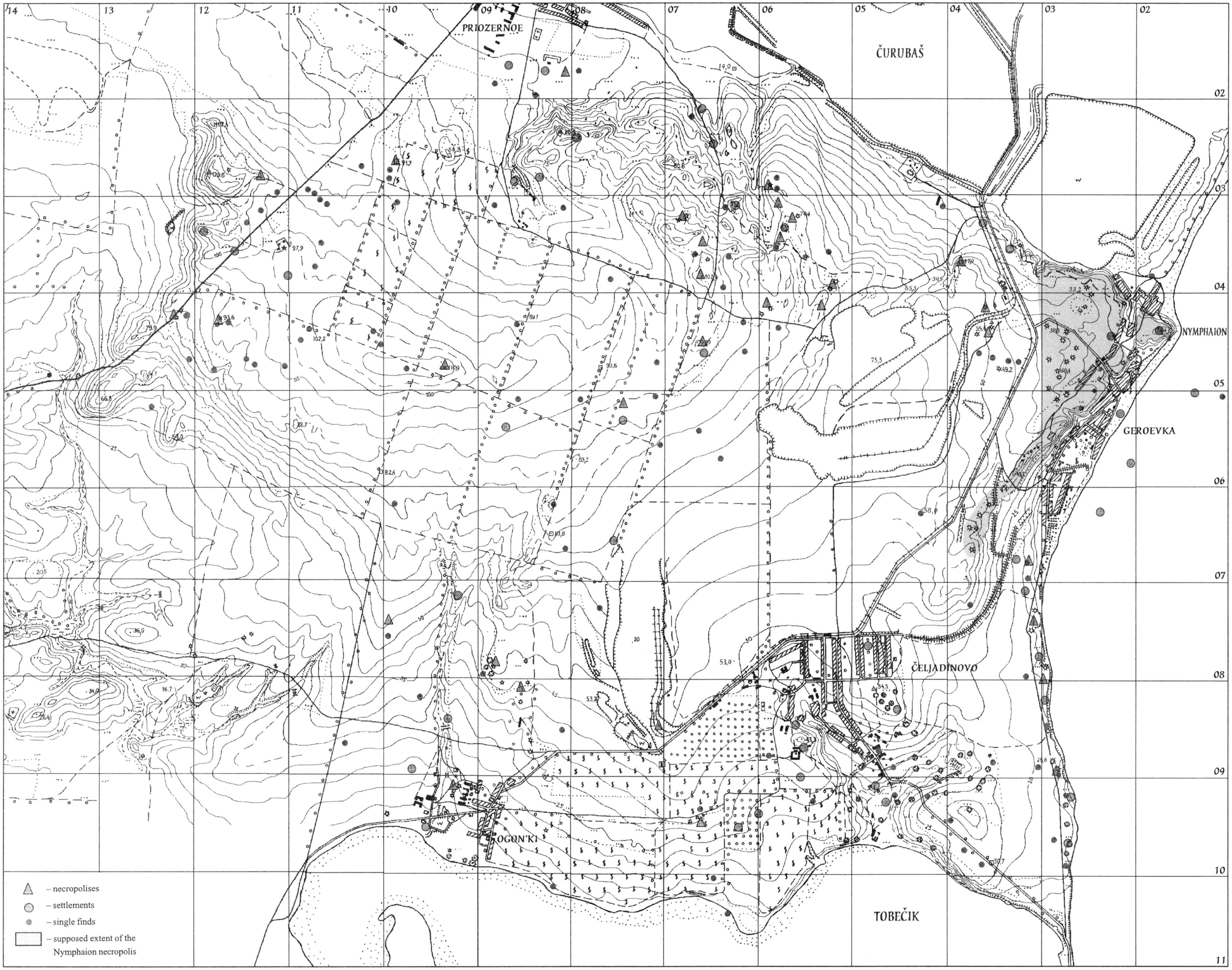

PRIOZERNOE
ČURUBAŠ
NYMPHAION
GEROEVKA
ČELJADINOVO
OGON'KI
TOBEČIK
– necropolises
– settlements
– single finds
– supposed extent of the Nymphaion necropolis

2. Map of Ancient settlement the 6th century B.C. – the 4th century A.D.

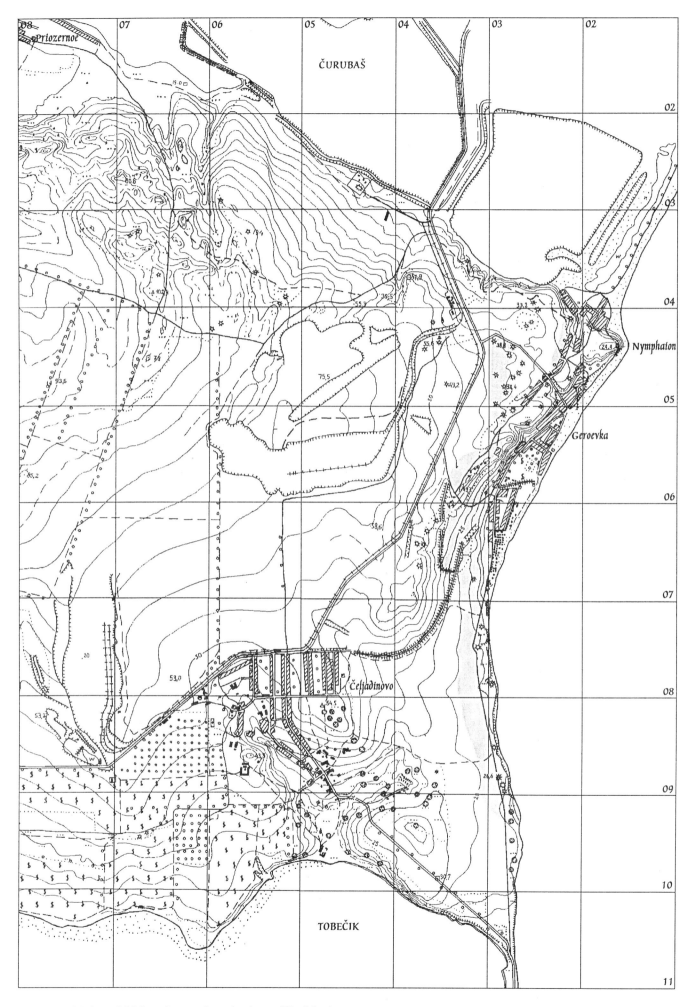

3. Extent of Saltovo-Majak settlement along the shore of Kerč Strait